ATLANTIS *of the* SANDS

ATLANTIS *of the* SANDS

The Search for the Lost City of Ubar

———————

RANULPH FIENNES

BLOOMSBURY

First published in Great Britain 1992
Bloomsbury Publishing Limited, 2 Soho Square, London W1V 5DE

Copyright © 1992 by Ranulph Fiennes

PICTURE SOURCES

Ali Ahmed Ali Mahash: pages 39 *bottom*, 43 *bottom right*, 44 *bottom*, 46 *top*, 47
Neil Barnes: pages 12, 13, 14, 15, 16, 32 *top*, 36 *top*, 42 *top*, 43 *top*
Bruce Blackney: pages 25 *top*, 49 *bottom*
British Aerospace: page 17 *bottom left*
Bryn Campbell: pages 18–19
Nick Clapp: page 35 *bottom*
Edmund Dulac: page 1
Andy Dunsire: pages 8 *bottom right*, 9, 10, 64 *top*
Ranulph Fiennes: pages 2 *inset top*, 2–3, 5, 6, 7, 8 *top & bottom left*, 11, 19 *inset*, 20 *bottom*, 21, 22, 23, 25
bottom, 27 *inset bottom*, 28, 29 *bottom*, 30 *bottom right*, 32 *bottom*, 36 *bottom*, 38, 39 *top*, 40 *top left & top
right*, 46 *bottom*, 48 *top left*, 50, 51 *bottom*, 53 *bottom*, 55 *top left & top right*, 59, 61 *top left*, 62 *top left*, 63
Kevin Fletcher: pages 54 *top*, 58 *top*
Terry Lloyd: pages 20 *top*, 24 *top*, 30 *top*
Ministry of Information of Oman: pages 4 *bottom*, 34
Nigel Moss: pages 3 *inset*, 4 *top*, 31, 40 *bottom*, 42 *bottom*, 43 *bottom left*, 61 *top right & bottom*
Sebastian Munster: page 37 *top left*
Mohomed Mustapha: pages 58 *bottom*, 62 *top right & bottom*
Kevin O'Brien: pages 41, 54 *bottom*
George Ollen: endpapers, pages 26–7, 27 *inset top*, 29 *top*, 30 *bottom left*, 33, 35 *top*, 44 *top*, 45, 48 *top right*,
49 *top left & top right*, 51 *top*, 52, 53 *top*, 55 *bottom*, 56 *inset top*, 56–7, 57 *inset top*, 60
Said Shanfari: page 64 *bottom*
Mike Stroud: page 24 *bottom left & bottom right*
Bertram Thomas: page 2 *inset bottom*
Image enhancement on page 37 by Drs R.E. Crippen and R.G. Blom, JPL/Caltech. Original data provided
by the Earth Observation Satellite Co. (*bottom left & bottom right*) and by SPOT Image Corp. (© CNES)
and the Earth Observation Satellite Co. (*top right*)

Maps on text pages 8, 30, 31 and 144 by Neil Hyslop

A CIP catalogue record for this book
is available from the British Library

ISBN 0 7475 1327 9

Designed by Fielding Rowinski
Typeset by Hewer Text Composition Services, Edinburgh
Printed and bound by the Bath Press, Avon

CONTENTS

Chapter One 9

Chapter Two 19

Chapter Three 26

Chapter Four 34

Chapter Five 46

Chapter Six 55

Chapter Seven 67

Chapter Eight 80

Chapter Nine 98

Chapter Ten 115

Chapter Eleven 126

Chapter Twelve 145

Chapter Thirteen 156

Chapter Fourteen 166

Postscript: The Lost City 174

Bibliography 183

Acknowledgements 185

Index 189

Where there is no water, 'tis the Empty Quarter, none thither goes.

Suwid al Azma

The spade may yet disclose the identity and history of Ad.

H. St J.B. Philby

A lam tara keif fa'ala rabbuka bi 'Ād Irama dhāti il 'imādi Al tali lam yukhlaq mithluhā al bilādi.

Qur'an

This the treasure of Shadaad son of Ad, him who laid the base of the many-columned Irem, the like of which was never made in all the land.

The 996th tale of the *Arabian Nights*

Other Arabs in my previous journeys had told me of Ubar, the Atlantis of the Sands, but none could say where it lay.

Bertram Thomas

Bedouin ways were hard, even for those brought up in them and for strangers terrible: a death in life. No man can live this life and emerge unchanged. He will carry, however faint, the imprint of the desert, the brand which marks the nomad; and he will have within him the yearning to return, weak or insistent according to his nature. For this cruel land can cast a spell which no temperate clime can match.

T.E. Lawrence

The finest, bravest people I have met are Arabs of Oman. This book is dedicated to two of them, Sheikh Nashran bin Sultan of the Bait Shaasha and Hamed al Khalas of the Bait Kathir, who first inspired me to search for Ubar.

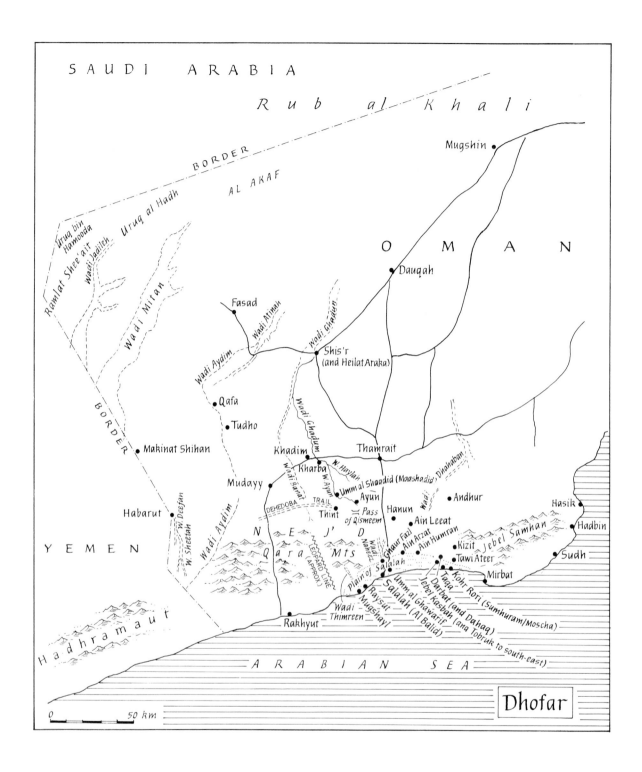

SAUDI ARABIA

Rub al Khali

BORDER

AL AKAF

Mugshin

Uruq bin Hamooda

Ramlat Shee'ait

Wadi Jaailteh

Uruq al Hadh

O M A N

Dauqah

Wadi Mitan

Fasad

Wadi Atinah

Wadi Ghadun

Wadi Aydim

Shis'r
(and Heilat Araka)

Qafa

Tudho

Wadi Ghadun

Thamrait

BORDER

Makinat Shihan

Khadim

Wadi Barat

Kharba

W. Haylah

W. Ayun

Umm al Shaadid (Maashadid)

Wadi Dhahaban

Mudayy

DEHEDOBA

TRAIL

Thint

Ayun

Pass
of Qismeem

Hanun

Wadi

Andhur

Hasik

Habarut

W. Deefan

W. Sheelah

Wadi Aydim

N E
Qara
Mts

J'
D

LEOPARD LINE
(APPROX)

Ain Leeat

Ain Arzat
Ain Humran

Kizit

Jebel Samhan

Hadbin

YEMEN

Wadi Naheez

Ghaur Fazl

Plain of
Salalah

Tawi Ateer

Sudh

Mirbat

Kohr Rori (Sumhuram/Moscha)

Raysut

Wadi Thimreen

Mugshayl

Umm al Ghawarif

Salalah (Al Balid)

Jebel Kasbah, (ana Tobruk to south-east)

Darbat (and Dahaq)

Tuqa'

Rakhyut

H a d h r a m a u t

A R A B I A N   S E A

0   50 km

Dhofar

CHAPTER ONE

For twenty-four years I searched for a lost city, a fabulous legend of Arabia. This is the story of the search, the interruptions and, remarkably, the eventual success. To hunt diligently for the relics of the ancients is the work of the archaeologist and historian, but this book is no treatise for specialists. It is the record of an addictive fascination with an Arabian mystery to which I was introduced by the will of Allah and an early inability to pass exams.

Unable to enter Sandhurst Military Academy and become a regular Army officer, I joined a cavalry regiment on a 'short-service' engagement and accepted chance secondments whenever possible. After a short spell with the Special Air Service (SAS) I applied in 1968 to join the Army of the Sultan of Oman, Said bin Taimur. At that time Marxist ambitions threatened the status quo in many countries, including Oman, where armed insurrection thrived in the southern province of Dhofar. Muscat and Oman were eventually combined to form the Sultanate of Oman in 1970.

The Sultan fielded an army of three hundred volunteer soldiers armed with old bolt-action rifles against some two thousand insurgents supported by the Soviet Union. The Sultan's men were Muslims from Oman and Baluchistan with a smattering of Zanzibaris.

The troubles had started in 1965 as a purely nationalist business with local Muslim Dhofaris wanting a better life than they were then getting from the Sultan.

My reconnaisance platoon consisted of thirty men and six stripped-down Land Rovers. With twelve light machine-guns and a plethora of white phosphorus hand grenades, our unit was able to penetrate the enemy-held Dhofar mountains, provided we moved only by night, leaving the vehicles out of sight and sound of the foothills. To drive or deploy in or near the mountains by day was to invite death. There were no helicopters and often no ground assistance from other hard-pressed troops to help evacuate a casualty. All water, food and ammunition had to be carried by the soldiers, there was little or no information from Intelligence and the entire Sultan's Air Force consisted of two single-seater Piston Provost fighters backed up by a propeller-driven Beaver.

Only the coastal plain around Salalah, the capital of Dhofar and seat of the Sultan, remained free of Marxist control. To the north of the mountains, vast wastes of gravel and sand, the home of wandering *bedu*, stretched away to the borders of Yemen and Saudi Arabia. By the summer of 1968 the Marxist forces were ready to attack our last safe bastions, the Plain of Salalah and the outlying Sultanate forts at Mirbat and Taqa.

That August three companies were deployed in the mountains, leaving only ninety armed men at the coastal headquarters, Umm al Ghawarif. At 07.36 hours on 7 August, under the cover of monsoon clouds, an enemy force attacked the *Beau Geste*-like fortress of Mirbat with its garrison of two dozen Sultanate militiamen. Mirbat's lone signaller managed to tap out an emergency call and by mid-morning all available soldiers from Umm al Ghawarif were trucked along the single coastal route running east towards Mirbat.

The track was often mined and ambushed, so we moved with caution, arriving at dusk at a deep ravine, from where we advanced on foot along the beach. For eight hours we progressed with great care and at dawn, unlike the US cavalry, arrived just too late to help the unfortunate garrison. They had held out, but dead and wounded lay about within the fort and beneath the crenellated battlements.

The enemy forces had retreated an hour before our own arrival at Jebel Ali, from which outcrop, with a touch more speed, we could have cut them off from the mountains. For three days we searched the hovels of Mirbat for traces of collaboration between townsfolk and the enemy. There were no more than three hundred Mirbatis, mostly fisherfolk, in the town, but ancient ruins, including standing pillars, in the surrounding area suggested past times of greater glory and affluence. Unfortunately very little was known of Dhofar's history, for only one archaeologist had ever been allowed to work in the country.

Close by Jebel Ali I wandered over to a comparatively well-preserved tomb dated AD 1160. Plagued by fleas and prickly heat, I found the sticky humidity made sleep elusive and was glad when the British captain in charge of our convoy decided to go back to Salalah.

Fearing that our return journey would be waylaid, we scouted every step with minesweeping gear and camped, halfway back, at the ancient ruins of Kohr Rori.

Here, in 1962, the Sultan's American friend, the oilman and archaeologist Dr Wendell Phillips, after three seasons of excavation work, left behind a labyrinth of partially revealed ruins, defence towers and incense storage vats. In the moon shadows of racing clouds, the cliff-top metropolis held me spellbound. I forgot my worries of imminent attack and wandered through a black and silver landscape where, at the time of Christ, animists had performed sacrifices to the Moon God Sin.

A fat snake, startled by my clumsy steps through the diggers' detritus, moved across my path. I could easily imagine the great satisfaction that Phillips and his team must have experienced in discovering such a place. Although no amateur archaeologist, I was an avid reader of ancient history, particularly concerning mysteries of long ago and places different or remote.

Salalah, our signaller announced, was under attack. We drove on without lights and my thighs remained clenched tight in anticipation of mines. We reached Umm al Ghawarif at 02.00 hours to discover that our haste had been unnecessary. Mortars had been fired at the RAF camp north of Salalah but no ground assault had followed. So we slept until, a few hours later, two RAF vehicles were ambushed in the foothills. Our weary soldiers piled back on to the trucks and I was ordered to locate the attackers.

Like thirty lemmings, my men advanced over flat, open ground straight towards a well-sited enemy ambush. That we were not wiped out to a man was sheer providence. One of my sergeants was shot through the thigh and my signaller, in a panic, shot an inch of skin from one of my fingers. Otherwise all was well, and an hour later the enemy faded away.

Six miles to the south the Sultan heard the fighting, unpleasantly close to the Palace, and signalled his Defence Secretary to order automatic rifles for his army. Next day in Iraq, Radio Baghdad reported the fighting thus: 'An enemy Hunter aircraft and forty-nine imperialist troops have been killed.' The BBC said nothing, for the British public had never heard of Dhofar and much less did they know of the war going on there.

- - - - - - - - - - - - - - - -

In between operations there was time to relax but nowhere to safely ramble except within the wire boundary fence that surrounded the landward flanks of Salalah. One of my Sultanate guides was Nashran bin Sultan, a sheikh of the *bedu* Bait Shaasha tribe with whom I had worked on several operations. On a visit to the

Salalah *sooq*, the open-air market, Nashran and I bought some bananas and drove to the beach, an endless stretch of coconut palm and empty white sands. He then took me to Al Balid, a place of imposing ruins, overgrown and snake-infested, that fronted the Indian Ocean and included a silted-up lagoon that once had harboured trading boats from China and the Indies. Marco Polo called the city Zafar when he visited the area in the thirteenth century. He described it as a great, noble and fine city from which many horses were traded to India.

'What other ruined cities are there in Dhofar?' I asked Nashran.

'Only Salalah is now of any size,' he replied. 'But in days past, when frankincense was in demand, there were many great centres for trade.'

'Were all of them here on the coast?'

'Who knows?' Nashran smiled, and scratched at the sand with his camel stick. 'Some say the finest city in all Arabia was Ubar, built like Paradise with pillars fashioned from gold. Allah destroyed the place and no man has been there for a thousand years. Ubar is not on this coast but over there – he pointed his stick north towards the distant Qara mountains and west towards the Yemen – in the Sands beyond the Wadi Mitan.'

'Will you take me there, Nashran?' I asked.

'*Insh'allah,*' was his reply: 'God willing.'

From that moment on, through the fears and hopes of the war, a Walter Mitty-like desire grew in me into a self-imposed but undeniable quest: I would find the golden pillars of Ubar however deep they lay buried within the sea of sand and however long it might take. I must interrogate each and every *bedu* of the Sands, speak better Arabic, learn about Islamic and Arab history. But I must never reveal my aim to my fellow officers, for they might inform the Commanding Officer, who could forbid any forays into non-operational areas. A further worry was that one of them might be equally fired by the thought of making a similar discovery.

Many a hot, sleepless night passed by the more productively for planning my secret endeavour and my spare time at Umm al Ghawarif was filled with reading. Until that time I neither knew nor cared about the history of Oman or Islam. Now I read whatever I could lay my hands on that gave an insight into Arabia. In my initial ignorance I was not alone. Few of my fellow officers, mostly from Britain or Commonwealth countries, were able to tell me a single detail about the Prophet Muhammad.

Before Muhammad, the fierce and predatory Arab tribes had constantly expended their aggressive energies on internal struggles. Now, under the banner of Islam, they were for the first time united and surged out of Arabia as unstoppable as the hordes of Genghis Khan. Within the span of a single century they had conquered a region greater than and including a great deal of the Roman Empire. Syria, Mesopotamia, Egypt, Libya, Palestine, Persia and Armenia all succumbed to the Arabs.

When the Mongol forces disintegrated, only the horror of their excesses was remembered: they left no language and no culture. The Arabs created brilliant civilizations across the world from the Taj Mahal to the Alhambra. And just as the language of a tiny island, Britain, was to spread far and wide, so too did Arabic, the dialect of the desert *bedu*.

- - - - - - - - - - - - - - - - -

Since the dawn of civilization trade between the West and the mysterious East had been monopolized by seafarers, Phoenicians and Muscat Arabs, and the keystone of their commerce was incense, primarily *olibanum*, or frankincense. Historians initially believed that this scented gum originated from Somaliland and the Hadhramaut. But recent research has shown that, while frankincense trees were indeed abundant in both countries, the one and only source of superior-quality frankincense was Dhofar. The guardians of the frankincense orchards possessed a monopoly on a commodity, more valuable even than gold, which for six thousand years provoked an insatiable worldwide demand.

My early, superficial studies led me to the ready conclusion that some fabulously wealthy city was likely to have existed, because of the inescapable need for a watering place for the thousands of men and beasts involved in transporting frankincense from Dhofar to the northern markets.

Historians stress that the incense travelled from Dhofar by sea and by land. The ocean routes were at risk from storms and pirates while the desert trails involved passage through different tribal lands, with middlemen levying taxes all the way. The routes that were chronicled in greatest detail all led west from Dhofar's northern borders into Yemen, and this made me conclude that Nashran's missing incense city, Ubar, must lie on or close to that border. Somewhere there was, or once had been, a great deal more water than might be drawn from a single desert well.

In the month of fasting, Ramadan, which fell in December that year, my reconnaissance platoon was posted to the north of the Dhofar mountains and for some months my work was interrupted by no contact with other Army units. Indeed there was nobody in all the land between Yemen, the Sands and northern Oman save for ourselves and the wandering *bedu*. With six Land Rovers and a thousand miles of desert to our northern flank, I was superbly positioned to search for Ubar.

My only problem was the regimental CO, Colonel Peter Thwaites, a Grenadier Guards officer who worked from Umm al Ghawarif, our Salalah headquarters, but was wont to involve himself personally in the operations of his sub-units. He would not, I realized, look kindly on his most mobile force disappearing from operational duties on what Americans called a boondoggle, an unproductive jaunt on the company payroll.

At the time Colonel Thwaites had me on a very loose rein and, apart from the unpredictable need to respond to sudden emergency operations, I had only to block enemy incursions to the north of the mountains. So long as I maintained a strong force under my sergeant in the danger zone and remained in radio contact with headquarters in Salalah, I reasoned that nobody would be unduly concerned. In retrospect, I realize that I felt very guilty, and for many years told nobody of my irresponsible course of action. Had I acted in such a way during, say, the First World War the penalty – for what was, after all, desertion – would have been the firing squad. In my present role as a soldier of the Sultan, I might merely have received a reprimand. However, earlier my pistol had been stolen in camp and I was warned by the Commander of the Sultan's Armed Forces, Brigadier Coran Purdon, that any future black mark would mean my removal from the army.

Furthermore, only weeks before I had come within an ace of heavy censure from on high. I had received a signal from headquarters ordering a search for tracks in the waterless wastes to the south-east of Habarut, our only garrison on the Yemeni border. A camel train carrying arms was expected to cross from Yemen in the near future. If we found any likely infiltration trail, we were to ambush it.

From Habarut a maze of deep valleys zigzag southwards, chasms in a moonscape of nameless escarpments. Travelling in dust and blinding sunlight and never certain that our vehicles were following a gainful route, since so many valleys were sheer-sided culs-de-sac, I selected a major valley which my map called Wadi Sheetah. Caching all but the lightest equipment, we bounced our way into a trackless nothingness plagued by wide rifts of soft sand.

After two days, with a couple of the vehicles still serviceable, we came to a place of white boulders that blocked further progress. There had been no sign of a camel trail, so I decided to advance on foot. Filling our waterbags we moved south-west for six hours until, at noon on the third day, a ridge of high ground revealed a great valley that curved south to the distant Qamr mountains. No camel could cross such an obstacle, I felt certain. We turned back.

Two *bedu* goat herders intercepted us and from them I learnt our exact location, the Wadi Deefan, well into enemy territory. Since the Sultan had given the strictest orders against any form of border incursion, not wishing to provoke the Yemeni government, I was thoroughly alarmed and withdrew with some haste. All the same, on the principle of 'out of sight, out of mind', and having got away with this incursion, I felt relatively safe in making an exploratory foray into the Sands to the north of our patrol zone.

Leaving all but seven men under the able command of my sergeant, I took two Land Rovers to the well of Tudho, where we filled all our water containers. We then drove north through gravel deserts once we had left the main track running east to Thamrait, our rest-base at a deserted oil camp. Travelling to the eastern flank of the Wadi Aydim, a dry watercourse with many reaches of soft sand, we came to the wreck of a Dodge power-wagon. My Omani corporal explained that this had been destroyed by the Sultan's Forces in 1965 when Musallim bin Nuffl, the original leader of the Dhofari insurgents, had crossed the Sands from Saudi Arabia with four Dodges loaded with men and arms. 'This place is called Qafa,' he said, with a gesture that embraced the entire visible landscape.

My map, originally surveyed by the oil prospectors of the 1950s, showed an oil camp, now abandoned, some forty miles to the north. For two days we struggled across the Wadi al Atinah after losing an originally promising camel trail. Thrice one or both of the vehicles became enmired in soft sand or stretches of *sabkha*, a chalky layer of powder often hidden beneath the gravel crust.

I nursed a growing fear of a breakdown which could only be repaired by signalling for some spare part to be parachuted to us from the Sultan's Beaver. One vehicle could tow another in most places but certainly not through the many difficult areas we had already crossed. To call for any assistance would reveal to my colonel that we were miles from any zone that I could find a reasonable excuse to patrol.

By the time we came to Fasad, two burst tyres and one split half-shaft to the north-east from Qafa, I gave myself at most two more days' outward travel before it would be sensible to turn back. My sergeant had confirmed that all was well with the main body of the platoon, but a further six days without some form of emergency call was a lot to hope for.

As we left the scattered shacks of Fasad, a place of wind and spiders, my sense of guilt increased, but so did my curiosity. We were now within forty easy miles of the Wadi Mitan, the only place-name Nashran had identified in association with the lost city.

I wished above all else that Nashran was with us, for he would have known where to locate a *bedu* with knowledge of these parts. As it was, we had seen not a soul, not even a camel, since leaving Tudho.

From Fasad, using the sun and the passage of time, we headed due west wherever the terrain allowed and, after twenty-four miles of largely flat, stony plain, passed over a dozen or so well-trodden camel trails. 'Very old,' the men in my vehicle commented, nodding sagely. I had the idea that no member of the platoon was particularly desert-wise but I may have been wrong. Their heads were all mummy-wrapped in green Arab headcloths from which only their dark eyes emerged, their eyelashes dusted with white *sabkha*. They were all quite unconcerned as to whether or not we traced the lost city, being happy simply to be free of their habitual fear of landmines and ambush. My own fear of discovery by the authorities did not touch them. In a narrow defile, which my Baluchi driver Murad had unwisely entered by way of an intended short cut, we lost another half-shaft and replaced it with our only remaining spare. This was especially worrying, since the same was likely to happen again, given the difficult country we were expecting. While wisdom dictated an immediate return, the Wadi Mitan had a powerful allure.

Late on the third day from Qafa we reached the wadi and crossed it, after dark, at a point where the sand and the scrub of low saltbushes stretched for nearly a mile to the far bank and a firmer surface.

The men, mostly Kolbani tribesmen from the Jebel Akhdar in northern Oman, lit a fire of *hatab*, the dead wood to be had in every wadi bed, and prepared our supper from rice and a goat which Murad selected and killed from the half dozen which travelled with us live. Everybody made a great pre-dinner clatter, with much slapping of rifle butts and hearty laughter.

After the meal, eaten as usual in groups squatting round two large tin dishes, one of the Kolbani began to sing a long and tuneless dirge. Others followed suit and from time to time, by chance, achieved a sort of harmony. I had never seen them so full of the joys of life, but then any chit-chat above a low whisper was expressly forbidden in our operational camps.

In the morning Murad shook me awake with a mug of tea and a fried chapatti. '*Bedu*,' he said, nodding to the east. We walked over a hillock and were greeted by two old Rashidi. They shook the hand of my corporal and then mine, Christians being at the bottom of the social pecking order. Their women and children watched from close by and chattered excitedly among themselves. They were abjectly poor yet seemed happy enough. The older man offered us camel's milk, which we drank, warm and topped with a head of frothy scum, from a battered alloy bowl.

After extended greetings, the corporal asked if either man knew of a lost city named Ubar. A terrific babble ensued, joined by the womenfolk, and the elder Rashidi at length gave us a distilled version of all the family input. I understood very little and judged that my corporal, from the intensity of his frown, was making as heavy weather as would a Cockney listening to a tale of folklore from a toothless Devon farmer.

We thanked the Rashidi and, ignoring their protests that they lacked for nothing, left them a sack of flour and replenishment for their water carriers: the crudely modified inner tubes of tyres probably obtained from a mined and abandoned army truck.

The Rashidi did not know Ubar's location but they knew a man who did. He was a relation who could be found at or near the head of the Wadi Jadileh, less than two days by camel to the west.

I resolved to turn back after one more day's search whether or not we found a guide to Ubar. It was already likely to prove highly embarrassing if an order should arrive requiring instant reaction by the platoon.

Murad halted at midday in a dry watercourse with a pleasant bower of tamarisk giving shade and the sound of sieved desert breeze. We ate tuna fish on dry biscuits. These were timeless British Army biscuits available in two types, Biscuits Plain or Biscuits Sweet. There was absolutely no detectable difference in taste or texture between them, but the soldiers managed nonetheless to argue heatedly over their respective merits.

Among my companions a certain interest had begun to stir as to the reason for our northerly excursion. The corporal, in relating the Rashidi's comments on Ubar, had sparked his comrades' curiosity and now, when I announced we must turn back on the morrow, there was an immediate show of disappointment.

'But Bakhait,' they cried, using the nickname they favoured when away from an official atmosphere, 'we have come a long way and the city is made of gold. We must press on.'

That evening, after four hours of easy driving over a shiny black stone waste, we reached the Wadi Jadileh and followed its course with the orange glimmer of distant sand dunes closing in across our northern horizon. When the wadi petered out into a low pan of *sabkha*, there was no longer anywhere specific to head for. A needle in a haystack would have been as easy to find as Rashidi somewhere in the sands of the Rub al Khali, the Empty Quarter.

CHAPTER TWO

My first attempt to find Ubar failed dismally, but the lesson was well learnt: I would never again head for the Sands without a guide. Unable to locate the Rashidi or anyone else at the head of the Wadi Jabreen, we returned, luckily without further breakdowns, to our patrol zones further south.

We laid ambushes, constantly changing areas in order to confuse the enemy and so avoid counter-ambush. For every successful operation there were many wasted days: for every minute of sudden terror, of bullets, explosions and dead men, there were hours of waiting with the crawling flies and the sticky heat of the *nej'd*, the gravel wasteland between the plains and the mountains.

A venerable leather suitcase travelled in my Land Rover and, wherever our mobile rear base happened to be, I immersed myself in the books I had brought with me, some on extended loan from the library of the Royal Geographical Society. I learnt that Ubar was not merely a figment of the imagination of Nashran and his *bedu* kinsfolk; nor was I the first to search for its location.

The first geographers to map the Arabian Peninsula were based in Alexandria, and using information received from merchants and seafarers they produced treatises giving the positions of the main Arab cities and trade centres. By AD 200 Alexandrian professors had recorded the existence of a major market town well into the region now known as the Empty Quarter, the greatest sand desert in the world. They located this entrepôt in the lands of the Iôbaritae, close to the Sachalitae (men of Salalah Plain), and gave it the name Omanum Emporion, meaning 'coastal market centre of Oman'. This was the first time the word Oman had appeared in writing: until then most references to the country used the Persian name Mazun.

The Qur'an (Koran) was written some four centuries later and mentioned neither Ubar nor Omanum Emporion (later Latinized into Emporium). The word of God, as passed on by the Prophet Muhammad in the Qur'an, told of desert cities whose inhabitants had behaved badly and as a result incurred the wrath of God. These doomed cities were named as Thamud, Ophir, Ad and Irem. The locations of the first three were clearly not in Oman but Irem's identity, past or present, was unknown. The Prophet, in the Qu'ran's Chapter of the Dawn, stated that Irem was destroyed in the same way as Ad. 'Irem of the columns, the like of which has not been created in the land' is the exact Quranic description.

The tenth book of Genesis gives the names of the original rulers of Arabia and states that Joktan occupied the south-western region, while his cousin Ad settled to the east between the Empty Quarter and the Indian Ocean. King Ad's son, Shedad, according to *bedu* legends, written and spoken, built Irem in a fertile area of the desert where he attempted to imitate the wealth and splendour of Paradise.

At the time of the Norman Conquest of England, the Arab historian al-Himyari wrote: 'Wabar is the name of the land which belonged to Ad in the eastern parts of Yemen and which is today an untrodden waste owing to the drying up of the desert. There are to be found in it great buildings which the wind has smothered in sand.'

During the First World War, T.E. Lawrence (Lawrence of Arabia) urged the Air Ministry to route the R101 airship, Britain's answer to the Germans' Zeppelins, over the Arabian Empty Quarter *en route* for India, the intended goal of its maiden voyage. He stressed the publicity advantages to be gained through crossing over one of the last unexplored parts of the world.

When the traveller Raymond O'Shea visited T.E. Lawrence in 1934 at Clouds Hill, his Dorset retreat, E.T. Shaw, as Lawrence then called himself, said he was intensely interested in the legend of the lost city reputed to exist in the middle of the Rub al Khali. 'I am convinced that the remains of an ancient Arab civilization are to be found in that desert,' he told O'Shea. 'I have been told by the Arabs that the ruined castles of the great King Ad, son of Kin'ad, have been seen by wandering tribes in the region of Wabar. There is always some substance in these Arab tales.'

Lawrence's desert deeds inspired many of his countrymen of later generations, two of whom, not much younger than himself, were to bring Ubar to the attention of the public in the West for the first time.

Bertram Sidney Thomas, an administrator in Palestine, was selected by the Sultan of Muscat in 1925 as his personal financial adviser. Oman was then a forbidden place for foreigners, especially Christians, and only a handful had penetrated even the edge of the great deserts of the Interior. Thomas's dream was to cross the length of the Empty Quarter from south to north and he discussed his plans in secret with the Sultan's heir, Said bin Taimur. No one else knew of his intentions when he slipped aboard a dhow that took him from Muscat to Salalah and, in the closing days of 1930, he set out with Murra and Rashidi guides into the great and waterless unknown.

The subsequent nine-hundred-mile camel journey took Thomas fifty-eight days. He received the personal congratulations of King George V, the Founder's Medal of the Royal Geographical Society and the eternal chagrin of Mr H. St J.B. Philby, the father of one of Britain's better-known spies. Philby senior was an adviser to His Majesty King Abdul Aziz of the Saudis and, with a secrecy equal to that of Thomas, had for a dozen years nurtured the grail of being the first non-Arab to cross the Empty Quarter.

When he heard of Thomas's successful traverse he was so upset that he spoke to nobody for a week. Nonetheless, a year later, he made the crossing from east to west by a far more difficult route, during which he claimed the discovery of Wabar.

In the debating forums of the Royal Geographical Society and the editorial pages of the *Journal of the Central Asian Society*, the two explorers exchanged terse letters on various differences of opinion. What seemed to especially niggle both men was the name used by the other for the lost city.

Philby, who favoured Wabar, wrote: 'Who can have a better claim to know how the word was spelt than myself, for I have actually been there?'

Thomas, who described Ubar as the 'Atlantis of the Sands', pointed out that Ubar was in south Arabia, a region never reached by Philby and one where every member of every tribe he had met used the term Ubar and had never heard of Wabar. Thomas had unearthed evidence indicating that the lost Quranic city was well into the southern reaches of the Empty Quarter.

Philby's Wabar was a legend among the northern *bedu* and Ibn Jiluwi, the influential governor of Al-Hasa, the stepping-stone to the Empty Quarter, told Philby's appointed deputies that they must, on the king's orders, take him to Wabar.

On reaching Jabreen oasis on the northern fringe of the Sands, Philby was told local legends of how King Ad of Wabar had attacked Jabreen from the south and destroyed the village. Heading into the Sands, Philby believed he would locate Wabar at or close by to a desert well named Umm al Hadid (Mother of Iron).

When, in 1918, Philby had first been told of Wabar, his informant described a great 'piece of iron' in the Sands and he had taken this to refer to some as yet unburied statue. Ali, one of his guides, described ruins with 'walls as of castles'. The search ended at a 'low line of ruins riding upon a wave of the yellow sands'. Philby wrote:

I looked down not upon the ruins of an ancient city but into the mouth of a volcano whose twin craters, half filled with drifted sand lay surrounded by lava outpoured from the bowels of the earth . . . I knew not whether to laugh or cry but was strangely fascinated by a scene that had shattered the dreams of years. So this was Wabar! A volcano in the desert and on it built the story of a city destroyed by fire from heaven . . . So far as I was concerned the search for Wabar was over. I could now honourably bequeath the task to my successors – to younger men or women who may not be deterred by my barren search for the fabled ruins.

Philby further concluded:

There is little likelihood of ancient ruins being found anywhere in the *Rub al Khali*. I think it has been unsuitable for human occupation except by nomads since long before the beginning of civilization . . . What then of the legend? So far as the *Rub al Khali* is concerned, it is a myth and no more. We must seek elsewhere the site that gave rise to it . . . The spade may yet disclose the identity and history of Ad.

The passage of time cannot have dulled Philby's fascination with the lost city since in London in the early 1960s, by which time his son was a KGB general in Moscow, he told the American explorer Wendell Phillips that he believed: 'Wabar and Ubar both refer to the same ancient city of tradition which still remains to be discovered.'

Bertram Thomas's answer to Philby's Wabar discovery was well reasoned:

The tradition of Ubar – a golden city lying beneath the sands – was told to me not in answer to my enquiries but as a spontaneous outburst on passing definite archaeological remains of extensive caravan tracks leading straight into the great southern bulwark of the sands.

It is clear that this may be said in favour of a *southern* site for a buried city, if such exists, that the *deepest* sands are in the south . . . They are comparatively shallow near Philby's site, where nonetheless no trace of any exposed building was found. As a discovery of great scientific importance and interest, I envy and applaud Philby's find but, as the site of Ubar, it is a mirage!

Thomas disagreed with Philby's understanding of Wabar as a lost city. He emphasized that Wabar, like Ad and Thamud, was the name for an entire region and for the tribe that dwelt there. He also chided Philby over his dutiful translation of biblical folklore into real and acceptable historical data.

According to the Bible, there was a great flood which destroyed all of humanity except for Noah and his three sons. The first son, Shem, fathered the Arab (Semitic) race through his descendants, including Joktan and Abraham. The second son, Ham, was responsible for the African races and Japheth, the third son, for everybody else. Thomas suggested that all this was unscientific hogwash, and merely a primitive attempt by the Bible's writers to present history in an intelligible, readable fashion.

Thomas himself never found ruins that he claimed were Ubar but, somewhere west of the Wadi Mitan in 1930, one of his guides had shouted: 'Look, there is the road to Ubar.' Thomas described the feature as 'well-worn tracks, about a hundred yards in cross section and graven in the Plain.'

Four years after Philby's great journey the inimitable traveller and writer Freya Stark met the Yemeni Sultan of Qatn, who told her: 'Wabar is a deserted city which spirits took over when Ad and Thamud were destroyed. It lies between Hadhramaut and Oman.' Freya Stark pointed out that Arab geographers had variously situated Wabar inside Yemen, between Yemen and Jabreen, between Najran, Shis'r and Mahra, between Shis'r and Sanaa and in numerous other locations. 'With such evidence,' she concluded, 'it seems quite possible for Mr Thomas and Mr Philby *each* to find Wabar in an opposite corner of Arabia.'

After the Wabar searches of Thomas and Philby fourteen years elapsed before another explorer penetrated the Sands. Wilfred Thesiger, born in Ethiopia in 1910, had served with the Sudan Political Service until, following the outbreak of war in 1939, he soldiered in Syria, Abyssinia and, with the SAS, in the Western Desert. At Oxford he read *Arabia Felix* by Bertram Thomas and *Revolt in the Desert* by T.E. Lawrence. He began to dream of the Empty Quarter, of the *bedu* way of life, and so joined the Middle East Anti-Locust Unit purely as a means to enter Dhofar with some sort of official blessing.

Two years later, by dint of arduous camel journeys, he had achieved two crossings of the Empty Quarter and seen more of the Sands than any man alive. Of lost cities he had found no sign but, in the southern Aradh region of Saudi Arabia, local tribesmen told him of the ruins of Ad. They were convinced that the city had been 'destroyed by God for arrogance', as related in the Qur'an. Thesiger's chief guide told him that the ruins were definitely buried in the sands to the north of Habarut, naming an oasis astride the Omani–Yemeni border. There were, he said, many clearly defined camel trails that had once led to the city and they all converged on the Sands at its site.

The same story of ancient trails was prevalent nine hundred miles away at the other end of the Empty Quarter. In Kuwait in 1943 the Arabist Colonel H.R.P. Dickson made enquiries about King Ad of Ubar and was told by Murra tribesmen that many tracks from the old times still ran through the Sands, being especially visible in rocky areas, and that all of them led to the buried city.

In 1953, five years after Thesiger's Dhofar-based travels, the American oilman and archaeologist Wendell Phillips travelled one hundred miles inland from Salalah to the only permanent watering place in the central steppes, the well of Shis'r. Thence, with three vehicles, Bait Kathir guides and the blessing of Sultan bin Taimur, he crossed the Wadi Mitan and, travelling along the rim of the Sands of Mitan, which form an outcrop of dunes to the south of the Empty Quarter proper, he spotted what he believed to be the tracks that Thomas had reported in 1930. Phillips's description was the more detailed: 'Rows of parallel tracks incised deep in the hard surface and covered with glazed pebbles. I counted eighty-four such tracks running side by side.'

I realized that my own unauthorized and feeble excursion had crossed the Wadi Mitan some fourteen miles to the south of Phillips's sighting. Next time, I resolved, I would repeat his route and approach the Mitan from Shis'r instead of Qafa.

Wendell Phillips, while working in Dhofar in 1955, had met a guide from the Bait Imani tribe who showed him shards of pottery found in the great dunes five days by camel to the west of Shis'r. Again the Sultan bade Phillips find the city, so, with sixteen companions and five days' supplies, the party headed west from Shis'r. They used aerial photographs to navigate the Wadis Ghadun and Atinah and then the Bait Imani took over. Phillips's descriptions of quite where the party then travelled are vague and they do not appear ever to have left the Wadi Atinah. At some point, presumably to the north-west of the wadi, they picked up the ancient trail and followed it north-north-west for four miles into the dunes.

The Sultan had loaned Phillips a number of his beefy slaves, whose strength allowed the three vehicles a certain amount of progress in the soft sand. But not for long: the following morning and probably no more than a mile or two into the dune belt, the expedition turned back. Phillips summarized thus:

> The mystery of Ubar remains unsolved. In a completely inaccessible area where today there is little or no camel traffic, a well-marked highway centuries old, made by thousands of camel caravans, leads west for many miles from the famous spice lands of Dhofar and then, on a bearing of N75°W, mysteriously disappears without a trace in the great sands. A dozen Ubars could well be lost among these high dunes, unknown even to the present day bedu. I firmly believe some day some explorer will solve the mystery of Ubar, Arabia's most intriguing lost city.

CHAPTER THREE

Late in 1968 my regiment was recalled to northern Oman and, while on leave in Africa, I led a six-man expedition to ascend the White Nile, a tributary of the longest river in the world, from mouth to source. We used two-seater hovercraft and encountered all manner of problems in Egypt, Sudan, and especially within the Sudd Swamps, where a war raged between the Muslim government troops and the Christian–pagan amalgamation of southern rebels.

The three-thousand-mile journey began in Alexandria, situated at the western mouth of the Nile and for two thousand years the greatest city of Egypt and the centre of world commerce. Under the Ptolemies the sciences thrived as never before, based within the Alexandrian Library where, luckily for subsequent scholars, the Ptolemaic historians determined to record what they could about Arabia.

Without the sages of Alexandria, no references to Omanum Emporion or the Iôbaritae would exist to confirm the oral legends of the *bedu*. Ptolemy has these Iôbaritae as neighbours of the Sachalitae (of the Plain of Salalah). In the game of jumping to conclusions this suggests that Ubar is close to Salalah. Although Hellenistic Alexandrian science was gradually eroded, enough survived to establish at least a skeletal framework of Oman's history.

Even the most learned of modern archaeologists needs an all-embracing knowledge of human history if he or she is to make worthwhile discoveries in any part of the world. Cambridge University PhD and archaeologist Paul Bahn, author of *Images of the Iron Age*, dispensed with the standard humbug of his profession when he wrote:

Archaeology is like a vast and fiendish jigsaw puzzle invented by the devil as an instrument of torment since:
   a) it will never be finished

b) you don't know how many pieces are missing

c) most of them are lost forever

d) you cannot cheat by looking at the picture.

Much of the time, archaeological evidence is so patchy that anyone's guess is as valid as anyone else's. You cannot prove anything. Where the remote past is concerned, nobody *knows* what took place. The best that can be offered is an informed guess . . . Some eminent archaeologists have built their entire careers upon convincing bluff.

To locate a lost city that might have been the key to the routing of Oman's most valuable commodity over a period of six thousand years or more could involve a search for clues to be found within the annals of Oman, her neighbours and her various conquerors. If Ubar were to prove merely a myth I would be surprised, since references to its existence have kept recurring over a period of more than fifteen hundred years. Before that there were excellent reasons why outsiders were purposely kept in the dark as to the secrets of Arabia. The Arabs were well aware that their geographical position astride the trade routes of the world was the key to their wealth. They did not intend to give up the sources of their riches by allowing access to trade routes or information about the locations of key commodities inside Arabia or in the Far East. The main threat to their monopoly came from the Greeks and the Romans.

Around 5000 BC Mesopotamia and Egypt were the earliest seats of civilization. Pagan burials in both centres created a huge demand for spices, incense and slaves. Around 6000 BC the Arabian Peninsula was too hot and arid for human habitation, so 5000 BC can be taken as the dawn of world trade.

It is probable that much of the Gulf and eastern Arabian trade was conducted by Indian vessels. In the interior of Arabia, Arab writers distinguish between an indigenous population called the genuine (Ariba) tribes and Arabicized tribes claiming descent from Ishmael. These latter would have included the Thamud, the Ad and the Wabariti, all of whom built cities in southern Arabia which, according to the Qur'an, were destroyed by God.

According to the Old Testament, the Ariba tribes inhabited the peninsula before Ishmael was thrown out into the desert on the birth of Isaac. The discovery of Ubar could well reveal what happened to them and help establish the historical identity of today's Dhofari tribes. For example, perhaps the people of

Ad, whose prophet Hud is still venerated at his tomb in the Hadhramaut, are one and the same as the modern Shahra tribe.

At about the time Rome was established, in the eighth century BC, the Joktanite Yarabi conquered the Joktanite Azdites. The great grandson of the first Yarab chief was named Himyar and his dynasty ruled the southern coastal districts of Arabia from Yemen to Muscat until the time of the Prophet, the seventh century AD. This Himyarite dynasty gave way from time to time to a number of Persian invaders, including Cyrus the Great.

At some stage the seafarers lost their monopoly on trade, owing to the opening of land routes, where goods were not endangered by storms or pirates, and the book of Genesis establishes that by 2000 BC caravans traversed Arabia with supplies for Egypt.

As early as 500 BC the Persian Gulf route began to lose trade to merchants using the Red Sea route up the west coast of Yemen, despite the vigorous attempts by Babylonians such as King Nebuchadnezzar, around 561 BC, to attack Red Sea centres and thereby retain the Mesopotamian monopoly.

If, throughout all the early years, Oman had been able to transport Indian goods overland towards Egypt she would have gained far greater power and wealth. Historians believe that the great sand deserts to her west isolated her and made such trade impractical. Any discovery of a major Omani trading city on the edge of the Empty Quarter – Ubar or otherwise – would add a new dimension to such reasoning.

When the Mesopotamian dominance waned, Omani trade and wealth followed suit. Through the millennium of Roman and Greek power, the advent of Jesus Christ and until the rise of Islam, Oman's documented history is only fragmentary. The only useful records, following Alexander the Great's conquest of Egypt in the third century BC, come from the scientists of Alexandria.

When Alexander died, one of his generals, Ptolemy, made himself king of Egypt in 304 BC. His family ruled Egypt until the last Ptolemy, the son of Queen Cleopatra, died in 30 BC. The first three Ptolemies encouraged Greco-Egyptian science and art and these were centralized in a museum and library established in Alexandria which can aptly be described as the first university in the world.

With the departure of the Ptolemies, Egypt became part of the Roman Empire and so added, to the caravan routes already won in Syria and Asia Minor, the direct sea route to the Far East via the Ptolemies' Red Sea outposts. The centre of world trade quickly shifted from Alexandria to Rome, but not the centre of learning. Among the many sages who were involved with work centred in Alexandria were Euclid, Eratosthenes, Archimedes, Apollonius, Hipparchus, Agatharchides, Artemidorus, Strabo and Ptolemy.

The latter, Claudius Ptolemy, unrelated to the kings of that name, was an Egyptian astronomer and cartographer from Alexandria who, among many other great works, produced his *Geography* in AD 150. This was the first attempt to map the then known world, giving locations based on observation of the sun's altitude. Ptolemy's *Geocentric World System* was accepted throughout the world for fourteen centuries and his *Almagest*, giving the theory for the movement of heavenly bodies, was only outdated by Copernicus in 1543.

Much of Ptolemy's information, apart from facts learned from his Alexandria Library predecessors, came from the many famous sailors and merchants who visited Alexandria. Ptolemy recognized that such sources were subject to inbuilt error. He wrote: 'the merchant class are only intent on their business and have little interest in exploration and that often, through their love of boasting, they magnify distances'. Nevertheless Ptolemy gave the world its first inkling of knowledge of a previously unknown geography.

The western powers, Greek and Roman alike, craved to trade direct with the Far Eastern sources of the expensive commodities for which they provided a bottomless market. But the Arabs zealously discouraged the dissemination of any information that might break their grasp on the trade.

Around AD 60 an unnamed ship's captain wrote a maritime log, known to historians as the *Periplus of the Erythraean Sea*, describing his voyage between Roman Egypt and India and this gave the West its first good description of the southern Arabian incense coast.

Some intelligence had also been gained from a Roman expedition under General Aelius Gallus whose legions, in 25 BC, had marched down the arid coastal reaches of western Arabia almost to within reach of Marib, the legendary seat of the Queen of Sheba. Running short of supplies, the Romans retreated but coastal information derived from their sortie may have helped subsequent voyages such as that by the famous Greek captain Hippalus to navigate all the way to the spice ports of India. This, for the first time, would have cut out the Arab traders and their Persian Gulf route.

Great shifts in national power followed the new trading patterns set by the *Periplus* and Hippalus voyages and altered the subsequent history of Oman.

Legend relates that the fabulously wealthy Queen of Sheba, around 930 BC,

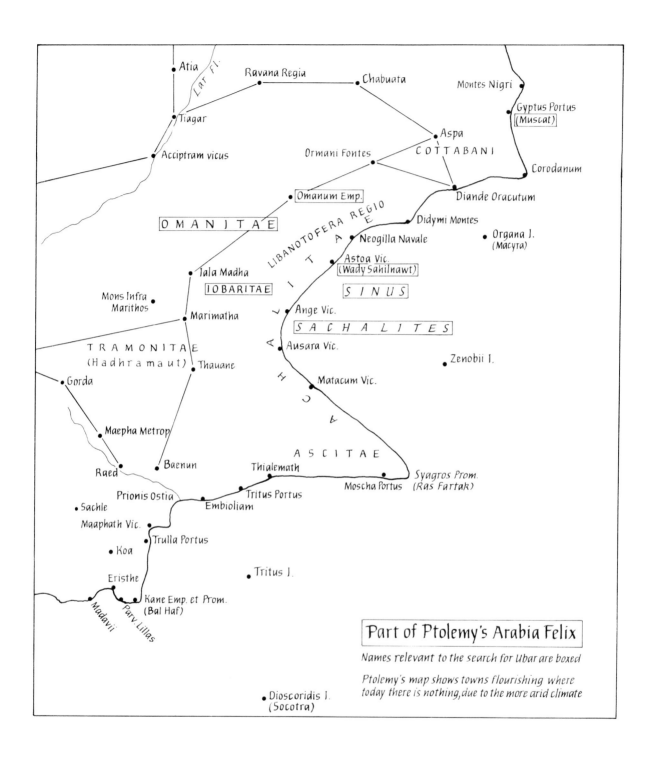

Atia

Lar Fl.

Ravana Regia

Chabuata

Montes Nigri

Gyptus Portus
(Muscat)

Tiagar

Acciptram vicus

Ormani Fontes

Aspa

COTTABANI

Corodanum

Omanum Emp.

Diande Oracutum

OMANITAE

LIBANOTOFERA REGIO

Didymi Montes

Neogilla Navale

Organa I.
(Macyra)

Astoa Vic.
(Wady Sahilnawt)

Jala Madha

IOBARITAE

SINUS

Mons Infra
Marithos

Ange Vic.

Marimatha

SACHALITES

TRAMONITAE
(Hadhramaut)

Ausara Vic.

Zenobii I.

Thauane

Matacum Vic.

Gorda

Maepha Metrop

ASCITAE

Raed

Baenun

Thialemath

Syagros Prom.
(Ras Fartak)

Prionis Ostia

Tritus Portus

Moscha Portus

Sachle

Embioliam

Maaphath Vic.

Trulla Portus

Koa

Tritus I.

Eristhe

Kane Emp. et Prom.
(Bal Haf)

Madavii

Parv. Lillas

Part of Ptolemy's Arabia Felix

Names relevant to the search for Ubar are boxed

Ptolemy's map shows towns flourishing where
today there is nothing, due to the more arid climate

Dioscoridis I.
(Socotra)

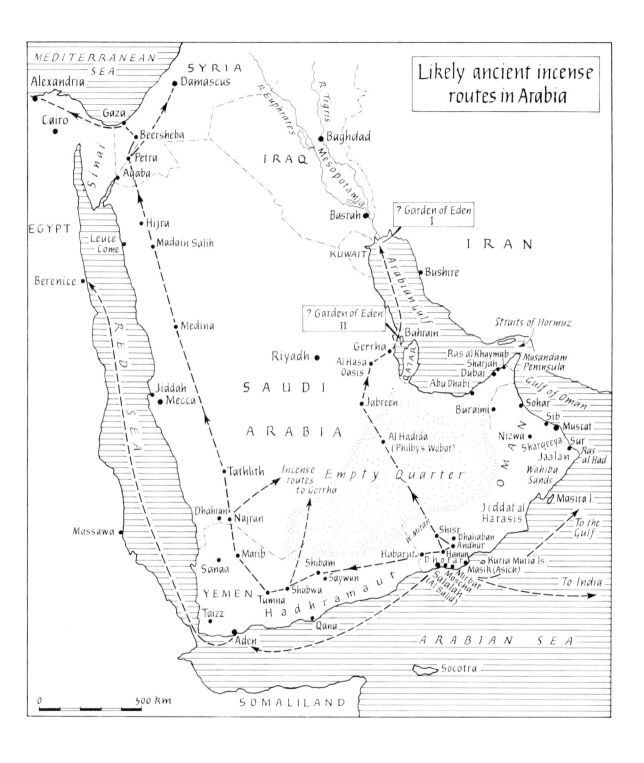

Likely ancient incense routes in Arabia

left her capital of Marib in Yemen to visit King Solomon, son of David, third monarch of Israel and builder of the famous Temple in Jerusalem.

The land of Sheba may indeed have been the south Arabian incense kingdom referred to in the biblical Book of Ezekiel *or* the more northerly Sheba referred to in Genesis. In the sixth century BC a great Yemeni engineering feat raised a six-hundred-yard-long dam, one hundred and twenty feet high at its centre, across a storm wadi. Allied sluices and irrigation systems allowed a rich agricultural community to thrive and the local Azdites were able to subjugate the entire south Arabian incense trade for many centuries.

Between the third and fifth centuries AD new Persian invasions into what is now Syria and Saudi Arabia unsettled the inhabitants, the Adnanis, who emigrated to Oman, where they were to clash in bitter civil wars with the Azdites until the present century.

Until the advent of Islam in the seventh century AD, Omanis and Yemenis had mostly practised stellar worship, although in coastal towns and trading centres there were many Jews, Christians, Brahmins and Hindus.

Stellar worship involved the heavenly bodies, natural features such as prominent rocks or trees and certain animals, while each family had their own house-angels, through whom they prayed to the supreme God. They practised trial by oath, circumcized their children and sometimes buried girl babies alive. All these things disappeared as Islam spread slowly but surely through the veins of Oman. Over the following centuries the religion and culture of Islam were consolidated and successive waves of invaders, notably Persians, Turks and Portuguese, repulsed.

- - - - - - - - - - - - - - - -

In 1968, when I first arrived in Oman, the Sultanate began to receive oil revenues, at which point the British Government cancelled their centuries-old agreement to provide free assistance in times of trouble. From that time loaned equipment or personnel had to be paid for, but the Sultanate revenues, £2 million a month, were insufficient to stave off the Marxist takeover of Dhofar which, in the pre-monsoon months of 1969, seemed imminent.

When I returned from my leave spent hovercrafting up the Nile, Colonel Thwaites gave me instructions to ambush the foothills region of the Salalah Plain in an attempt to hinder the infiltration of camel trains loaded with Marxist weapons.

The fabulous lost city of Ubar as imagined by Dulac in the illustrated Arabian Nights. *Ubar's legendary demise parallels that of Sodom.*

During Thomas's 1931 crossing of the Empty Quarter, the explorer discovered important clues in the search for Ubar.

Bertram Thomas with his exploration team prepare to venture into the Empty Quarter in 1931.
MAIN PICTURE: *The great dunes of the Uruq al Hadh in the Empty Quarter as Thomas saw them in 1931.*

Charles Weston-Baker, a rival to the author in his search for Ubar, seeks the lost city from a balloon.

His Majesty Sultan Qaboos bin Said, Sultan of Oman, in the early 1970s. The Sultan assumed power in 1970, after a bloodless coup.

Omani girls in ceremonial dress.

A Kathir family in a dry valley of the nej'd.

A plains woman of the Bait Tabawq.

Jebalis, *mountain tribesmen on the Plain of Salalah.*

The Nasser al Bahr, *a formidable component of the navy of Sultan Said bin Taimur.*

The author, who served with the Sultan's Armed Forces in the late 1960s, with part of the Reconnaissance Platoon at Thamrait.

On the secret route we discovered from Thamrait to Ayun, we had to bring the big guns up an improvised ramp.

Four Strikemaster jets of the Sultan's Air Force patrol the skies over the western edge of Dhofar's Salalah Plain.

A position held by the Sultan's Armed Forces in western Dhofar comes under attack.

A sandstorm threatens Thamrait.

LEFT: *The Intelligence agent Said bin Ghia, of the powerful Bait Qatan tribe, was a great asset in covert operations against guerillas in the desert, because of his extensive knowledge of the area.* RIGHT: *Hamid, one of the Reconnaissance Platoon's machine-gunners.*

The pools of Ayun. The water, we were to discover, led to Ubar.

The fast-moving hooded malpolen, one of the many species of snake indigenous to Dhofar.

The lethal and extremely aggressive carpet viper is found in large numbers in Dhofar.

Prized at the table in Dhofar is the dhab *lizard of the* nej'd, *the gravel wasteland.*

The common Dhofar chameleon.

The common Dhofar scorpion.

A scorpion with its young at Thamrait.

A male wolf spider photographed at the excavation of the Oracle of Diana. It is poisonous and has two fangs under its head.

The camel spider can inflict an impressive bite and eats flesh.

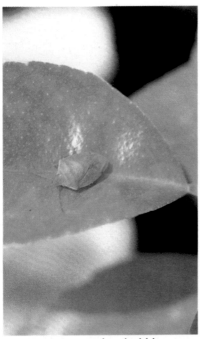

An encounter with a shield bug can result in a painful bite.

The mantis occurs throughout the mountains and the plains of Dhofar. This is a young specimen.

An unidentified species of large moth found at Thamrait.

A delicate butterfly found in the nej'd.

The great danger of ambushing, as many Sultanate officers had learnt to their cost, was the inherent risk of counter-ambush. The slightest error of judgement, poor navigation by night or noise and movement by a careless soldier could give away the platoon's presence in the enemy-held mountains.

The Colonel accompanied me on a three-day mountain ambush above Taqa and saw for himself how easily things could go wrong. A *bedu* goatherd chanced upon us deep in the mountainside undergrowth and, before we could seize the man, he yodelled, ostensibly to his goats but more probably to local enemy patrols. The following day we withdrew silently from our positions but on reaching the open 'killing ground' beneath, we were subjected to intense automatic fire from our own previous redoubt. Only luck and instant reaction from covering machine-guns averted a disaster, but we had long since counted off our nine lives and I vowed to be more careful.

The monsoon turned the mountains into a miserable hell for the soldiers. Permanent drizzling fog cut visibility to a few yards and the soil underfoot became a slippery quagmire. To climb or descend any gradient without slipping and falling was well-nigh impossible. Noise was unavoidable, for we were always heavily laden with weapons and equipment. The enemy would then close in unseen with their Soviet automatic weapons. If we survived the monsoon, which most years lasted from June until September, we could breathe again. With luck the Colonel would send us back to the north together with a *bedu* guide; someone who could identify enemy activities through the *ethe*, or trail, that they would leave. Such a man would prove my key to Ubar.

CHAPTER FOUR

The monsoon cocooned the mountains in early July. From then on they were seldom visible. A nightmarish period followed and I often wished myself well away from this God-forsaken land of eternal damp, dripping foliage and the maddening bite of the monsoon fly.

For a week or more before the true monsoon settled over the land, tattered banks of cloud raced over the Plain of Salalah. My sergeant and a number of the soldiers caught colds. A single untimely cough in the mountains was inadvisable so I selected only sixteen men for our first operation of the monsoon. The target area was the village of Darbat, the birthplace of the Sultan's wife, the mother of the heir apparent, Qaboos.

As we began to climb the foothills, before ascending the thickly wooded slopes east of the village, our lead scout Said Salim moved ahead through a region of man-sized molehills animated by the moon shadows of scudding clouds.

After a while Said knelt down, avoiding rocks and branches with the snub snout of his Bren gun. I stopped likewise. So did the fourteen men behind me. We listened and heard only the soft susurration of thorn branches in the breeze. Then Said lifted a hand and motioned towards the ground. One by one, in our snaking file, we lowered our bodies and loads noiselessly until we meshed with the shadows of the broken ground.

The sound of heavy movement came from above and increased until my heart was in my mouth. Then, all around us, a herd of Dhofari cattle trotted by. I exhaled with a hiss of relief. The sharp tac-tac of the herdsman's crook against branches passed by to our flank and when the man hallooed to his charges, I felt sure he was not sounding the alarm, for there seemed no way he could have seen us.

Said disagreed. 'He smelled us in the dark,' he whispered, his tone carrying no further than the gentle rubbing together of hands. 'He called to the watchers of Darbat, *not* to the cows. The wind is from the sea now and towards the village.'

On his bidding and feeling distinctly dubious, I rubbed the liquid dung of the cattle over my trousers and shirt. Said passed the word back to all. With another machine-gunner, the Zingibari Mubarreq, Said again pressed ahead. The ground climbed steeply and an approach to the target that would have taken an unladen Dhofari twenty minutes lasted three hours.

To avoid slipping and causing the consequent tell-tale sounds, every soldier – burdened as we were with weapons, five hundred rounds and, in some cases, with bombs for the mortar – climbed hand over hand from branch to rock hold with many pauses to stop and to listen. The faint slurp of the water within our waterbags and the beat of our hearts against the cloth of our chequered green headcloths sounded huge in the void of the valley ahead.

When we came to the upper rump of the Darbat escarpment we edged in a cautious traverse to the vantage point of a rock tumble immediately above the village. I pressed the switch of my National walkie-talkie twice and heard the muted double-blip of my corporal's acknowledgement.

In moments he passed me, followed at intervals by his seven men. With binoculars I watched them split into two groups that disappeared to either flank of the village. My own section, including the two lead scouts, then did likewise.

Finding a tangle of rocky undergrowth and carefully siting our machine-gun towards the village, we set about placing protective rocks on the vulnerable flank of our hide. The men checked as best they could for scorpions or snakes before removing each rock.

From time to time the scream of wild cats punctured the quietness. Once Mubarreq turned and whispered to me: 'That is no cat. It is the enemy. The people of this village are for the most part former Zingibari servants from Salalah. Their night calls are those of our forefathers from the rain forests of Usumbara and Ukambani.'

'They *know*, Bakhait,' Said Salim added. 'In the morning they will come behind us. This is a bad place to defend.'

As a general rule, officers do not alter their tactics on the whim of their soldiers, and in the Royal Scots Greys I made a particular point of never doing so. But I trusted Said's judgement beyond my own and quickly recalled the corporal's section.

When we were all together I explained the change of plan. We must continue at once to the far side of the village. From there we could again overlook Darbat but without the current risk of being cut off from a safe retreat to Salalah Plain. Our immediate problem was the five-hundred-foot vertical cliffs of Dahaq, a limestone-fronted abyss whose sudden barrier stretched for a mile between the two mountain features, Jebel Darbat and Jebel Nasheeb, which flanked the village. The thatched rondavels and the cultivated fields of Darbat were perched atop the lip of the cliffs, the site of the greatest waterfall in Arabia, now active merely in response to flash-floods from the mountain uplands.

My corporal had switched off his transceiver before approaching me, to avoid the electronic screech of VHF feedback should either of us inadvertently touch his transmission button. We were all surprised then when a rapid whispering sounded from my National.

'It is Zingibari,' Mubarreq cursed.

He leant over to listen, but there were no further calls. The incident lent wings to our advance. The corporal, deciding upon a position that we could see across the valley, left first. I tensed each time I saw some movement by his men as they crossed the often open ground to the north of the village. But there was no sharp crackle of gunfire, no cry of wounded friends: only the stillness alternating with a distant roar from thermals up the face of the abyss.

In a while I heard clicks from my corporal on the National. He was in place, and none too soon, for the sky was already responding to approaching dawn. We crossed the elevated meadows of Darbat close to the rim of the cliffs. No dogs barked from the darkness of the conical mud huts, for a powerful smell of burning dung vied with the odour of our body sweat. At one stage we passed along the very brink of the Dahaq. I lay flat on my stomach and peered down to check for a possible escape route. No nook or crevice was visible. The white travertine walls fell away to a greyish channel far below, with truncated stalactites lancing downwards in tangled columns. At the distant base of the cliffs a dark confusion of giant castor-oil plants curled and swayed in the wind.

With the increasing light I saw the shape of the mountain ahead and noted a high ridge with thick vegetation. Rejoining the corporal's men, we climbed again in double file, racing the dawn. Crawling on hands and knees over many stretches of the ascent, we reached the chosen place and dragged our gear behind a web of creepers just beneath the crest of the summit. A fissured rock formed the roof of a shallow cave above and we slept where we lay except for Said, who kept watch from close above the hide.

Woken by the discomfort of an insect bite and the humid heat of the cave, I drank some of my remaining water and then I noticed a smell of putrefaction. Somewhere close by an animal corpse was rotting and the buzz of feeding flies could be heard clearly. We opened a tin of corned beef and spread the pink meat on our army biscuits. Flies from the unseen carrion appeared to prefer our food, for we were soon hosts to a swarm of bluebottles.

I could see, through a veil of mimosa, activity in the village below. There were men with weapons, but only ancient matchlocks which served as virility symbols. No Soviet automatics were in evidence – indeed nothing suspicious.

Along the banks of the Nile I had seen many villages similar to Darbat. It was difficult to think of Arabia when contemplating the immediate scenery. The Bait Maashani of Darbat were Qara mountain men, with loose, shoulder-hung cloths and leather thongs about their wild black hair. They had turned Darbat into an idyllic and productive garden. Cotton, maize and other vegetables had been planted and a lattice of irrigation channels cleared right up to the rocky limits of the cliff edge. The occasional bleat of goats and the cries of children, both unseen below our hide, took our attention from the bites of the large black ants and the nearly invisible monsoon flies.

The pools of water upstream of Darbat village were shallow and rimmed with margins of dry mud, but within three months I knew the valley would be a Garden of Eden, a necklace of lakes teeming with heron, widgeon, mallard and coot. Great fig trees, and whispering willows, hummingbirds, dragonflies and outsize butterflies ascend the curving valley to higher waterfalls and other smaller villages, until the forested ravines meet with the wild-flower-filled meadows of the mountaintop world.

Twice during that long, hot day a herd of goats passed over and beside our cranny and each time the women who drove them could clearly be seen to search every thicket and hollow. Distracted perhaps by the stench, neither goats nor women entered our hide, but the second herder, a hag in tattered clothes, cast several covert glances at our thicket. For a while I lost sight of the old woman, although her goats continued to mill around us. Then a rock rattled over the cave's roof and a shadow flickered across the lattice of thorns. My blood ran thin as the woman screamed shrilly from above us. Then, when all the goats had passed by, no more herders came our way and even the village appeared empty.

By dusk I knew the ambush had failed – whether through compromise or bad luck, I could not tell. At any rate the Intelligence report that armed men met daily in the village had not proved true and the likelihood that our presence had been detected was too great to risk another day of observation.

All day my corporal had watched our escape route to the Plain. When we met up after dusk he assured me the enemy had laid no ambush. But at noon a herd of cattle had been driven to the base of the ravine down which we must descend, and they were still there.

'Good,' said my signaller. 'They never take cattle to an area they intend to ambush.'

Said Salim shook his head. 'We must wait and listen,' he counselled. 'It is wrong to leave cattle outside the village byres by night. The wolves and hyenas will kill them. *They* know this well enough. We must be careful.'

Although keen to depart quickly, I agreed with Said and we stayed at the upper neck of the ravine, from where, with binoculars, we could see the cattle far below. In a short while there was a commotion and I made out at least a dozen figures moving among the cows, driving them further up the ravine towards us. Then all was quiet again.

Leaving Said Salim and Mubarreq well hidden, the rest of us headed north towards the inner fastness of the mountains, away from safety. We made more noise than usual and trod where our prints would be seen. At a suitable point we waylaid our own trail but nobody followed and in two hours we were back with Said and Mubarreq. Said handed me back my telescope. He whispered quietly enough but could not hide his excitement. 'When you left, we could hear you for many minutes. All of Darbat would know that you were heading north. One hour after your move the cows began to move again directly below us and many men were among them. They are all gone north now and our way is clear.'

We reached the edge of the Plain in two hours, made aware once again of the mettle of 'the enemy', as we conveniently described all Dhofaris who took up arms against our Sultan.

No amount of reading reveals a clear picture of the Dhofaris' origin. Some day, when a lost city of pre-Christian dating is discovered in Dhofar, many an intriguing mystery about these people and their past may be cleared up. The most persistent explanation, and one which most of my brother Sultanate officers held dear, was that the Dhofari mountain tribes arrived with the Queen of Sheba when she colonized the frankincense orchards before her legendary journey to, and courtship of, King Solomon. The Bible's Book of Kings, when concertinaed, runs: 'When the Queen of Sheba heard of the wisdom of King Solomon of Israel she travelled to Jerusalem with gifts and he showed her the Temple . . .'

In the Qur'an she is called Bilgris, Queen of Saba, and her burial place is recorded as a temple near Marib. The Ethiopians believe she was their own Queen Makeda of Sheba and that she had a son with Solomon who later stole for Ethiopia the Israelis' Ark of the Covenant.

Both Quranic and Ethiopian versions are based on the Bible and the only biblical reference to the Queen's identity is in Genesis, connecting her with Ophir, a city of gold that is probably in western Saudi Arabia.

Archaeology has to date produced no proof of Sheba's origins but some scholars believe that she was ruler of a Sabaean state in northern Arabia which may or may not have held sway over Marib and other south Arabian regions.

The four different languages spoken by Dhofaris – Mahra, Shahra, Harsusi and Botahari – are linguistically different from Arabic. Whatever the complex truth, the main reason for the ethnic differences between the Dhofari tribes is the frequently changing foreign dominations throughout their history. Most of the invaders originated from the Yemen or the Hadhramaut and not from Oman, but the tribes have nonetheless divided themselves into the same two confederations, the Ghafiri and the Hinawi, as have the tribes of northern Oman. Dhofaris from the arid lands north of the mountains are mostly Hinawi and, with few exceptions, the mountain and coastal tribes are Ghafiri.

One of the reasons that Dhofari history can only be guessed at is the paucity of their ancestral remains or written records other than scattered arrangements of rocks and occasional graffiti in caves in a script as yet undeciphered.

- - - - - - - - - - - - - - - - -

When, in the early 1960s the first Army patrols probed into the deeper *jebel* valleys and marvelled at the unique and luxuriant paradise they found there, they were often the first outsiders to do so. There were still many limestone ravines, wrapped in jungle, interspersed with cave systems and peopled by hostile tribesmen, where white men were talked of by wandering *bedu* to marvelling audiences of little Qara folk.

In July a new Intelligence officer took over in Dhofar. His predecessor, a South African, was an enthusiastic amateur botanist who garnered much hitherto unknown information about the corms and tubers of the monsoon region. One plant is even named after him. But this gentleman's success with any non-floral intelligence work was minimal. With Tom Greening, a Canadian with a British Army background, things changed dramatically. He learned to speak the language of the mountain folk, he acquired informants and he worked hard.

Soon after Tom's arrival I received instructions to ambush the spring of Arzat, the source of the Sultan's own water supply and reputedly the sweetest water in the land. Using plastic explosives, the enemy had taken to blowing up sections of the concrete aqueduct taking Arzat water to the Sultan's private gardens at Mamoorah. Each time servants repaired the damage, the saboteurs struck again, usually close by the spring itself.

At that time a visiting VIP was granted an audience with the Sultan and I escorted him to the Palace, the only occasion when I met my nominal ruler, whose water supply I was to guard and whose personal safety I would certainly have risked death to ensure. The Palace squatted dazzling white on the Salalah beachfront. The glare turned nearby coconut palms to dark outlines and the boom of breakers numbed all other sounds, for monsoon waves crashed on the shale yards from the seaward wall of the Palace.

Corporal Salim's Land Rover slewed to a halt beside mine as a Sultanate officer passed by between the quarters of the heir apparent, Qaboos bin Said, and the house of Bureik, Wali of Salalah.

Qaboos, the Sultan's only son, had grown up in Salalah, then been educated privately in England. After training at Sandhurst he became an officer in the Cameronian Regiment. Following street fights leading to the murder of German citizens in the garrison town of Minden, the regiment was disbanded.

Back in Salalah, Sultan Said placed his son under virtual house arrest, ostensibly to study the Qur'an, and allowed him very few visitors. Friends from many parts of the Omani community managed to make covert contact with Qaboos at this time. They shared a common purpose: to remove the Sultan and install the half-Dhofari Qaboos as ruler of Oman. They believed that if such a change was not implemented very soon, Dhofar would be taken by the Marxists. They saw the Sultan as reactionary and stubborn in his refusal to use his new oil revenues to improve the lot of all Omanis, north and south. Qaboos, they were sure, would prove an enlightened ruler who would somehow stem the tide of Marxism, despite the fact that elsewhere, from Asia to Africa, Soviet-sponsored rebellions were proving unquashable by the old order.

One day, not long before the overthrow of Sultan Said, I was on escort duty at his palace in Salalah. We were lined up in a passageway leading to the royal courtyard. Black servants guarded all the doorways, massive men in turbans and long white skirts bunched about their paunches by the ornate belts of their silver daggers. They stood impassively at the entries to the inner recesses of the royal quarters. White shrouds covered the Sultan's fleet of armoured cars parked about the courtyard and a cine camera whirred quietly from an upper window slit.

A servant approached, leading two robed Arabs, the Royal Secretary and His Majesty Sultan Said bin Taimur, who greeted me with a smile and handshake. He moved slowly along the line of the platoon, speaking to each of the men. After an English education at a college in India, he had ruled Oman wisely for thirty-five years in the days when the country was impoverished and caution was his watchword. An impressive aura of dignity surrounded him even though he was small in stature, and I felt a respect and loyalty which were difficult to reconcile with the widespread misery of his subjects. My thoughts about the man were decidedly confused but, since my duty clearly lay in his service, I believe I would without question have obeyed his orders to arrest anyone suspected of plotting a coup.

Whatever the present state of trust between Britain and Oman, it cannot be denied that the original reason for British solidarity with the Al bin Saidis was of course self-interest, and chiefly to keep the French influence to a minimum. By the 1960s, being seen to help a reactionary dictator, however benign in person, drew a hysterical clamour from the international protest factory and black marks in the halls of the United Nations. It was claimed that Britain, with the Sultan as its puppet figurehead, was keeping Omanis oppressed to ensure the safe passage of its oil through the Omani-dominated Straits of Hormuz from the Persian Gulf.

The reality was otherwise. The few hundred Britons in Oman were all there as mercenaries paid for by the Sultan and subject only to his direct orders. Some were there for fun and diversity, some to earn untaxed salaries or escape soured marriages, others by fate or, in a few cases, an active dislike of communist aggression.

By mid-July the mountains were in the thrall of the monsoon. The pall of gloom that hid them extended some way south over the Plain. Grass grew thinly everywhere but the profusion of flowers, blue and pink and yellow, which appeared from the dead summer dust served only to accentuate the dank and miserable mien of the gravel wastes. Visibility, often less than a hundred yards, meant the intermittent grounding of the two Air Force fighters, while, along the coast, the churning seas ensured that no ship could call for shelter. The Plain was cut off from the outside world on all sides since the only track that crossed the mountains was a quagmire quite impassable to vehicles.

The mist provided cover for enemy minelayers, who prepared the few serviceable vehicle tracks with British anti-tank mines abandoned by Her Majesty's forces on leaving Aden two years previously. Although we laid sandbags on the floor and under the seats of our Land Rovers, we knew the likely result of a mining. Some drivers had their feet or legs amputated, their spinal cords twisted and buckled and their eardrums split. Others were flung clear: a mile from the RAF camp we found the body of a Pakistani truck driver over a hundred yards from the impact point with the Mark VII mine that destroyed his vehicle.

The enemy also laid plastic Soviet TM6 mines, the size of bananas, which were designed to blow a man's foot into his stomach, tear off his genitals and blind him. Often the two types of mine were laid in tandem so that would-be rescuers of the crew of a mined vehicle would detonate the TM6s. There were many scenes of writhing, pleading torsos watched by helpless colleagues who knew that to give help would entail certain suicide.

I took nine men to ambush the Sultan's water source from a deep cave in the mountainside above. We carried enough water for four days and, early in the morning of the third day, suspect movement about the aqueduct's most vulnerable point prompted me to call in one of the Sultan's two Strikemaster fighters. Within minutes a pod of Sura rockets slammed into the fig trees beside the concrete water channel. Since there was no visible human reaction, we stayed put in the cave and, although we neither heard nor saw an explosion, the aqueduct had been destroyed in two places by the morning of the fourth day.

Another observation group spotted four figures sprinting from the area, wearing dark cloaks and bearing large bundles. Again the Strikemaster fired rockets and this time reported a hit. We found two bodies, both female, with their clothes blasted off.

The enemy included many women and the war split many families. When Tom Greening, unlike his predecessor, told me to ambush a particular place the results often proved worthwhile. In the evenings at Umm al Ghawarif, safe within the camp confines, ringed with wire and searchlights, we would often join the soldiers in the compound to watch a film projected on to a whitewashed stone wall. If the film went on too long my duty corporal would appear briefly by the screen and wave his arms. The members of the reconnaissance platoon would then leave the action of Bonnie and Clyde and get ready to face the possibility of real-life excitement. Collecting weapons and equipment we would meet by the vehicle yard, cock rifles and drive without lights as quietly as possible out of the gates.

On moonless nights our route towards the foothills involved one soldier jogging ahead with a white cloth. All the Land Rover drivers would strain to avoid collision with each other and the lead driver kept his eyes on the cloth. This way we avoided heading like lemmings over the many sudden cut-banks and the sides of dry stream beds.

Once they had dropped us within half an hour of the foothills, the drivers would find a hidden gulch and wait there, sometimes three or four days, until, in response to green flares, they would collect us at the end of the operation.

One of the original drivers had to leave and a new man, unaccustomed to the hazards of such driving, turned his vehicle over trying to avoid a sudden gully. My best machine-gunner was crushed and killed and two men seriously hurt.

The best of the Sultan's Intelligence agents in the southern reaches of the mountains was a portly gentleman named Said bin Ghia. He was a sheikh of the powerful Bait Qatan tribe who had emigrated in the 1950s to Bahrain, where he became head gardener to the American Forces Golf Club. Coerced into joining the Dhofar insurgents in 1963, he was sent with a hundred others to train at an Iraqi Army camp. Two years later a force of thirty fighters, including Said, set out in six Dodge trucks to cross the desert from Dhahran to Dhofar.

'Those three weeks in the Sands were difficult,' Said told me. 'Always grit in the rice. All cooking gear was soon lost in a sandstorm, two Dodges had to be towed and I repaired a third by battering our coffee-pot to replace a piston ring. I fixed radiator leaks with flour and sand mixed and when all our water ran out we shot gazelles. Then we shared out portions of their stomach water and urine.'

When they arrived in Dhofar they were betrayed to the Army by their leader's uncle. Said managed to escape and surrendered to the Government. He still retained contact with his tribe and knew of any event in his part of the mountains within days of its occurrence.

Said guided some of our ambush operations into the areas he knew best such as the Wadi Naheez, where we split into groups of four, each with a machine-gun, hidden in various rock-littered caves.

The Naheez valley was an enemy stronghold. Villages nestled in clearings deep within its forests of acacia, tamarind, jasmine and sycamore. Clear streams ran down rocky gorges decked in fern and tropical flowers. Camels, cattle and goats, often it seemed on automatic pilot, wandered along jungle paths, free to graze anywhere except in the cultivated patches. Maize, cotton and alfalfa flourish alongside melons, potatoes, chilli peppers, papaya and mangoes. All this luxuriance was difficult to appreciate from the recesses of a cave, the only visible scenery being a carefully selected 'killing ground'.

On one night approach to the Naheez, we had just entered the foothills by the *fadhl*, the mouth of the valley, when Said seized my shoulder in the darkness. 'Take care,' he warned me. 'This is a place of the people of Ad.' His action saved me from a nasty fall since I was about to lead the platoon into a large sink-hole known as Ghaur Fazl, which was seventy feet deep and at least thirty feet wide. That night we based ourselves in a series of caves and Said warned me of cave ticks. Some cause raging irritation and fever, others deep ulcers and lesions. They are hosted by the foxes, goats and leopards that frequent the caves. Other denizens include hyenas, civet-cats and lynxes. Wolves, Said said, usually keep to the more open places but are the worst predators of cattle.

In our zeal to avoid treading on 'scrotum-thieves', as the smaller enemy mines were nicknamed, we often chose a route in the darkness through snake-ridden places. The mountain wadis are home to numerous species, including the spotted rocksnake, which glides up almost vertical surfaces, the tiny threadsnake and the carpet viper, which can kill in six seconds.

We had many a memorable skirmish in the Naheez and the success of the platoon's nocturnal activities did not go unnoticed by our enemy. Said bin Ghia took me aside one evening in camp and gave me a warning. The enemy, he said, were satisfied that the companies were kept under permanent surveillance; their every move noted and so easily countered. However, as our platoon moved only by night to ambush a wide and unpredictable front, we were less easy to avoid. Certain regional groups, Said said, had recently been tasked to eliminate us during the course of our operations. Since Said was very often with us I could understand his eagerness to ensure that I continued to exercise maximum caution. I thanked him but dismissed his advice, for the Intelligence agents were thought to be alarmist.

When I asked Said about Ubar his initial response was: 'Where and what is Ubar?' When I explained, he was full of mirth and ribbed me about it for many months. I would be wasting my time to search for such a place in the Great Sands. Of course he had heard the *bedu* stories! Tales of three-toed monkeys with a single arm protruding from their chests and of golden pillars buried in the dunes. All rubbish! He had travelled through those dunes and knew that no city could ever have flourished in such a waterless hell.

If I was determined to find a lost city of his ancestors, then I should look in the mountains and on the Plain. He could show me a dozen likely spots.

CHAPTER FIVE

Tom Greening summoned me to his office one morning and, without being specific as to my target, suggested that I keep a night-time watch over the garrison of the Dhofar Force and the hamlet that huddled on the beach to its immediate south.

The Dhofar Force was a military anachronism founded by an ex-Arab Legion officer, Major St John B. Armitage, on the Sultan's orders. The Force was recruited entirely from local Dhofaris, and equipped with formidable armoured cars which we envied, but not allowed involvement in the fighting. There was a good deal of apprehension at Umm al Ghawarif lest this so-called allied force murder their Pakistani officers and mount a frontal attack on our camp to coincide with a full-scale uprising in the rest of the country.

Three years earlier, while the Sultan was inspecting the men of the Dhofar Force, they suddenly cocked their weapons and attempted to kill him. The Pakistani commander and two of the Sultan's servants were hit but not a bullet touched the royal personage. Thirteen of the garrison, presumably the guilty parties, fled to the mountains and the Sultan's subsequent failure to disband the Force astonished his advisers. 'If they see us outside their fort they will shoot us,' my men warned me, 'and afterwards say they thought we were the enemy.'

Each night for a week the platoon spaced out in groups in a semicircle about the fort and the village, forming a cordon all the way to the sea on both flanks. Night followed night and nothing happened. My faith in Tom Greening's information sources took a tumble. Then, four nights *after* we were called away to a task in the mountains, I found out the reason for our deployment.

The village of Arzat consisted of a scrappy tangle of huts put together with lengths of coconut palm, rusty oil drums and wattle fronds. The place stank of drying sardines and in my opinion did not warrant an attack by enemy forces.

Six men armed with AK47 rifles skirted the Dhofar Force fort in the small hours of the morning and approached the shack owned by the family of Naseeb, an Intelligence aide of Tom Greening. The men were led by Naseeb's brother, Said Mistahayl, who was naturally recognized and welcomed by his mother when she responded to a knock on the door. When Naseeb appeared with a lantern he was murdered by his brother in front of their parents. Villagers tried to help but were shot down and the killers returned to the mountains, probably to Darbat.

Early in August Radio Aden announced that the insurgents of Dhofar had located a group of British propaganda specialists attempting to bribe and seduce the plainsfolk of Dhofar. They were following these specialists and would soon eliminate them. Said bin Ghia assured me that my platoon were the 'specialists' and we would do well to take extra care. In fact the 'seduction' had been unsuccessful in obtaining any information about the enemy but had certainly made those Dhofaris who received the food and medicines that we now provided, more friendly towards the Government.

Taking Said's warning to heart on this occasion, I began to lay carefully sited ambushes to overlook sites from which we ourselves could be ambushed during our increasingly frequent village visits to dole out supplies.

The non-stop drizzle and the dank monsoon air caused many of the men to develop coughs. No longer able to spare people to man protective cordons, we reverted to our previous, less cautious tactics.

In late August we paid a visit by night to a huddle of mud and thorn huts at the mouth of the Wadi Thimreen. Reduced to only twelve men, including our guide, Said bin Ghia, we carried heavy packs of food and medicines through the thorn forest around the village.

When both our six-man groups were ready in the sparser foliage that rimmed the village clearing, I signalled the corporal to advance to the eastern flank. I gave him a few minutes then stood up to move forward with my machine-gunner and Said. Said was sweating and his brow creased with unease. The village was too quiet. As we left the last shred of cover, a withering burst of machine-gun and rifle fire erupted, echoed by the crackle of breaking thorn branches immediately behind us and the hammer of Soviet RPD automatics, nicknamed 'woodpeckers' for their rapid fire and their high-velocity bullets.

Said bin Ghia screamed and fell to the ground. I twisted and lurched back to the nearest anthill. The machine-gunner was already there. Said rolled over, very quickly for one with so large a belly. Flour spilled out of his backpack, reddened with his blood, but he reached our earthen redoubt. The woodpeckers homed in on the anthill and seemed determined to rip it away until we were exposed. A bullet tore through my loose shirt tail, and earth sprayed in my face.

The corporal's five men saved us with effective fire from the east, killing six of the enemy. When all was quiet we dressed the wound in Said's arm and resolved to do no more food runs without an adequately sized force.

Information began to reach us of powerful new weapons and large, well-trained forces that had come through Yemen under cover of the mist. Once the monsoon was over the enemy would be in an ideal situation to conquer Dhofar. The Sultan's Armed Forces were puny by comparison and the Plain very vulnerable by night. With no helicopters, no outside assistance other than two dozen foreign officers and an army inferior in numbers and ground equipment, the Sultan's Forces were in no shape to resist a determined and coordinated attack from the mountains.

The colonel pinned his hopes on a linear barrier, the Leopard Line, that he hoped to position all the way from the foothills in the south to the northern desert. As soon as the monsoon lifted, my platoon was to form the northern end of that line.

The cave ambushes, lasting up to four days at a time, were a testing experience not merely because of the danger of discovery by a larger force of the enemy but also because of the tiny monsoon flies, similar to the 'no-see-ums' of northern Canada, which make life miserable throughout the hours of daylight. Too small to be baulked by mosquito netting, these virulent midges suck the blood of any living animal and leave behind a frantic irritation which, when scratched, easily goes septic.

I remember a heavily built Baluchi soldier, a brave and energetic man, who was reduced to silent tears during one of our longer cave vigils in midge country. The result of even a short sojourn on ambush duty was a body rash of angry red pimples that retained their itch for up to a week.

The colonel, perhaps prompted by the irritable state of some of his officers, decided to hold a Sunday barbecue on the beach east of Salalah. The natural beauty spot he selected was the creek of Kohr Rori to the east of Taqa village.

My platoon provided protective cover on the high ground north of the beach and eight or nine officers, British, Omani and Asian, enjoyed a day of peace and the cool relief of sea water on sore skin. The beach below the cliffs was of white sand, rich in seashells, and the boom of monsoon waves filled the air, shutting out the distant sounds of war from the mountains.

I settled back on an outcrop of rock above the beach after taking sandwiches and squash to the platoon positions. The rock was marked with the rough cuts of some ancient mason's tools and the cliff had once housed an outpost of a city built above the creek to the west of the beach.

Quite what went on in south Arabia before the arrival of Islam remains mostly a mystery. This dark hole in time is referred to as the Jehaliya, the Age of Ignorance, and is that much darker than the corresponding period in Western Europe, owing to the lack of conquerors who kept written records.

Kohr Rori is an exception to this rule because in the 1960s inscriptions were unearthed there by Wendell Phillips's team which, when translated in tandem with records found in the Yemen, tell the story of the creek in 100 BC.

Five hundred miles to the west, in the Yemeni city of Shabwa, King Il'aud Yalut, also known as Eleazus, decided to colonize the frankincense groves of Dhofar. He enrolled troops and sent them to Kohr Rori, then the best harbour of the entire incense coastline, where the Shabwans built a fine city, which they called Sumhuram.

They left behind graffiti chipped into rock tablets which agreed with early literature that a region called the land of the Sachalites (almost certainly the Plain of Salalah) included Dhofar, that the Shabwan settlers worshipped Lord Sin, the Moon God, and that the overall aim of the colonizers was to control the incense trade at source.

The creek that I lazily observed in 1969 was little more than a lagoon fringed with coot-infested reeds and paddled by camels. Since it was cut off from the sea by a sandbank and a receding coastline, it was difficult to picture a once-busy harbour penetrating inland for over a mile and alive with trading boats of many strange shapes and mast systems. Beside the creek seafarers and traders had thronged in the shanty port of Moscha and above them, brushed by the cliff-top breeze, stood the citadel of the Moon God, still thriving in the third century after Christ, by which time an efficient system of inland trails and storehouses produced many tons of top-quality frankincense, then the most expensive commodity in the world.

Had the Dhofaris kept in their own country the riches derived from their precious resource, that land would not have remained so obscure. However, south Arabia's rulers were nearly always based in present-day Yemen, and that is where the money went. So much so that, at the height of the Roman Empire, the richest people in the world lived in south Arabia and over seven thousand tons of frankincense left their borders by land and sea every year.

Successive Yemeni or Hadhraumi rulers and traders successfully hid from the Romans and Greeks the true identity of the frankincense lands, with the result that centuries of historians mistakenly recorded the Yemen as the chief source of the commodity.

What is known of the history of Dhofar, Zafar or the biblical Sephar? Merely that, in biblical terms, Noah begat Shem, the first Semite, whose kindred included Joktan, whose tribe settled in the Sephar area.

After the Shabwan settlement of Kohr Rori nothing is known until, in AD 570, the early Dhofar capital of Raysut was overrun by troops of the Persian general Wahriz.

In the seventh century, after defeating pagan Oman at the battle of Dibba, the Muslim general Ikrima marched south to Dhofar, where he nominally established the Faith, at least along the accessible coastline. In 819 Muhammad bin Ziyad re-established Islam and his family ruled Dhofar for ninety years from Mirbat, which possessed a harbour giving shelter from the north-east monsoon winds.

During the tenth century the Persian Minjui dynasty held sway and built their capital at Al Balid, or Zafar, now a wired-off wasteland of pillaged ruins along the eastern coastline of Salalah. Robat, a more recent suburb of Zafar, is a small appendage a mile north-east of the ruins. Both Al Balid and Robat are ripe for the archaeologist's spade, although neither shows pre-Islamic traces.

The Minjuis were still about in 1145 when Ahmed bin Muhammad, then a dependant to temporary Omani hegemony, ruled from Mirbat.

In 1200 a Hadhraumi attack was repulsed but, seven years later, a Yemeni merchant named Al Haboodhi killed the last Minjui and started his own dynasty, one of whom destroyed then rebuilt both Al Balid (then called Mansura) and Mirbat. In 1278 the latter's grandson, the last Haboodhi, was replaced after the battle of Auqad by another Yemeni family, the Rasoolis, who survived well into the fifteenth century.

The Al Balid of the Minjuis, Haboodhis and Rasoolis was a fine Islamic port almost surrounded by sea, since natural inlets on either seaward flank were kept dredged and negotiable by trading boats. In addition to the outward trade of incense, the city was an important outlet for horses from central Arabia bound for Iraq, Egypt and the Far East.

A relic of the Rasoolis can still be seen at London's Victoria and Albert Museum: the tombstone of the King of Zafar, who lived from 1292 to 1311.

The Rasoolis lasted until 1516 when another Hadhraumi tribe, the Kathiris of King Bed'r bin Tuwairiq, came to power.

Noted events of this period in Al Balid's history were visits by the Venetian Marco Polo in 1285 and then by Ibn Batuta, the famous Arab traveller and writer. History records great hurricanes in 1286 and 1325 which killed many people and battered the port. In 1692 the Portuguese pillaged Al Balid and their sea power caused a loss of trade that led to its decline. Dhofar's economy dwindled, coming to rely instead on small-scale agriculture and offshore fishing. The people of Al Balid moved out to rural settlements which later became modern Salalah.

In 1692 the English traveller Ovington visited the Dhofar coast and, twelve years later, a naval officer, Captain Hamilton, noted that an English ship, landing for supplies, had been burned and the crew massacred. In 1860 the pirate Muhammad Akil took over the Dhofar coast, built a fort at Mirbat and subdued the mountain tribes for two years until they caught and killed him. This displeased Sultan Said of Muscat, who sent a force to Dhofar, which then became his dominion and has remained an integral part of Oman ever since.

With Sultanate support, the Indian Navy sent ships to Dhofar in the 1830s and 1840s, thus gathering miscellaneous information from reports by the likes of Haines, Wellsted, Cruttenden and Carter.

While Consul in Muscat in the 1870s, Colonel S.B. Miles twice visited Dhofar and described conditions on the coastal plain. At the time an Indian merchant, Mopla Said Fadhl, ruled from Salalah for two years. Various troubles were quelled by Muscat troops in 1881 and again after the murder of their Salalah garrison in 1896. Sultanate authority, and indeed the influence of all previous dynasties, seldom reached further than the edge of the Salalah Plain – a fact of which I was painfully aware as the time grew near for our move over the enemy-held mountains.

The *khareef* clouds dispersed on 14 September, and a week later all available army units, about a hundred and fifty armed men, approached the mountains with justifiable trepidation. The enemy had, during the three monsoon months, planned a suitable response in readiness for the inevitable army attempt to reuse the track over the mountains.

Boulders were rolled down on to the road at especially hazardous points, mines were laid, steep ramps blown with explosives and successive ambush positions prepared. Many of our men were killed or wounded, trucks were destroyed by high-explosive bullets from new long-distance Shpaagin machine-guns and morale was so dented that one company mutinied and refused to operate until the Royal Marines officer commanding them was replaced. But at length we crossed the mountains. The road was used only once again that year. It was to remain in enemy hands for the next four years.

Our guide, for the new work of the Leopard Line, was Hamed al Khalas of the Bait Maashani tribe, a gentle *bedu* and an expert tracker. From the freshwater pools of Ayun we scouted west for many days over a lofty escarpment. There had been no rain for fifteen years but Hamed knew of isolated water-holes where both the enemy and we ourselves must go in order to survive. Such wells as Thint, lost in a God-forsaken wilderness of lava valleys, where we filled our water *chaguls* and stumbled on in the heat until we came to a bottleneck ridge where Hamed was at last content.

'Here,' he said, indicating the deeply incised escarpment on all sides, 'is the narrowest neck of the Dehedoba Trail.'

All enemy infiltration routes accessible by camel must converge in order to pass west at this point including the main Dehedoba, a trail used through the *nej'd* over hundreds of years of trade between the Hadhramaut and Dhofar. Apart from ambushing the Dehedoba Trail and denying known water points to the enemy, we were tasked with finding a track cutting north from the *nej'd* to the desert base of Thamrait. This work would involve many long patrols into the unmapped maze of vertiginous escarpments immediately contiguous to the gravel fringes of the Empty Quarter. I determined to seize any chance of a further search for Wabar.

Various translations of the Qur'an gave differing histories of the lost city of Irem but, as with Ptolemy's lost Omanum Emporium in the land of the people of Ubar, they all dealt with 'the people of the Al Akaf'. The region of the Wadi Mitan and the wastes of that latitude are still called Al Akaf by local *bedu*, and since the beginning of remembered time these people have always described the lost city of this area as Ubar or Wabar.

Circumstantial evidence strongly points to the lost city having three separate names Ubar (Wabar), Irem and Omanum Emporium. The inhabitants are referred to either as the Ubariti or the people of Ad. These last were, according to Quranic history, a tribe descended from Ad, son of Uz, son of Irem, son of Shem, the son of Noah. Following the Tower of Babel event, the tribe settled in Al Akaf, where Ad's son, King Shedad, prospered and built Irem. The inhabitants became idolatrous and did not respond to warnings from Prophet Hud (or Heber), with the result that Irem was destroyed in some manner.

What form the destruction took is not immediately clear from the Qur'an, which gives no clue to Irem-searchers. Some relevant passages are:

'The prophet Hud, brother of Ad, warned his people of Al Akaf and when they saw a cloud approach, he told them it would destroy everything.'

'And into Ad was sent a desolating wind that turned all to ashes.'

'As for Ad, they perished with a violent cold blast to which He subjected them for seven days and nights.'

'The people of Noah called him a liar as did they of Ad, Thamud, Abraham, Lot and Moses . . . and we destroyed their cities . . . All these cities, too big with pride, we did destroy. Against some we sent a sandstorm, some were seized by a great noise. For some we cleaved open the earth and some were drowned.'

In other words Ubar may have ended in a sandstorm, flood, earthquake or volcanic eruption. The only detail given of Irem – Consider how the Lord dealt with Ad, the people of Irem, adorned with lofty buildings the like of which has not been seen – is again too open to interpretation to be of any help with identification. Some of the early Muslim authorities interpret the key word '*amud*' as meaning pillars or buildings and others point to the Adites themselves who, in all legends, are extremely tall.

If the classical records of Ptolemy and other Greco-Romans are of little help and the Qur'an not much better, the Arab geographers and historians only muddy the water. Al Hamdani, in the sixth century, reported that Shedad built Ubar 'to imitate paradise'.

Bin Ishaq around 750, Al Kalbi some fifty years later and Yaqut around 1200, all state that Wabar was a fertile place in south Arabia with plentiful water, fruit and palm trees. Yaqut, in adding 'Wabar lies between Sana and Shahar, a broad land three hundred farsakhs long by three hundred wide', is limiting the search to a region almost as long as the whole of south Arabia.

References to Wabar in Yaqut's *Wonders of the World* and in *The Arabian Nights*, in which the fictional cobbler Maruf visits the Sands, are so fanciful that later generations of Arabs were brought up on a legend of a marvellous city of sparkling spires and tapered pillars of gold hidden in the midst of giant dunes.

More recent respected sources include Landberg, who deduces that Wabar 'includes a cave area in which troglodytes live'; and the *Encyclopaedia of Islam*, which puts Wabar 'north of Mahra country and within the Rub al Khali'.

Of the available Wabar references garnered from over two thousand years of records, only a loose summary is possible here. The apparently large tribal area of Wabar seems cognate with the Ubar of Ptolemy and other classical sources. If so, Wabar was the region containing the cities, including Irem, referred to in the Qur'an as 'destroyed by God'.

Arab historians are agreed that Wabar and Ad and seven other tribes all gave their names to the regions of Arabia in which they lived and, in some cases, also to their central town or city.

Many of the historians' records are written in the form of legends but this does not indict them as baseless myths. Rather they are the surviving memories of ancient peoples which have over centuries become legends, and the early history of most if not all countries has been sieved through the same process. With such a wealth of Quranic comment, biblical clues and local legend to indicate the presence of a once magnificent lost city named Ad, Ubar, Wabar and/or Irem, the evidence for its existence somewhere in or close to the Empty Quarter was considerable.

Atlantis, Noah's Ark and the lost City of the Incas have no greater wealth of historic reference behind them yet all have been sought by many expeditions mounted by explorers from all over the world. Ubar, the Atlantis of the Sands, has remained one of the world's great riddles for two thousand years, but up until 1969 only two expeditions had been allowed into Oman to search for it, those of Bertram Thomas and Wendell Phillips, and my employer the Sultan had subsequently ordered Dr Phillips never to return to Oman. My belief was that he would be extremely angry if I were found to be planning private expeditions to Ubar unannounced and while on his payroll. I had no intention of risking my colonel's refusal or the Sultan's wrath by even asking for permission. My hope remained that ignorance would ensure bliss so long as I could find a suitable time when nobody would notice my absence from the *nej'd*.

CHAPTER SIX

The heat of the *nej'd* was leaden. Searing winds from the great oven of sand to our north blew grit into each item of clothing and equipment. Every morsel of food, seasoned with fine sand, crunched between the teeth. Our eyes stung and watered and tiny sores began at night as I tossed and turned naked under a single blanket. The sores attracted the flies by day and grew into festering wounds especially on my hands and feet. On days when there was wind the heat was all-powerful, affecting my ability to think clearly.

Our patrols away from the Dehedoba Trail were concerned mainly with water-holes and conformed to no set pattern beyond the monthly need to visit the *nej'd* camp of Thamrait to replenish our stock of food, ammunition and fuel. On the way back from the camp, which was manned by a single British officer and a dozen Baluchis, we called at the pools of Ayun for our monthly wash. I seldom noticed any offensive body odours emanating from the soldiers or the *bedu* we met. This may have been due to my own equally unwashed state. There was no way of knowing.

Sometimes we met my old friend, the guide Nashran bin Sultan, at Thamrait and he came with us on visits to regions where he was, through his tribal connections, more likely to pick up information than Hamed al Khalas, our more permanent companion.

Close by the water-hole of Kharba in the Wadi Ghadun Nashran stopped by a herd of goats. They seemed to be untended but Nashran headed unerringly for a thicket of *ghaf* scrub in the shade of which we found the goatherd, a lone girl of great beauty. Perhaps eleven years of age and slightly too young to wear the hooded black *burka* first donned in adolescence, she was nevertheless within a year of eligibility for marriage.

Her light-brown skin, dark eyes and slim, supple body affected all the men. Unusually silent, they simply stared at this desert angel in the wide white wadi.

Nashran rubbed noses with the girl, who was a cousin of his. He said her name was Landon. We left a bag of rice for her and there were sighs and laughter in her memory for many a day afterwards. We did revisit Kharba but never saw Landon again.

The *nej'd* appeared lifeless even within the scrub of the wadi beds where we often camped, for the soft, pliable sand made an excellent bed, but in reality every crack in the crumbling surface of the *nej'd* concealed something that crawled or slithered.

I often wore no shirt or shoes, for it was cooler without them, there were no other Europeans to object and the soles of my feet had grown sufficiently coarse not to mind the hot sand or uneven ground. I was thankful for the sharp eyes of Said Salim more than once. He held up a six-inch-long sand-coloured scorpion at one midday halt. He had killed it within striking distance of my ankle as we squatted about a plate of rice. On another occasion, while I was searching for anti-personnel mines I had laid on a suspect trail a year before, Said saved my legs if not my life.

Because the Sultan's Army possessed no mines of any sort but was suffering increasing casualties from the communist variety, one of our contract officers, a Rhodesian named Spike 'Muldoon' Powell, formed a mine production line in his office using AA torch batteries, electrical wire, detonators and plastic explosive contained in Coca-Cola or beer cans from the Officers' Mess trash dump. The devices were known as 'muldoons' and at that time only two had claimed victims. One was an armed enemy and the other an own goal: a soldier who had gone to urinate where he had been told not to go. His officer, a friend of mine named Eddie Viturakis, personally dragged the mangled man clear of the minefield, displaying commendable bravery or a liking for Russian roulette. Some weeks later poor Eddie was murdered at night by one of his own men, a drug addict, who then fled to the enemy.

In the trackless wastes of the *nej'd* there were no mines of course, but it was as well never to forget the snakes nor, before sleeping, the spiders.

Hamed al Khalas was a practitioner of desert first aid, and often knew of remedies to be had from nearby vegetation. Sometimes, however, he would shrug his shoulders, smile and say: 'Only God can help you if that should bite you.'

There were several types of scorpion, mostly green, black or brown and none was deadly, although their sting could be painful and incapacitate a strong man for a day. The snakes we saw most frequently in the *nej'd* were the African puff-adder and the horned viper, both of which have a dust-coloured camouflage. 'If they bite,' Hamed advised me, 'kill an oryx and apply the blood to the bite. Then you might live.'

A number of large spiders of evil aspect exist in the *nej'd*, the most notorious being the camel spider, which can jump a metre or more. It is difficult to squash, being squat and very robust, and has large eyes and a beak which allows it to eat flesh, be it camel or human. My sergeant explained: 'They do not wish to cause pain when they eat your flesh at night so they first inject you with their drug, then, when they eat, you continue to sleep.'

We sometimes left the vehicles close by Ayun and marched overnight to the Pass of Qismeem at the northern extent of the foliated region. Here many footpaths criss-cross through a natural bottleneck, an obvious place for an ambush. Two mountain men of the Bait Tabawq tribe stumbled into one of our positions and we gave them food. They were no lovers of the Marxists and warned us of a group designated to watch our movements. It was well known, they said, that we blocked the Dehedoba Trail. Once a pattern was established of our movement routine, we would be ambushed and our tracks mined.

This information lent urgency to our attempts to locate a route over the moon-like country north of the pools of Ayun and leading down to one of the great wadis that flowed out to the open *nej'd*. In all the weeks that two or more of our Land Rovers scoured the endless maze of interlocked ridgelines we saw not a single usable route. Yet in the northerly sector of the *nej'd*, all the way to the Yemeni border, many old trails bear witness to the fruitless oil searches of the 1950s and early 1960s.

In 1953 the Sultan sanctioned the building of a gravel track from the Plain to the *nej'd* and hundreds of labourers, mostly from Aden, hacked their way north between monsoons until the road was ready and drilling began. Despite seven years of costly effort no oil was found in Dhofar, although Shell began to produce oil commercially in 1965 at Fahud in northern Oman.

Many of the oil trails were useful to our patrols to places such as Mugshin, Dauqah and Fasad but often a compass bearing or Nashran's directional wave were quicker to follow where there were no natural obstacles to negotiate.

The colonel sent me a message which boosted my hopes of finding Ubar. We were tasked to find a new route from Thamrait to the border garrison at Habarut avoiding the roundabout route based on old oil trails. This new route should head between known water-holes, thereby covering many of the necessary ports of call of enemy arms caravans.

Hamed helped us with the search, starting at Umm al Shaadid. 'The sweetest water in the land,' he called it. He boasted that he could tell the source of any water by smell and taste alone. Shaadid water, he said, came from the pools of Ayun then flowed on via the springs at Hayla, Kharba and Khadim to the distant desert well of Shis'r.

Thomas and Thesiger had called at Shaadid in the 1930s and 1940s *en route* to cross the Empty Quarter. I was curious to see how the *bedu* watered their camels since the water was forty five feet down a narrow shaft.

'Be careful,' Hamed warned me. 'There are snakes in there.'

Wearing shoes and carrying a torch, I cautiously let myself down a tattered length of hemp. The heat was stifling and the shaft descended in leaps, with three intervening bottlenecks where the original diggers had gone off at a tangent to avoid boulders. The daylight from above soon disappeared and by the time I reached the last narrow funnel I was full of admiration for any *bedu* having to work in such a place to fill heavy leather bags for their camels. I was pleased to see no snakes, but on reaching the water level I struck a rock with my torch and broke the bulb.

Straddling either side of the shaft with my legs, I felt above my head only to realize that there were *two* shafts heading upwards. Unable to find one of the hemp ropes, I began to climb by feel alone and disturbed a colony of bats. Their leathery wings and the foul stench of their dung further disorientated me and I slithered back down into the water. A second attempt led me to a rope fixture and, greatly relieved, I climbed back to the well-head and the wonderful taste of fresh air.

West of Shaadid we probed a circuitous way through broken hills to a gravel plain stretching all the way to the Wadi Banat. I calculated I could count on ten spare days at this point, for my sergeant was in charge of the Dehedoba blocks and the senior corporal with both guides could finish off the new Habarut approach track. The colonel was fully focused on the teething troubles of the Leopard Line at Raydah in the mountains: enemy groups there were creeping up on David Bayley's ridge-top outposts, killing the soldiers and taking their weapons.

With two of our less ancient Land Rovers laden with fuel and water, ten live goats and plenty of rice but minimal weaponry, seven of us followed an oil trail north to Bait Masan territory.

Neither Hamed al Khalas nor Nashran had any idea where Ubar might best be sought. Both had heard that the city lay somewhere west of the Wadi Mitan and well within the dune country.

'Which side of the border?' I asked.

'Which border?' asked Nashran, who liked others to be precise. 'The Saudis' or the Yemenis'?'

'Either,' I replied.

'Where are these borders? Are they marked with *burmail*?'

Burmail is the Omani word for oil drum, the ubiquitous desert markers. Originally most drums were marked Burmah Oil and the corruption slowly entered the language.

'There are no markers,' I told Nashran.

'Ubar likewise,' said Nashran with a smile that eased the fierce fine lines of the desert aristocrat.

Nashran's own tribe, the Bait Shaasha, were related to all the other Kathiri tribes and his recommendation carried weight, for he was by adoption the son of the paramount sheikh of all the Shaasha. His advice was to seek out an elderly member of the Bait Masan, kin to the Shaasha, since they were always to be found in or near to the water-hole of Shis'r.

'They will give you help if they can,' Nashran assured me, 'but it is really the Rashidi to the west that you need.'

The Rashidi and the Kathiri were distant relatives but they had often raided and killed one another over the years.

Shis'r was easy to locate because a great limestone bulge rises just east of the Wadi Ghadun and the Sultan, aware that Shis'r held the only water source in the entire central steppes bordering the Sands, had in 1955 built a fortress atop the mound to guard the spring. The water flow was a continuation of the Ghadun aquifer which I knew so well from the pools of Ayun and Umm al Shaadid. *Shis'r* means a cleft in the dialect of the Kathiri and obviously stems from the limestone cliff that abuts the spring immediately above it.

There was nobody there on our arrival so we took our empty cans down into the sandy depression at the foot of the cliff and slid down a slope of dirty sand that disappeared under the cliff until, some twenty feet below, we came to the water level.

The Sultan's fortress, manned until a year before by eight Omani militiamen, according to my corporal, was above and set back from the cliff face by thirty yards, but another edifice, of unknown age, was perched on the very edge of the cliff top and consisted of a heap of crumbling rubble.

Could this be an original fort from the time of Ad? The soldiers shrugged and

Nashran, whom I later quizzed on the subject, told me the old fort was about a hundred years old. Wendell Phillips, setting out from Shis'r in 1953 to find Ubar, heard a legend that attributed the building to the sixteenth-century Hadhraumi sheikh Bed'r bin Tuwairiq, a previous conqueror of Dhofar.

My driver, Murad, searched the area in one of the vehicles and came back with an old sheikh, Abdulla Salim Mugtot, who assured us that none of the Masan knew where to find Ubar and that, since there was a curse on the man who did, he wanted no part in our venture. With much muttering he suggested we find a Rashidi, for they were forever boasting of the place as though it was theirs.

Another old oil trail took us to Fasad, where we found no sign of life. Not wishing to waste time, we continued directly across the Wadi Mitan, where some thirty camels grazed in low *ghaf* scrub. Casting about, we found the owner and his family camped under a ledge cut into the western bank of the wadi by some long-forgotten flood.

I had seen a great deal of poverty in many countries but this family, who appeared destitute, stand out in my memory for their sheer *joie de vivre*. I counted four children in dirty rags who were playing, amid a great show of excitement, with other dirty rags. Two old hooded women, seemingly in their sixties, were seated in the sand engaged in a round of delighted gossip that stopped for nothing and seemed oblivious to the frequent stomping of one or more of the children grasping the rags and using the crones as shelter from each other. The resulting happy hubbub all took place in an open desert where the temperature in the shade must have been in excess of 100°F.

The patriarch was assisted in hosting us with camel's milk of great saltiness by a boy of perhaps eleven years as ragged as his younger kin who, when not busily fetching and carrying, stood behind the old man and, almost protectively, certainly with affection, put his hands on his shoulders.

Apart from their rocky ledge, two tins bowls, an inner tube of water and a goodly supply of rags, the whole family had no belongings save for the camels and each other. Yet I have never met such a contented group of people. They had probably met few or, in the children's case, no Europeans before, yet such was their self-containment that I was totalled ignored by all but the two elder males.

Were we after the Bag'r Waheesh, they asked. With my basic Arabic I translated this as wild cows, so I assured the Rashidi that we were not hunting cows, nor had we seen any in the *nej'd* where we came from.

A swift exchange of queries led to laughter. No, no, said the Sheikh. Not wild cows, but *bin Sola, Bag'r bin Sola*: the oryx.

At this I tried to explain to the sheikh that it was bad to shoot oryx because they were on the verge of extinction. After his visit in the thirteenth century, Marco Polo was probably the unwitting originator of the unicorn legend after seeing golden oryx, which, in profile, look like large African antelopes but with sloppy, almost bovine, rear ends. Too slow to escape from camel-borne pursuers and a poor breeder, the oryx had suffered the consequences of tasting delicious.

The Rashidi ignored my lecture on conservation and turned down my offer to let him guide us to Ubar. He did not actually say he knew the location, but he gave every impression of doing so while explaining that he must stay with his family and camels and that it would take too long.

'How long?' I asked.

'Three days by camel.' His reply was impressive for its alacrity.

'And by Land Rover?'

'No vehicle can go there.' He scoffed at the very idea.

We left the little camp after treating one child, loath to be dragged from the rag-game, for a filthy and pustulating wound on her foot. I left ointment and bandages behind while the corporal supplied them with water and rice.

I left the happy camp with spirits raised but still guideless and convinced that no *bedu* alive had actually seen Ubar. Surely, if they had, the secret would have quickly leaked to the oilmen. If a Rashidi who had lived all his life around the Wadi Mitan would, and probably could, not lead me to Wabar, then nobody could. Guesswork was the only answer and, like Wendell Phillips sixteen years earlier, I concluded that the answer must lie in the 'old road' sighted by Thomas and probably – although his description of it differed – by Phillips. By simply following its course far enough into the Sands, or at least up to the border, we would come upon any trace of ruins not obscured by sandstorms.

My study of Wendell Phillips's own account of a day spent following the Thomas road led me to suspect that he travelled somewhere between ten and twenty miles in a straight line along its length within the Sands. Better equipped in terms of men and vehicles, I saw no reason why we should not progress a good deal further than Phillips.

It should be easy enough to find the road by simply travelling due north from the most northerly point of the Wadi Mitan. Phillips's search apparently began less than a dozen miles north of the Wadi Atinah, which is a good way south of

Fasad and nowhere near the true dunes. The American ended his search by stating: 'The last we saw of the ancient tracks, they were bearing N75°W in the direction of Saudi Arabia within a mighty mountain system of billowing immeasurable sands stretching like a vast ocean as far as the eye could see in its cruel and sublime grandeur.' Unfortunately he gives no mention of his own location at this point of turning back, thus leaving his successors no useful point of reference.

Thomas left explicit enough details of his own sighting of well-worn tracks, about a hundred yards in cross section and graven in the plain. They bore 325° at approximately latitude 18° 45' North, longitude 52° 30' East, on the verge of the Sands.

After reaching that point where the Wadi Mitan was no longer visible as a geographical feature distinguishable from the surrounding wastes, we continued for ten miles on the odometer. It was impossible to maintain a direct northerly bearing as dunes and areas of bad going forced us to the north-west.

We crossed a number of well-worn camel tracks heading in various directions, including 325°, but none which suggested a once-great highway that had borne thousands of tons of incense on countless camels. Leaving one vehicle beneath a prominent dune, the rest of us completed a three-hour search to the west, often travelling fast on flat gravel until brought up short by dunes. In most cases we had little difficulty penetrating from one line of dunes to another, simply driving parallel to the obstacle until a passageway appeared. Some of these were narrow sandy passes between two high dunes, but often enough the gravel plain itself continued to be negotiable on the far side.

Some time that afternoon we crossed both the longitude and latitude of Thomas's 'road' and, in all probability, drove within a mile of his recorded grid reference. Yet no trails that resembled his or those of Phillips were ever visible.

Assuming that shifting winds covered certain areas only to be blown away by storms from a new direction, it seemed best to examine the Thomas area more minutely since we had no guide to lead us to any specific sighting and since the only other twentieth-century report, from Phillips, was so diffuse as to be useless.

At the stated reference point, within a few miles of our own position, Thomas's lead guide, who was a *bedu* of the region, said: 'Look, there is the road to Ubar . . . a great city rich in treasure with date gardens and a fort of red-silver. It now lies buried beneath the Ramlat Shee'ait, a few days to the north.'

'A few days' was a very rough guide to distance, since the rule of thumb for camel travel in desert stretches from seventeen to seventy, depending entirely on the terrain. However, Thomas's 'most intelligent Rashidi' had personally found pottery and notched stones too heavy for him to lift in the Sands between Mitan and Fasad. He remembered that this had been within two days' march of the dune edge.

Although it seemed likely that blown sand could temporarily cover surface tracks and low features, I doubted at that time that an entire city could be consumed for ever without trace.

The twelfth-century Arab archaeologist Nashwan Said wrote: 'Wabar is the land of Ad in eastern Yemen but is today an untrodden desert owing to the drying up of its water. There are to be found in it great buildings which the wind has smothered in sand.' But archaeology at that time was on a level with geography: full of misconceptions, especially where the mysteries of Arabia were concerned. It was believed by many Muslims that: 'The world is the shape of a ball and floats in the circumambient ocean like an egg in water. The exposed portion is inhabited. The other half is the Empty Quarter located in the barren wastes of Arabia.'

Since the *nej'd* winds were mostly northerly, except when the monsoon southerlies were blowing, I assumed the dunes were also heading south if they were indeed in motion.

Further west, in South Yemen, I had heard stories from ex-mercenaries that old trails through mountain passes were now completely blocked by dunes up to one hundred and fifty feet high and the old routes still existed on either side. To the north, in the Wahiba Sands, I had been told, the dunes moved at an average annual rate of five inches to leeward of the prevailing winds.

The dunes of the Empty Quarter are reputed to reach seven hundred feet in height but in the region to the immediate north of the Wadi Mitan they were nearer two hundred feet or less. Since the original gravel plain could be seen in most areas between the dunes, it seemed a safe conclusion that a sizeable city, though perhaps partially covered by blown sand, would still retain some exposed suburbs or satellite villages in its immediate vicinity. Buoyed up by this belief, I sought the opinion of my corporal, who made an unconvincing show of interest in my theories about sand dunes.

'How long will we remain in the Sands?' he asked.

'How long will the stores last?' I countered.

'There is good *hatab* not far to the south and we have stores for eight days. If we do not use too much petrol, we have six days to spend . . . What are we looking for? Tracks?'

I nodded. We were always looking for tracks. It was our job. The men were, as usual, totally content to be far away from the dangers of the mountains and mined tracks. There seemed no point in briefing them to look for old dwellings or artefacts. They would latch on to anything unusual, however trivial, without being asked.

In the *nej'd* we were accustomed to supplementing our goat rations with the occasional gazelle, ibex or partridge, for they were all to be seen in abundance, especially in the wadi beds between the mountains and the plains. In these sands we saw no animals or birds other than colourful lizards, some of them two feet in length, and a variety of strange insects. The sky was ever cloudless. Ravens, larks, buzzards and vultures fly over the desert, but we saw none. There were a good many tracks, mostly in the lower reaches of the dunes and often emanating from the many straggly thorned bushes known as *gai'sh*, which find water from God knows where.

Lizards, snakes and beetles left clear trails where the ground was flat. But the larger animals, which sometimes roamed even the steeper ridges of the high dunes, were difficult to identify from their spoor as the sand spilled over to blur all imprints so that foxes could leave wolf-like trails and vice versa.

The windward side of certain dunes were scooped out into deep horseshoe-shaped amphitheatres, in which we often camped. Few plants were flowering at that time but many bore withered fruit, including the miniature Sodom apples that the *bedu* heat and use for poultices.

At night, lying in the still warm sand and contemplating the dune-framed sky of a billion stars, I felt a powerful urge to stay in the Sands until I was successful.

For three days we searched up and down deep valleys, climbed to the summits of high dunes and scanned ever more new panoramas through binoculars, but all that we found, on the third afternoon, was a *bedu* encampment with signs of recent habitation, human and camel. On the fourth day we attempted to follow the tracks of the *bedu*, but a high sandy pass proved too steep for the vehicles and various detours failed to relocate the trail further west.

That evening a radio signal from my sergeant bade us return to the *nej'd* without delay. This we did despite running into far more trouble with vehicles getting bogged down in soft *sabkha* than on our more methodical outward route.

As we bounced and jolted through the floating mirages and our own dust

Mrs Thatcher and the author at the Petroleum Institute's 1986 Dinner.

His Royal Highness The Prince of Wales, British Aerospace staff, Mike Stroud and the author in 1989.

The late Dr Armand Hammer and the author in Paris.

Charles Burton during his Antarctic crossing in 1980. MAIN PICTURE: *The ship and the team of the first journey round the Earth's axis.*

The author meets Soviet long-range bomber pilots during the Siberian Arctic expedition of 1990.

Mike Stroud and his fellow expeditionists in the Arctic in 1986 had to haul their equipment across seven hundred miles of moving sea ice.

Mike Stroud prepares to cross sea ice a mere centimetre thick in the Siberian Arctic.

One of the problems faced by Mike Stroud was that as the improvised sled-boat smashed a way through the thin ice, the ice instantly refroze in the supercool air.

Mike Stroud resolutely drags a sledge weighing three hundred pounds towards the North Pole during the 1990 expedition.

Mike Stroud in a pressure pack in the Siberian Arctic.

Having no weapons, we were constantly on the alert for polar bears on the Arctic pack ice.

After his ski binding broke on the 1990 expedition, Mike Stroud sank up to his thighs in soft snow - an incident which caused a great delay.

Mike Stroud and the author at the beginning of the Siberian Arctic expedition of 1990.

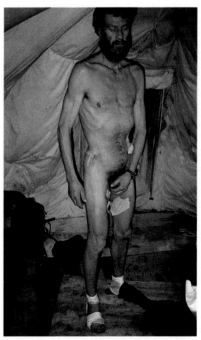

LEFT: *By the end of his 1990 polar journey the author was suffering from the extreme weight loss usually caused by sustained exertion in a hostile environment.* RIGHT: *On their return to England, tests were carried out on the expedition members at the RAF's Institute of Aviation Medicine at Farnborough in Hampshire.*

The 1991 search for Ubar benefited greatly from satellite images of the area. Here Dr Ron Blom of the Jet Propulsion Laboratory in Pasadena, California, Nick Clapp and the author are seen with a satellite image that was used as a map in the Uruq al Hadh region.

Ron Blom, together with his colleagues Dr Charles Elachi and Dr Robert Crippen, provided invaluable satellite mapping to assist the search for Ubar in 1991.

A Discovery finds its way through soft sand dunes. MAIN PICTURE: *In the desert a vehicle with the ruggedness of the Land Rover Discovery is indispensable.*

Our sponsors plastered the Discoveries with their logos - a ploy that sometimes backfired.

The great cave in the Wadi Naheez.

Dhofari mountain men, or jebalis, *in a round-house.*

The ruins at Al Balid, Salalah.

Andy Dunsire and the author descend into the Oracle of Diana.

Nick Clapp and the author, with Kevin O'Brien, the cameraman, in close attendance, during the attempted clearance of the Oracle's shaft.

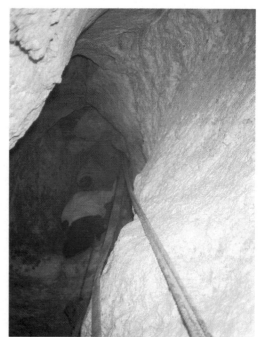

Hamed al Khalas talks the author into the well of Maashadid, from where the Ghadum aquifer flows to Shis'r.

Shis'r in 1959. The site may well be that of Ubar, the Atlantis of the Sands.

The first dig of the Ubar expedition of 1991 took place at the Oracle of Diana.

Dr Ron Blom at the incense storage vats of Andhur.

clouds I came to a rueful conclusion. My chances of finding the city through any number of random surface searches were minimal. Somehow I must obtain air support, locate Thomas's road from above, which would be easy, and follow it by aircraft until it led to signs of ruins. This, after all, was how archaeologists working near my brother-in-law's Yorkshire farm had located some of their most promising sites. I knew two of the Sultan's pilots well enough and I resolved to take the more adventurous man into my confidence.

The reason for my sergeant's summons turned out merely to be connected with his own return from a long and unsuccessful search for a new track from Ayun and Thamrait. Sheer cliffs had sooner or later blocked all his attempts. We took over from the sergeant and this time my section struck lucky. Just east of Ayun, Murad found a hidden incline which looked steeper than it really was.

We unloaded one Land Rover and roared up the side of the mountain, spitting gravel spumes into the void. There were three separate mountain shoulders and the last was the worst. At times we all dismounted and watched as Murad powered upwards, crashing over rocks and skidding around boulders before disappearing over the top.

The next week was unforgettable. There was no sign of man, past or present, on that high escarpment. Roraima, the Lost World of Conan Doyle, came to mind. For a week we travelled this wild new region. Gazelle and ibex were everywhere. Twice we saw wolves, great shaggy beasts and surprisingly unafraid of man. Said Salim showed me the spoor of a large cat, twice the size of the wild cats so common in the mountains to the south.

All about us were sheer-sided ravines, some being mere splits, like polar crevasses, but deep and dark. One false trail followed another, each ending in crumbling dead-end drops to the gravel steppes and the distant shimmer of the northern plains. Once a vehicle slipped sideways off a high rock bridge spanning an abyss. Boulders and rubble fell away into space and only quick-thinking Murad saved the day, with linked tow ropes and all available manpower.

Finding I was running short of supplies, I sent a section back to Thamrait to collect our supply truck. They made heavy weather of our new ramp and their load broke free. A four-hundred-and-fifty-pound fuel drum crushed our meat rations, eight live goats, which the men then refused to eat, since they had not been killed by *hellal*, the Quranic cutting of the throat.

Three weeks later another of my sections found a way off the northern rim of the escarpment.

'Allah was good to us to show us the way,' the corporal proudly explained, 'and *I* was always correct in choosing the right route.'

For several days four of our sections worked in gangs. We rolled boulders down to widen a natural rock ledge and Murad was at length able to skid his vehicle all the way down to the wadi bed below. This we later identified as an arm of the Wadi Harazon which led us back to Thamrait.

We signalled the colonel and not long afterwards the Leopard Line force was able to withdraw along our new 'road' and so avoid the overlooked and dangerous Valley of Haloof.

I bided my time, awaiting a supply drop by the friendly Beaver pilot: the key, I believed, to locating Ubar.

CHAPTER SEVEN

Tom Greening, the Intelligence officer, realizing that the Sultan's Government in Dhofar was in grave danger of imminent military defeat by the Marxist forces, alerted them to the fact. As a result, Omanis and some expatriates decided to act to save the situation. They planned to replace the Sultan with his son in the hope that a new and enlightened style of government would cause many Dhofaris to desert the Marxists.

Since they knew the time for a coup must be exactly right and that all was not yet ready, they also decided that Intelligence and the Sultan's Armed Forces should unsettle the enemy by encouraging distrust between the mainline Marxists and those purely nationalist fighters who disliked communism. Most of the latter group lived and fought in that region of the mountains that lay to the east of the Thamrait track and many were of eastern Mahra stock.

Intelligence and the Army needed a breathing space of some six months during which they could try to delay the strongly rumoured major enemy offensive that was likely to take place the following June, as soon as the monsoon arrived to hinder the activities of the Sultan's Air Force.

My Ubar plans were shelved, for a welter of activity kept the platoon on the move. An armed squabble at the border village of Habarut threatened to escalate into a shooting match between the Omani and Yemeni garrisons, whose twin whitewashed forts faced each other across the oasis.

Taking all the vehicles and men, we stocked up with mortars and ammunition at Thamrait and drove non-stop to Habarut, ignoring the possibility of mines. Having made contact through a neutral villager, I invited the Yemeni garrison commander to meet me halfway across the wadi at noon. He arrived with two soldiers of the Hadhraumi Bedouin Legion and I offered an official apology from the Sultan for the behaviour of his villagers together with the personal gift of four hundred Rothman cigarettes. I added that any retaliatory attack on the Sultan's fortress would be considered an act of war.

The commander accepted the apology and the cigarettes. Soon afterwards the Yemenis razed the Sultan's fort to the ground and imprisoned the garrison.

From Habarut we were summoned by an Operations Immediate signal to Thamrait, where Tom Greening briefed me to capture two political commissars from the centre of the eastern mountain region. The army had not previously operated in the area and little was known about the enemy there, but Tom produced a Mahra informant who would lead us by night to the correct village, where we would find the communist leaders.

Leaving two sections by the Dehedoba Trail, I took twenty-six men, Tom's guide and all available light machine-guns to the Mahra water-hole of Leeat. We moved southwards all night, arriving in the epicentre of the enemy's most secure eastern zone shortly before dawn.

The commissars walked by the four-man hide that we had quickly prepared beside an approach path to the village. I asked them to drop their weapons but they spun their Soviet automatics towards us. Both were killed and the noise of our fire alerted all enemy forces to our front and rear.

Seizing only the dead commissars' document case, we fled for four hours, throwing caution to the winds, and reached the edge of the *nej'd* before the enemy caught up with us. The names and ranks of many of their leaders were revealed by the captured papers, along with their intended policy for the immediate future.

As Tom had hoped, the ambush of the two communist leaders in their eastern stronghold had far-reaching effects. The enemy were suddenly less confident within their own territory, for they could no longer discount the possibility of betrayal by informants. They became inward-looking and the impetus of their planned counter-offensive was blunted by a fierce purge of suspects from their own ranks.

On 23 July 1970, after a well-executed and all but bloodless palace coup, the Sultan was exiled to the Dorchester Hotel in London where, two years later, he died a sad but charming old man and a victim to his own deep-rooted sense of economic caution.

The new monarch, Qaboos bin Said, at once declared an amnesty, which triggered a trickle of deserters from the Marxist front. These he rearmed and redirected against their former colleagues with advice from British SAS men.

By 1975, with help from Iran and Jordan, the tide turned in favour of the

Sultan and Islam. In three years Qaboos defeated Marxism in Oman and used the increasing oil revenues to drag Oman from medieval obscurity straight into the twentieth century.

After further operations in the eastern area we returned to the *nej'd* and before leaving the Sultanate in the spring of 1970 I made one further attempt to find Ubar. On this occasion we were led by a Rashidi guide, whom we met at the spring of Tudho. In response to our promises of rice, flour and medicines the elderly *bedu* agreed to show me 'the pillars'. This, after close interrogation, turned out to be a single stone pillar surrounded by many pieces of pottery which he had seen somewhere in the Uruq bin Hamooda.

I was convinced of success this time and greatly disappointed when, after three days' travel, including some very hard work in soft sand, we came to the long, narrow valley between two dune lines which our guide avowed was the place of the pillar.

'Where is it, then?' I asked.

'It *was* here,' he said with a Gallic shrug which gave me the impression that whoever's fault it was that we had so fruitlessly struggled to this God-forsaken spot, it could not be his. It was *he* who had been badly let down.

The Rashidi was taken back to Tudho and left with his bounty. I never again met the Beaver pilot on whom I had counted for an aerial search, and in the spring of 1970 my contract with the Sultan's Army came to an end. I hated to leave the Arabs I had come to know so well but, as a short-service officer, my time was irreversibly over with the Sultan's and Her Majesty's Armed Forces.

For a while I lived in London, squatting in the flat of my fiancée, Ginnie, where I haltingly began the process of making a career out of expeditions. Not knowing anybody who had ever explored by way of making a living, I could not be certain that, mathematically speaking, it was a feasible proposition.

My first self-imposed rule was never to pay anybody for anything where expeditions were concerned. Every item and every activity must be sponsored one hundred per cent, not merely at a generous discount.

The Nile hovercraft expedition had been a poor start. Because the Sultan's Army was paying me at the time, the project did not lead to bankruptcy, but I had spent over half my entire savings to buy one Land Rover for the journey. By good fortune I had sold the vehicle at a profit in Nairobi, yet there had been a definite risk I did not intend to repeat on future expeditions.

Sponsorship does not grow on trees. Company directors and publicity executives did not regard altruism as reasonable grounds for hand-outs in cash or kind. They wanted to be sure that their company would reap some tangible benefit from any help they gave and their standard yardstick was an estimate of how much publicity the particular expedition might expect to achieve.

Over fifteen hundred major expeditions, in addition to many smaller school and university endeavours, left Britain's shores each summer at that time and all but a few used considerable effort and ingenuity to attract sponsors. It had become a rat race and as a result many a worthy project failed to get off the ground.

The secret was to find a skilled literary agent who specialized in expedition books, newspaper articles and television documentaries. Ginnie located Britain's most successful such agent, George Greenfield, whose authors included Vivian Fuchs, John Hunt and Francis Chichester. From George I learned a great deal, including what projects were never likely to get off the ground simply because, however worthy they might appear from a scientific point of view, they would never be attractive to those editors who commission adventure stories whether in book or news feature form.

I ran a number of projects past George's kindly but critical ear in the early 1970s. Those he disliked received polite nods whereas items with promise were given a thorough inquisition. Ubar struck no chords at all and I knew it would be senseless to push any project likely to involve many thousands of pounds which would not, in George's opinion, 'interest the public'.

I married Ginnie in 1971 and we lived in a basement flat behind Earls Court tube station, earning a basic living from lecturing, for £18 an evening, at town halls and Women's Institutes. My topic was normally Dhofar or the Nile, or other small journeys, illustrated with colour slides.

A letter arrived from Tom Greening. He had put my name forward to raise and lead a raiding group to be based in the Shis'r region of the Dhofar steppes and consist of Mahra anti-communist tribesmen with a sound knowledge of the border region.

The job fell through but it rekindled my fond memories of Arabia and in the autumn of 1972 I was sent by the Director of Independent Television News, Don Horobin, to interview His Majesty Sultan Qaboos for the first time on Western television. After some hasty instruction by Sandy Gall on television interview techniques I flew out to Muscat with an ITN film team. Our brief was to stay for a month and cover all aspects of war and peace in Oman.

Despite letters of authority from His Majesty, when we reached Dhofar the British Intelligence chief would not give me permission to film the SAS in action. Since ITN had specifically asked for this, we filmed a fierce-looking band of ex-communists charging downhill with weapons blazing and headcloths covering most of their faces. My commentary clearly suggested, without actually saying so, that the men were SAS-led. At the time I was a captain in the London Territorial SAS Regiment and for a while afterwards I anticipated trouble from on high. As it turned out, no feathers were badly ruffled, and at the end of the month my interview with the Sultan went ahead without problems.

Afterwards he asked me about my years working for his father and the conversation veered to Ubar. He showed an immediate interest and quoted from the Qur'an: 'Irem of Ad of the many pillars.' He wished me good luck in my attempt to find the city and expressed interest in expeditions generally. This, as I was to discover, was no idle talk.

Ginnie took on various assignments with *Woman's Own* magazine, one of which took her to Oman, where she lived for some time as the nominal third wife to the sheikh of Ulyah, a beautiful village in the Jebel Akhdar. She dressed and lived as her hosts did and quickly grew to love their friendly, generous ways.

We found that expeditions could only keep us afloat if we mounted one every spring and then returned to write and lecture about it for the rest of the year. To begin with I kept to mostly hot countries with jungles, rivers or deserts as the background to our travels, but at some point in the early 1970s George Greenfield indicated that if we were ever to progress beyond amateur status we should seriously think of the polar regions. I disagreed, for I failed to see how the book-buying, Sunday-supplement-reading public could prefer to learn about white wastes of frozen nothingness rather than the many remote but fascinating regions of the tropics and the temperate zones. So I decided to present George with an Ubar expedition that was, so to speak, fully paid up, a *fait accompli* with a sponsor and no loose ends.

Ginnie was all in favour of Ubar and hated the idea of freezing her toes off in icy places just as much as I did. Sadly, economics intervened and, after thirty-seven letters to carefully targeted corporate chairmen, supported by telephone calls and subsequent visits, we found ourselves contemplating the dole or submission to George's suggestion of an expedition with a polar theme.

Quite why the British populace, or at least that segment of it that buy Sunday newspapers and watch television documentaries, are not statistically switched on to deserts, lost cities and quests to fill gaps in our human history, was and is a mystery to me. The conundrum is emphasized by the undeniable zeal with which these same people imbibe any and every story of journeys through the polar wastes. I imagined the hypothetical task of writing a book about an Antarctic traverse. Two thousand miles of white snow and ice topped with a sky of blue or grey. But what else? At either coast the mountain scenery, the birds and sea animals would provide scope for description but nine tenths of the journey would involve places where there was no scenery, no colour, no people, birds, animals or even insects, no history, no smells or sounds but our own and no buildings past or present. The only interesting matter would be the internal relationships between the individuals struggling to survive against such a grey backdrop. If, by bad luck, all the people involved liked one another and there were no *en route* dramatics, the resulting 'expedition book' would be virtually unwritable, and certainly unreadable.

Nevertheless, as George had predicted, our numerous attempts to raise support for an Ubar search with helicopter assistance came to nothing. We looked into cheaper forms of air transport – hot-air balloons, microlight and ultralight prototype aircraft (with different names at that time) and even military drones, or mini unmanned spy planes – that might photograph the dunes from on high and then land close by with the results. Even allowing for full sponsorship of all food, clothing and field equipment, our cheapest overall estimate for items for which no sponsor could be found came to hundreds of thousands of pounds.

At Christmas that year Ginnie suggested that, while we still had a roof over our heads and a serviceable mini-van in which to visit sponsors, we must make the break and 'go cold'. She suggested, for a start, an attempt to circumnavigate Earth via both Poles. This project eventually took seven years of full-time work to mount and three years to complete. During the course of it we crossed the surface of Antarctica and the Arctic Ocean via both Poles and navigated the entire North-West Passage in a thousand days of travel. The amount of support and sponsorship entailed by the entire endeavour was huge and the eighteen hundred companies who participated were, with few exceptions, hooked by the drama and the extremes of the Poles rather than the jungle, desert and ocean regions which were just as much a part of the whole journey.

A number of times since leaving the Army I had been asked to call at the Omani Embassy in London to give talks to young officers about to serve in Dhofar, where the war was escalating with increased sophistication on both sides. Over six hundred British officers and NCOs were involved by 1974, and thousands of troops from the Shah of Persia provided enormous assistance to the Muslim effort. King Hussein of Jordan also sent troops and a squadron of Hunter fighter aircraft. What advice I could give the usually apprehensive volunteers was soon outdated. I knew a good deal about extrication of casualties by mule but less by helicopter. I was *au fait* with night operations where the risks from friendly fire were non-existent, but I knew nothing of movement through terrain stiff with multinational troops on every hilltop.

By 1975 visits to the Embassy petered out but Tom Greening kept in touch and introduced me to Omar Al Zawawi, a wealthy Omani international businessman, who on many occasions over the years was to help financially with our polar expeditions. His only stipulation was that we should fly the Omani flag on reaching either Pole.

Sultan Qaboos, on a visit to London, hosted a reception for the expedition at Les Ambassadeurs restaurant, during which he exhorted an audience of businessmen to support our circumpolar project, which he described as a fine example of free enterprise.

Through the years it took to mount the expedition, we earned a living as and when we could and one of the books that I wrote required research into the background of two Dhofaris who had fought as ardent communists but later responded to Sultan Qaboos's amnesty. By chance my territorial SAS training one year consisted of a course with regular SAS troops in the Brunei jungles.

The RAF route to Brunei passed by Gan in the Maldives and Salalah was often a route-stop. With help from my former colonel, Peter Thwaites, I obtained a flight pass to Salalah and, through Tom Greening, a letter of permission to trace the relevant communists in the mountain war zone.

Once again the Intelligence officer in Salalah, Roy Nightingale, forbade me to enter the combat area. Back in England another SAS officer chuckled when he heard my complaints. Both the ex-communists that I had sought in Dhofar, he informed me, were learning English on the south coast. I soon found one in Bristol and the other in Bournemouth and obtained enough data to write the book about Dhofar. Sultan Qaboos helped me to promote the book in Britain and later had it translated into Arabic under a title that translates as *Dhofar, No Longer a Burning Land.*

Rumours from the Royal Geographical Society in London suggested that a British officer who was proficient with the workings of hot-air balloons had begin to search for Ubar. I could find out no further details and soon afterwards left

England for the three-year polar journey. The thought that others were hot on the Ubar trail made me distinctly envious.

Immediately before our departure Dr Omar, whose brother had become an influential minister in Oman, invited Ginnie and me to his Muscat seaside home at the time of the Queen's 1979 visit to Oman.

Frequent guests and close friends of Dr Omar included the Goan Felix de Silva, who was then Chief of Police in Oman, and Eric Bennett, who was Commander of the Air Force. If only we had not been tied up in the polar project I could, through Dr Omar, have canvassed the support of the Oman Police and Air Force, the key elements to a thorough search for Ubar. But the visit passed, as did the opportunity, and for the next three years we followed the axis of the world across the polar deserts, experiencing wind-chill temperatures down to $-122°F$.

The day the circumpolar expedition ended, ten years from the date of its inception, our voluntary organizers in London revealed debts of £106,000. As we were especially empty-pocketed after three years with no earnings, this was a major blow. Ginnie and Anton Bowring, the volunteer leader of the marine phases of the endeavour, spent the next two years working full-time and unpaid to pay off the debts. This they did and the book and lectures that I gave in the meanwhile enabled Ginnie and me to keep our London base.

One of the main expedition sponsors was the Chairman of Occidental Petroleum, Armand Hammer, who became involved at the suggestion of our Patron, His Royal Highness The Prince of Wales. Aged eighty-seven, the Doctor was nevertheless hyperactive and combined the post of Chief Executive Officer of Occidental with frequent flights to the Soviet Union and China to promote world peace. Since he had been a friend to many of the American Presidents and all the Soviet Secretaries General, including Lenin but excluding Stalin, he was well placed for his self-appointed role of international peace-broker.

In the autumn of 1984 Dr Hammer made me his personal representative in Western Europe, a full-time occupation which was not geographically limited since it included work in the USA, Africa and Moscow.

Many wealthy Americans believed Dr Hammer was a closet communist and their belief was somewhat strengthened by his father's history as a founder of the American Communist Party. In reality the Doctor was the ultimate capitalist wheeler-dealer and the years I spent as his consultant were an Aladdin's Cave of experience for me; an introduction to a world of high-fliers, big money and preposterous debts that I had never even sniffed from my previous existence as an expeditionist.

Ginnie and I were suddenly able to take a break from the circuit of expeditions, lectures and books. For the first time we were receiving a predictable income. Ubar now became an obtainable goal. Hammer had agreed, on signing my contract, to put up with four months a year of my absence on expeditions; truly a boss sent by Allah. I called an old friend from Dhofar days, Patrick Brook, who was at the time commanding the Sultan's Armoured Regiment. He assured me that neither the hot-air balloonist, Charles Weston-Baker, nor anyone else had yet discovered Ubar.

Patrick had given command of his first Chieftain tank squadron to Charles Weston-Baker back in 1980 and knew of his numerous attempts to locate Ubar.

In 1979 Weston-Baker had learnt about Ubar while researching for an expedition to Yucatan to find a lost Mayan city. Before arriving in Oman he met Wilfred Thesiger and read all he could about the country. He used Shis'r as his base for all his subsequent Ubar sorties. He questioned a number of Bait Kathiri and Mahra *bedu*. 'Some,' he said, 'shrank back in horror, not even wishing to speak the name of Ubar.'

On a great gravel expanse one hundred and thirty kilometres north-west of Shis'r, Weston-Baker found a section of the Thomas road and, in 1982, received the assistance of two of the Sultan's specially equipped desert-rescue Land Rovers to further his search. Later that year he purchased a one-man hot-air balloon small enough to pack in the back of a jeep and easy to inflate.

Because of high air temperatures and the rapid onset of thermal activity, he had to inflate the balloon before dawn and drift up to greet the rising sun. With experience he was able to follow the Thomas road from his first sighting of it for a further thirty kilometres into the dunes before the last faint track disappeared.

In between various assignments for Hammer I began to organize an expedition to locate the lost city by land and by air using Land Rovers with trailer-towed microlight aircraft.

An old friend from circumpolar days, Oliver Shepard, called me one day with a proposal that sparked off a good deal of anguished decision making. He suggested the ultimate polar journey, the grail of the international polar fraternity: to reach the North Pole with no outside support and no air contact. It was a journey long thought impossible but, with the advent of lightweight sledge materials and high-calory lightweight foods, Oliver now believed it to be feasible.

For a month Ginnie and I argued the pros and cons of the two expeditions and, as in the early 1970s, the cold quest won – although for a different reason this time.

Ubar had lain hidden from explorers and archaeologists for two thousand years and no man had reached the North Pole unaided since the world began to spin. There was no immediate reason to believe Ubar would be discovered, since Weston-Baker was the only other active searcher who had the Sultan's blessing. No archaeologist had been allowed to work in Dhofar since 1972 and I believed the Sultan would give me the go-ahead if I came up with a reasonable proposal, even if I delayed for a year or two more.

On the other hand there was a growing band of enthusiastic young men, increasing in numbers every year, from Britain, Norway, Canada, the Soviet Union and the USA, who were hell-bent on reaching the North Pole unsupported. Time was not on my side, nor Oliver's, since we were both in our forties and well past the ideal age to take on the enormous physical effort involved. Most of our potential competitors were between ten and fifteen years younger. If we were to go at all it must be sooner rather than later. This rationale finally convinced me to call off the Ubar search until we could complete our North Pole plans.

I contacted the thirty sponsors who had agreed to provide material assistance for Ubar and explained my reasons for postponing the search. Almost without exception they agreed to transfer their assistance, where still applicable, to the North Pole. As in the world of commerce, timing and the ability to adapt to changing priorities are the key to survival in a once-romantic niche that has become as cutthroat as any other business. Mountaineers vie with one another to reserve pole position on the official waiting lists to climb major peaks, yachtsmen and yachtswomen furiously court the known sponsors in their field to back great voyages over the world's oceans. Polar travellers have only the two Poles on which to focus their ambitions and the rivalry has become intense. Luckily, our Ubar sponsors understood this need to be first in the field and so switching targets was comparatively painless.

Polar preparations were soon under way when a rare chance to pay the bills appeared from nowhere in the shape of a contract from the American magazine *Departures*. I was to write an illustrated article about an obscure but bloody nineteenth-century battle which took place in Oman between the rebellious Beni bu Ali tribe and Anglo–Omani troops under the Sultan of Muscat.

The Beni bu Ali had remained obnoxious, certainly up until 1968, when I had tried to recruit in the Sharqeeya and Jaalan districts for the Sultan's Army. Heavily armed tribesmen had blocked my vehicles and prompted an ignominious retreat. Later that year they had clashed with another tribe, killing a hundred or more and even making the foreign news page of *The Times.*

Back in 1820 the Beni bu Ali had turned to piracy and when a British brig was sent to threaten them they murdered the envoy. A British captain was then sent with thirteen hundred men, the Sultan himself and six field guns: enough, it was felt, to subdue the tribe.

I drove into Beni bu Ali country with a British captain, two men, no Sultan, three rifles and Olympus camera gear, and located not one but five battlefields. In each place the local Beni bu Ali guide proudly assured me that the entire force of British *kafirs* had been wiped out and that the local wadi had 'run with their blood'. Unable to ascertain which if any of the five localities was the original battleground, I photographed all of them, in each case with the captain and one Omani soldier gazing at history from the squat position in the foreground.

The original clash had resulted in the defeat of the Sultan's British and Omani troops, leaving hundreds of dead and all their cannons as witness to the ferocity of the Beni bu Ali. The Sultan was later presented with a sword of honour, having been wounded while saving a British soldier in the heat of the fray.

After photographing the only tribesman who claimed to have heard tales of the battle direct from a survivor, his father, I took a month's holiday to locate and visit old friends from my reconnaissance platoon. Omani officers were slowly taking over from the British at all levels of the Sultan's Armed Forces, but Patrick Brook was still in Muscat and sent signals to detachments of his Armoured Regiment to look after me.

In the north the country had changed beyond recognition in a thousand ways. Where fifteen years before there had been one school, one hospital and a few roads of tarmac close to the capital, there were now four-lane highways, spaghetti junctions, schools and hospitals throughout the countryside, free bus services, supermarkets, magnificent Islamic style Government ministries, museums, aquariums, factories, street lighting, public gardens with fountains – indeed everything you would expect to find in a developed country had arrived as though at the touch of a magic oil lamp.

Yet the overall planning had been sensible, avoiding wasteful haste and ugliness. The apparent miracle was easier to comprehend when one bore in mind that *all* ministries and *all* major plans were subject to the approval of one man: the Sultan. Despite his western education, Sultan Qaboos was a strict Ibadhi Muslim and venerated the benefits of traditional values in architecture as well as in moral issues. Unlike Prince Charles in Britain, he did not have to fume in frustrated helplessness when he espied some atrocious concrete carbuncle rearing up in an Omani city: he simply ordered it to be pulled down and replaced.

I found myself regretting the passing of old ways and hating the Toyotas that honked with impatience in clouds of diesel fumes where I remembered only laden camels and spicy fragrances; views of once-majestic grandeur punctured by pylons and mountain-top repeater stations; road signs and wrecked cars in remote and picturesque valleys. But there were other memories of poverty, disease and cruelty by ignorance, of wasted opportunities and human talents, to make me ashamed of my selfish aesthetic reminiscences.

In Salalah the changes were in many ways more startling than in the richer, more populous north. If the northern Omanis had leapt in a single generation from the Middle Ages into the 1980s, then the Dhofaris had bounded from the Old Testament into the 1950s and were straining at the leash to close the remaining gap.

A young Dhofari lieutenant with a .22 rifle drove me down a muddy track to the coastal town of Rakhyut. The last time I had seen the place was from a Strikemaster fighter flying just beyond the effective range of anti-aircraft guns hidden on the cliffs three thousand feet above the town. At that time I would never have dared patrol within miles of Rakhyut even by night and heavily armed. But times had changed throughout the land. There were still mines awaiting the careless, but the last of the enemy had surrendered in the early 1980s.

Dhofar was no longer backward nor even deserving of its old epithet of mysterious, but thankfully, from my point of view, it was still special and would remain so as long as Government policy continued to disallow foreign tourists. With oil revenues a finite resource, tourism would sooner or later be actively encouraged and when that happened the Government would cry out for interesting ruins to advertise, never mind the benefits of an entire lost city to explore.

During my 1985 visit I was unable to further my Ubar plans and the closest I came to the Wadi Mitan was a cross-country trip from Thamrait – now a square-mile complex of Sultanate forces, including a hardened runway for Phantom jets – to the Yemeni border at Makinat Shihan, well south of any likely Ubar site.

Before leaving Oman I borrowed a vehicle from Patrick and drove for four hours from Muscat to a remote mountain village which had resolutely resisted the ugliness of progress while accepting the benefits. Despite the thick beard I was cultivating in readiness for polar temperatures later in the year, Said Salim recognized me as soon as I entered his low Omani house. We sat for many hours exchanging memories: it was as though the intervening years had never been.

CHAPTER EIGHT

Dr Hammer was a great admirer of Prince Charles and a supporter of many charities which the Prince had helped. I had for months tried to find a film company who would make a documentary about our circumpolar journey and when I failed Prince Charles mentioned the problem to Dr Hammer. He then contacted American documentary makers, all of whom said the journey would be too long and too costly to film.

Never one to accept no for an answer, Dr Hammer formed his own film company and later named it Armand Hammer Productions. Its specific task was to film the expedition and this went ahead without stint. Over one million dollars was spent on the production, including narration by Richard Burton shortly before his death. The film editor hired by Dr Hammer was Nick Clapp, from Los Angeles, who worked on it for nearly a year. We became friends and I learnt that Nick, normally a freelance director, had made a documentary in northern Oman about the reintroduction of the golden oryx from holding areas in the USA into a suitable region of Oman.

Nick had fallen in love with the country and decided to find a good reason to return and make a major documentary. He began to read all the classics of Arabian exploration, including, in 1981, Bertram Thomas's *Arabia Felix*. When he came across the author's description of camel tracks in the desert and the tale of the lost city, Nick knew that he had his film theme.

For the next two years Nick became a book-ferret, searching for any and every reference to the city and the frankincense trade which was likely to have been its *raison d'être*. During visits to the Huntington Library, the Oriental Collection of the New York Public Library, the British Library and many other well-known institutions he combed through over five hundred books and manuscripts, scribbling his findings in dozen of notebooks. Before long he was able to plot a great number of references to the lost city on to a chart of Arabia. Most of the references were vague and many were contradictory, but having Thomas's original grid references for Ubar provided a solid basis around which to consider other less concrete but feasible sites.

Despite never having set foot in Dhofar, Nick knew from his three-day oryx film visit to northern Oman that obtaining permits to film in that country could prove difficult or even impossible.

From reading the book *Unknown Oman*, Nick knew that aerial photographs had previously been used to navigate the Sands: by Wendell Phillips's Ubar expedition.

Reading about technical advances in space photography that had revealed watercourses underneath several metres of African sand, Nick decided to contact NASA to ask if similar techniques might reveal the locations of buried sites. He called a specialist in remote sensing at the Jet Propulsion Laboratory in Pasadena, California. Ronald Blom, after checking this was not just another crank 'space-call', agreed to look into the matter. A few months earlier Dr Blom had been contacted by Charles Weston-Baker with the same request, so he already knew about the lost city.

Some weeks later, in June 1984, Nick presented his case to Dr Ron Blom and his boss, Dr Charles Elachi, who was the Assistant Director of JPL, and Dr Robert Crippen. They were interested and agreed to help as best they could. The SIR-B (Shuttle Imaging Radar) system, which Dr Elachi had helped design, would be programmed with a desert search programme to take place during *Challenger*'s very next mission. The space shuttle duly blasted off and passed over the relevant parts of Arabia at three a.m. on 11 October during Orbit 96.4 and again at the same time the following day during Orbit 112.4

In a subsequent interview with *Time* magazine Charles Elachi said: 'The lost city will have to remain lost for another year or so due to problems with the radar array.' Nevertheless, seven months later, the SIR-B radar images became available and indicated possible sites of ancient streams and lakes which might once have supported habitation.

Nick's book-combing activities continued. The curator of rare books at California's Huntington Library, Alan Jutze, helped with archival research and the connection was soon made between the Quranic lost city of Irem and Ubar, since both places were clearly identified with the ancient description 'People of Ad': circumstantial if not definite evidence that the two names referred to the same place.

Ptolemy's original latitudinal coordinates for his Arabian map had been erroneously interpreted by subsequent map-makers and this had gone unnoticed until discovered by a German academic in the nineteenth century. When attempts were made to correct the error, Ptolemy's Omanum Emporium was still clearly positioned in the south-eastern sector of the Rub al Khali and so was potentially yet another name for the lost city.

On 28 January 1986 *Challenger* exploded after lift-off, killing all seven crew members, and all aspects of the *Challenger* programme were affected. Nevertheless Charles Elachi, Ron Blom and Robert Crippen agreed to pursue the lost city project by acquiring and processing images from the American LANDSAT and the French SPOT satellite programmes. LANDSAT coloured mapping images record terrain in visible light and otherwise invisible near-infrared wavelengths which geologists find revealing of soil and rock conditions. SPOT photographs, which are black and white, give the most detailed images obtainable commercially. SPOT satellites orbit at a height of eight hundred kilometres and can distinguish small objects through a principle known as teledetection. Unlike the Pentagon spy satellites, they do not transmit real photographs of the ground but signals of light intensity, which are then interpreted by sophisticated computers to highlight certain ground features. These include anything that stands proud of its natural ground setting. The programme shows up swellings of only a few feet in height in an overall flat desert setting, and to an experienced archaeologist such information can indicate man-made foundations.

Nick and I corresponded, mostly by telephone, from our separate positions within Dr Hammer's empire. We were both keen to locate Ubar and it seemed to make sense to join forces. With the primary aim of making a film, Nick decided to expand his documentary to two separate projects based on different features apparently visible on satellite photographs of Arabia. His most ambitious aim was to locate and follow the course of a river that appeared to flow from the area of Marib in Yemen and right through Saudi Arabia to the Gulf. This, he believed, might prove to be the River Pishon, mentioned in Genesis. He envisaged an expedition to follow the river to its northerly mouth then drive east to Oman and begin searching for Ubar.

Nick gave me an outline plan for his project entitled TransArabia. I advised him that the Sultanate might not look too kindly on an expedition that intended to operate in both Yemen and Oman, countries recently at war and still suffering from border clashes. We agreed to meet as soon as possible to discuss the possibility of fusing our separate search efforts into a single endeavour.

- - - - - - - - - - - - - - - - -

Meanwhile my more immediate expedition, to the North Pole, was already under way in two phases. In the permanent darkness of the Arctic winter no ski plane can land on the edge of the semi-frozen ocean where we needed to prepare our base. To get around this problem we planned to hire a Twin Otter bush pilot, from Resolute Bay in the North-West Territories, to fly our team and equipment north while there were still enough daylight hours to build and stock up a base. The travel team, Ollie Shepard and I, would then stay behind for a month to train on pack ice with prototype sledges. After closing the base down, we would fly out at the onset of permanent winter darkness and return as soon as the next year's sun returned to that latitude and travel again became possible.

In the autumn and early winter of 1986, Ollie and I accompanied the film-maker Paul Cleary to Resolute Bay, from where an Indian chief called Russ Bomberry, a polar bush pilot of great skill, flew us over hundreds of miles of empty and mountainous Arctic snowscape to Ward Hunt Island. Bad weather conditions dictated that Russ immediately take off again after unloading Paul and me and the cargo. Ollie went back with Russ: he would supervise the loading of the second cargo flight out of a total of eight. He would be back, he estimated, in ten hours.

In a forty-knot driving wind with blown snow and no shelter, Paul and I began to erect the prefabricated tarpaulin hut. We were soon extremely cold, so we dragged into a temporary shelter the single box of food that Ollie had left us. This, we discovered, contained eggs and tinned ham. There was no other food and a series of blizzards prevented Ollie and Russ from reaching us again for eight days.

For a film director, Paul produced an impressive succession of egg and ham meals, none of which was identifiable nor similar to its predecessors. In the past I had been confined with BBC film people for long periods in remote places and my opinion of them had lowered to ground level. Paul now revived it, for he was neither narrow-minded nor self-centred. Indeed he proved so adaptable that the polar base was soon completed, with wind-generating masts and a complex battery bank erected and all snow shelters finished on schedule, despite Ollie's absence.

In hot deserts isolated travellers can be exposed to the lethal effects of heat and thirst and unless their personal planning and awareness is up to scratch, they can soon get into trouble. Conditions of extreme cold, coupled with an environment of moving ice floes weighing millions of tons, are infinitely more hazardous and require a level of competence seldom needed in other equally remote parts of the world. Usually a novice expeditionist can cut his or her milk teeth and learn lessons the hard way during preparatory forays of controlled duration and limited risk. Out on the Arctic Ocean, especially during the dark period and early spring, learning a lesson can be fatal. Novices should keep off the ice until early March when the sun again shines on the fifty million square miles of shrieking, fracturing sea ice.

In darkness and mind-numbing temperatures, the simplest of errors can quickly lead to death by drowning or the loss of frozen hands and feet as a result of some small oversight. Modern clothing, rations and safety gear do not stop travellers dying. As the polar expert Wally Herbert puts it: 'even a man with perfect circulation and the best clothing designed by man will suffer terribly under the worst Arctic conditions.'

One problem caused by the extreme nature of Arctic hazards is the narrowing of choice when looking for suitable travel companions. To manhaul over polar pack ice involves many hours of great exertion dragging over three hundred pounds in dead-weight. You sweat like pigs despite outside temperatures of around $-50°C$. When you stop for breath, the sweat turns to ice in your underwear. Little people, however bold in outlook and determined of spirit, are simply not built to manoeuvre heavy weights. So you need men, not women, of hefty stature and good pulling power; carthorses not fine racers.

I receive many letters from aspiring polar explorers, but the risks involved in taking an unknown quantity on to the Arctic Ocean are too great to even consider. So, wherever possible, I take only those who have a known history of survival on polar journeys in winter. This is unfair on the young hopefuls, for it causes a chicken-and-egg situation where those needing polar experience find it difficult to make the break.

No such difficulties face the would-be traveller of the world's hot deserts. With basic skills such as photography, first aid or communications to offer, anyone can get in on the act and quickly become an old Saharan hand.

After many previous journeys with Ollie Shepard, both in Antarctica and the Arctic, I knew there would be no problems caused merely through ignorance or underestimation of the Arctic's awesome powers. Once the polar base at Ward Hunt Island had finally been set up and Paul Cleary had departed to prepare his film team for the following spring, Ollie and I settled in to the most northerly habitation on Earth. Our nearest neighbours, a hundred miles to the east, were eighty Canadian servicemen watching for Soviet submarines from their centrally heated base at Alert. Our only companions were Arctic foxes, hares and wolves. All birds had long since left for warmer climes.

We set up scientific recording gear, sledged through the darkness to measure ablation on a floating island of ice and carried out exhaustive tests of prototype sledging gear in temperatures below −50°C over fields of fissured ice blocks up to twenty feet in height. On a number of occasions we became separated many miles from our base and twice I feared for Ollie's life when he failed to return to Ward Hunt Island during long and fierce blizzards that came without warning.

The cost of the expedition was £70,000, payable entirely to the company operating the Twin Otter ski-plane that enabled us to set up the base. There were no other costs since all equipment, food and insurance had been provided free of charge in return for promises of publicity. Dr Hammer, in agreeing that Occidental Petroleum would pay the £70,000, had also stipulated that the expedition should acknowledge his help in news and television coverage.

To obtain the interest of a major newspaper and a television film producer we had to achieve a major physical challenge. In the 1980s expeditions to remote areas were two a penny. It was not enough merely to reach the North Pole without support or air contact. We must be the first to do so. This was an unfortunate but unavoidable fact of life and reflected the hard rule of sponsorship in a highly competitive world.

Success in reaching the North Pole would lead to my ability to mount the more expensive and, media-wise, less exciting Ubar expedition. But such success depended upon the failure of others to achieve the same goal before Ollie and I could do so. Although we appeared to have a head start, there were dangerous stirrings of opposition from several quarters. American, Norwegian, Soviet, Canadian and other British teams had all announced plans to reach the North Pole with or without support as soon as they were able.

The ability to persuade an individual or a corporate board to give away a large sum of money to an event that is not in itself a charity depends entirely on the publicity factor. In the days of Scott, Shackleton and Livingstone rich merchants may have been driven to support great endeavours into the unknown for purely altruistic or jingoistic reasons. Not so nowadays. Marketing directors need their pound of flesh. They need to know that they will receive greater media exposure by linking their company name and logo with the expedition than they would through spending the same amount on, say, a two-page advertisement in a newspaper.

So long as we held a demonstrable chance of being the first to reach the Pole without support, I could be confident of finding a sponsor. Neither Ollie nor I was happy with our winter trials. The sledges, when laden with enough food and fuel for ninety days' travel, weighed four hundred and sixty pounds each. Our progress rate with these loads was one mile in three hours, which meant we would never reach the Pole, four hundred and twenty-five nautical miles to the north, in ninety days.

So we played with mathematics. Could the journey be done in forty-five days, giving us less horrendous loads but half the time? There seemed no obvious answer. The optimum team strength for such a journey is generally believed to be a threesome. All non-consumable goods are of course shared among the team, since three people do not, for instance, require three radios. This means a three-man team can carry a smaller pro-rata total than two people require.

On the other hand the very nature of an expedition that sets out to be unsupported entails failure the moment any aircraft support is summoned, no matter for what reason, and the chances of three people remaining uninjured all the way to the North Pole would be correspondingly smaller than for our two-man team.

In mid-November we packed up the base, making it snow-proof by applying heated cloth-tape to even the tiniest of holes in the canvas walls and sealing the chimney and vents. Then we placed tins of kerosene-soaked rags at intervals along the plateau to the east of our hut, ready to provide an 'illuminated' runway.

Karl Z'berg, an Austrian polar pilot we both knew well from previous journeys, managed the hazardous, ill-lit landing, and three days later we were back in London.

Britain's most experienced polar-base leader and radio expert, Laurence Howell, a British Telecom engineer, agreed to join us. He knew of two other current North Pole attempts. A Minnesota-based dog-sledger, Will Steger, was about to attempt a much-heralded repeat of Peary's 1910 journey. Peary's claim had been treated with disbelief by many polar experts, including Wally Herbert, but the blind and fierce defence of their champion by *National Geographic* magazine (flying in the face of incontrovertible evidence) has to this day sustained the firm belief of the American public that Peary reached the Pole first. Steger, trumpeting his own faith in Peary, was heavily supported by the *National Geographic*. He intended to take seven men, one woman and some forty huskies to the Pole and he acknowledged with commendable honesty that his was no unique endeavour since he accepted that dog-power was a very real form of support.

Steger was due to set out from a temporary base twenty miles west of our own. He intended to depart about a week after sun-up, with temperatures still in the −50s and the sea ice as firm as possible.

Laurence also told us of a lone Frenchman, a Paris doctor named Jean-Louis Etienne, who had just announced a solo attempt to ski to the Pole with maximum air support and thus minimal encumbrance from sledge weight. He would set out from Ward Hunt Island the day the sun first appeared there. From the other side of the world, Laurence had picked up unconfirmed rumours of two or three separate Soviet attempts to reach the Pole with no outside help.

Laurence's Aberdeen home was peppered with as impressive an array of radio snooping devices and ham antennae as the Soviet Embassy in Kensington, so very few Arctic radio conversations took place that he could not tune into.

In London during the winter of 1985–6 I caught up with my work for Dr Hammer, contacted my Ubar sponsors to assure them that the search would continue as soon as the Pole was reached and tried to make time to spend with Ginnie at home. This was difficult, since Dr Hammer was a busy man and my workload had piled up. He liked to know he could contact me and receive a speedy reaction to his queries or instructions at all times of the day or night but usually between one and four a.m., as this suited his Los Angeles work schedule.

Ginnie was not exactly pleased with the frequent nocturnal business calls from the good Doctor, but we both realized there would never be another chance to earn a good salary and for the first time to put money in the bank. For years we had lived close to the breadline, which is especially difficult when one has a title, since most people equate hereditary titles with wealth and cannot accept that it is possible to inherit the one without the other.

For years we had ached to leave the bustle of London and head for some quiet rural wilderness where we could hear ourselves think. Thanks to the job with Dr Hammer this was working out and Ginnie had slowly rehabilitated our near-derelict farmhouse in the heart of the Exmoor National Park. It was surrounded by moor and gorse-filled fields and there were no man-made objects in sight for nine miles or more – not even a telephone pole. At weekends we tore down damp plaster, swept out layers of mouse droppings and multicoloured fungi and tackled rotten walls.

We listed the things we had both wanted to do over the years but, through lack of funds, had buried at the back of our minds. Ginnie loved cows, especially calves, and the thought of hillfarming on Exmoor was a wonderful dream to her.

All too soon the time came to return to the frozen north. I made contact with Nick Clapp and we agreed to meet in Montreal, a reasonable 'halfway point' between his home in Los Angeles and mine in London.

Ollie Shepard, Laurence Howell and Paul Cleary, along with Terry Lloyd of ITN, joined me in London with our newly designed Arctic sledges and we flew to Montreal overnight before the next leg to the Inuit (Eskimo) settlement of Resolute Bay.

In Canada we were joined by Paul's camera team, which consisted solely of the amazing Beverly Johnson. She was the first woman to climb solo El Capitan, the stark and vertical rock wall in the Yosemite National Park which she scaled over a four-day period, dragging her water and gear behind her. Together with her husband, the equally venturesome Mike Hoover, she had filmed our earlier circumpolar expedition, during which she had fallen through weak ice and suffered from ten badly frostbitten toes as a result.

While Ollie and the others visited a local Montreal nightclub famous for its nude dancers, I met Nick Clapp at the hotel and we compared notes on Ubar. In total we had spent twenty-four years hoping to locate the lost city: I had begun my search in 1968 and Nick in 1981. He had great hopes that space technology would reveal the burial site but, even if this was not to be, he hoped to make a fascinating film of little-known Dhofar based on the search.

I liked Nick's sense of humour and his ability to pinpoint a single target to the exclusion of all else. He wanted to film in Oman and had been utterly determined to find a theme on which to base a documentary. He later wrote: 'My wife and I very much enjoyed this first trip to Oman and then and there determined to find a good reason to return and make a major documentary.'

Nick and I agreed to co-lead an expedition to find the city. Nick would concentrate on raising funds, hunting for further historical references and on the most difficult of tasks: finding sponsorship and backers for a documentary film. I would organize the political permissions, find equipment, sponsors, fix schedules and lead the team within Dhofar.

Nick would stand no chance of getting permission to enter Dhofar with an archaeological team, for he was not known to the Sultan and since 1972 all archaeological projects seeking to work in southern Oman had been refused permits. But through my contacts with the Sultanate, this barrier might be removed.

On the other side of the coin, I had twice found it difficult in Britain to raise the necessary financial sponsorship to mount a search for Ubar but, with American involvement and the cachet of NASA technology, whether this turned out to be helpful or not, I felt optimistic that the necessary funds would soon be forthcoming from the USA.

The satellite image given to Nick in 1986 by the key Jet Propulsion Laboratory officers Drs Charles Elachi, Ron Blom and Robert Crippen was from the SIR-B mission launched by *Challenger* and clearly showed a short stretch of the 'Thomas road' as well as an L-shaped feature near by that looked man-made. Only by reaching the Thomas road and the 'L-site' could an expedition hope to gather further information about the features photographed from space, and then only if an experienced archaeologist was present.

Nick spent a great many hours searching for ancient references to the names of key places and people that might provide clues to Ubar's location. Among the five hundred or so references that he unearthed were the following:

'Ubar is the name of the land which belonged to Ad in the eastern part of Yemen. Today it is an untrodden desert, owing to the drying up of its water. There are to be found in it great buildings which the wind has smothered in sand.' (Nashwan bin Said al Himyari, eleventh century)

'Wabar is between the land of the Beni Sa'ad, El Shahr and Mohra.' (Yaqut)

'The wind that destroyed Ubar came from the Wadi al-Mughith.' (Al-Kisai)

'The land of the 'Ad is "from the sands of Alaj to the trees of Oman".' (Al-Baidawi)

'Al Akaf is a valley between Oman and Mahra land.' (Ibn Abbas, cited in Yaqut)

'Al Akaf is sand between Oman and Hadhramaut.' (Ibn Ishak, cited in Yaqut)

'Irem dhat al hmad [Irem of the towers] is in the wilderness of Abyan.' (Al Hamdani)

'Mahra. Their origin is Ubar.' (Al Hamdani)

'The origin of Mahra is to be sought in the remains of the people of 'Ad who retreated to the mountains of Zufar.' (Ibn al-Mujawir)

Nick's extensive researches in books had led him to the inescapable conclusion that only Thomas's siting of Ubar gave a clue that was at all precise. The fact that the road and the L-site were the only interesting features produced by satellite imagery and that both were close to the Thomas location, seemed hopeful.

My own searches had relied on local knowledge and current *bedu* gossip without reference to historical records. Yet, despite little or no overlap in our separate hunts, we had each independently ended up with the same basic indicators: Ubar should be sought in the Sands to the west and north of the Wadi Mitan.

Nick accepted the delay that my polar travels might cause, little suspecting how badly things were to turn out.

I promised to approach His Majesty Sultan Qaboos of Oman as soon as the northern journey was over. Nick returned to Los Angeles, leaving me doubly keen to reach the Pole that spring.

The Marketing Manager of Nordair, the company who sponsored our Arctic flights out of Montreal, summoned me to his office before our departure. 'I thought I ought to warn you,' he said with an apologetic grimace, and handed me a copy of *Macleans*, the main Canadian general interest magazine pitched somewhere between *Newsweek* and *Harpers*. 'They have a profile feature on someone every month. They are often critical but this is worse than usual.'

The feature was about as bad as it could be and accused me of gimmicry, scrounging, a long ancestry of Colonel Blimps and implied that there was no serious content to my expeditions. I posted a copy of the feature back to Ginnie and suggested she contact a libel lawyer. The author, Alan Fotheringham, was one of two Canadian journalists who, for seventeen years, had attacked me, my expeditions and books, usually on false grounds. I had previously ignored the problem since their acerbic ramblings were unlikely to be repeated in the British press. But now I depended on Canadian sponsors to the tune of many thousands of dollars' worth of equipment and transport facilities. The executives who would decide whether or not such support should continue were exactly the people who were habitual readers of *Macleans*. I needed a rebuttal of the inaccurate profile as quickly as possible, otherwise my Canadian sponsors would rapidly withdraw.

Over the past two years I had handled a number of libel cases for Dr Hammer, who was not one to leave unanswered even the slightest of allegations against his character. Only a month previously I had received a cheque for £25,000 from *Private Eye* on the Doctor's behalf.

If Dr Hammer could bite back at the inaccurate aspersions of the media, I thought it worthwhile to follow his example. Mr Fotheringham's press colleagues had last fired a broadside during our circumpolar expedition through suggestions of cowardice and desertion. The occasion had been the Falklands War, shortly after a helicopter of SAS soldiers crashed and were killed. Charlie Burton and I, both SAS Territorial soldiers, were at the time adrift on an ice floe in the Arctic. The Canadian journalist suggested that we had carefully planned our predicament as far away as possible from the theatre of war with the express purpose of avoiding call-up.

- - - - - - - - - - - - - - - - -

From Montreal we flew to Resolute Bay, where our bush-pilot friends were based. The sun had only just risen at that latitude after a four-month disappearance and we were grateful for accommodation on the floor of a backroom full of spare parts in a heated aircraft hangar.

While awaiting daylight we jogged along the single road between the airstrip and the Inuit village: everywhere else was buried under deep snowdrifts.

Laurence paid for our keep by repairing radios, toasters and antennae systems at the airbase while we waited for the ideal weather conditions necessary for the potentially dangerous flight north to Eureka, an isolated weather station, and on to Ward Hunt Island.

Four days after sun-up at the latitude of the Ellesmere Island coastline, we touched down in appalling conditions on a tiny freshwater lake half a mile from our hut. The pilot immediately took off again and we burrowed our way through a giant snowdrift which had formed around the hut.

The temperature was $-52°C$ but our kerosene heaters soon made the hut habitable. Sledging preparations began immediately, for a North Pole journey with or without support must take place within the narrow corridor of time between sun-up and break-up. Too early a start is likely to lead to frostbite or fatal immersion in the sunless gloom, and anyone lingering on the sea ice once the ultraviolet rays of summer have rendered it rotten, is vulnerable to the dangers of a sudden storm and fracturing floes. Each day of inaction after sun-up on 3 March sets the clock ticking in a countdown to failure. Within a week we had prepared all our equipment and began to carry out ice trials on the new sledges.

To the east the American dog teams of Will Steger set out on schedule and a Twin Otter brought the diminutive French doctor Jean-Louis Etienne to our base for his solo attempt on skis. As yet unready to go, we agreed to show Jean-Louis the best route through the chaotic pack ice that forms a high wall just north of the Ward Hunt ice shelf. Although this is in continual movement and sometimes gives way to many miles of open sea, there had been little change since our trials there the previous winter and we soon found the best passage through the tortuous fields of ice.

Jean-Louis shook hands with us and set off for his epic walk to the dull clicks of our freezing camera shutters. Twenty-four hours later he was back again, looking cold and mournful. In order to check his ever-changing location, for the floes might move him many miles even while he slept, Jean-Louis used an Argos satellite transceiver and this he had discovered, at his very first camp, did not function. So he had slogged his way back through the rubble zone to our camp. His only option was to call for a Twin Otter from Resolute Bay to deliver his spare Argos – a round flight that would cost some $14,000 and up to a week's delay.

'Shall *I* see what's wrong?' Laurence asked the Frenchman.

Even with the knowledge of our radio operator's technical skills, I had not given a thought to the chances of repairing such a highly complex electronic device *in situ*. Eight hours later Laurence had fitted the various circuit boards and wires back together and the Argos worked perfectly.

'Badly designed switch,' Laurence muttered as Jean-Louis expressed his gratitude with Gallic gestures and a great toothy grin. He slept soundly in our hut. We plied him with whisky and the best of foodstuffs from sponsors Marks & Spencer. We hung his sleeping bag from the drying wires along the hut ceiling and marvelled at the amount of ice that had dripped into the feather down. At least two pints of water had collected in our floor basins.

- - - - - - - - - - - - - - - -

As the Steger dogs and the lone Jean-Louis Etienne slowly battled their way north, each vital day passed and found us floundering about the ice shelf in fruitless experiments with our giant loads. Even the superior design of our new sledges did not enable us to drag the three-hundred-and-eighty-pound loads at a reasonable pace.

We pared down equipment to a bare minimum, even shaving the Teflon runners with Stanley knives. All to no avail. The blow came by radio in late March. Ollie Shepard received an ultimatum from his London employers, Beefeater Gin. Either he returned within four weeks or he lost his job. With a wife and home to look after, the latter course was no option, so with great reluctance he signalled for a Twin Otter to come north by the end of the month.

Ginnie immediately began work in England to find a replacement to take over from Ollie. This was not an easy task, since we needed somebody who had undergone recent polar acclimatization and was fresh from a manhauling journey; preferably a heavily built person in good trim. There were only a dozen individuals in Britain whom she knew would be experienced enough, but none had been on polar expeditions for months if not years. The only exception was the three-man team of a South Pole expedition whose leaders were Roger Meares and Robert Swann. The latter was in Cape Town and the third man was in Antarctica, but Roger Meares told Ginnie he would consider it. However, he reluctantly succumbed to book-writing pressures and suggested in his place the first reserve of his expedition, Dr Mike Stroud, of the Emergency Unit of Guys' Hospital.

Mike Stroud was startled by Ginnie's call but agreed to come to the Arctic at once. Four days later, with clothing Ginnie had rustled up from our sponsors, Mike left Heathrow and reached Ward Hunt Island two days before 1 April, which was my deadline for departure for the Pole. Even then I knew we would be cutting things dangerously fine.

I received a shock when Mike climbed off the Twin Otter. Sensibly, Ginnie had not warned me by radio that Mike was small in height for a manhauler, *extremely* small. I am around six feet tall and lean, without visible muscle. Mike's head came to a level with my shoulder but he was built like a brick outhouse, with the biceps, chest and thighs of a bodybuilder. Swallowing my disappointment at the new arrival's appearance, I waved goodbye to Ollie.

Two days later the outlines of Laurence, our film crew and the hut slowly disappeared into the distance of the Ellesmere mountains as we dragged our sledges north. The film crew had dubbed Mike 'Mighty Mouse' after his first trial manhaul on the ice shelf. He pulled like a husky, digging his boots in and leaning so far forward that his nose seemed to scrape the ice. He dragged his sledge completely oblivious to its size and weight – more than twice his body weight – and trudged on relentlessly for hour after hour.

For the first two weeks I would stop at the end of each hour and follow my trail back to find Mike. I would help him for a while, and this he was sensible enough to accept. At the end of each day we compared our position with that of the other two expeditions, for Laurence's radio spy system enabled him to keep a precise log of their progress.

Travel through polar pack ice is not merely a matter of brawn and the correct equipment. The greatest bonus is experience, which brings an awareness of the ever-changing ice conditions, where to avoid, where easy corridors might best be sought, how to detect zones of open water before reaching them, what colour and thickness of wet ice can safely be crossed even though it screeches and bends at every step. Such knowledge can save hours, even days, and is the greatest single factor in the success or otherwise of any expedition, save only for the matter of luck.

Each of us towed a load of three hundred and eighty pounds, while Jean-Louis towed eighty pounds and Steger's dog handlers nothing. Of course, dog teams need help and persuasion but, in a given day, there are long periods when a handler can head north with nothing to pull, push or drag.

Jean-Louis' sledge weighed four pounds and could not be used as a canoe. Ours, which were amphibious and weighed seventy pounds when empty, were unbreakable. When the Frenchman's sledge developed a crack in its thin fibreglass shell, he merely signalled for a replacement on his next replenishment flight. Since our expedition was above all else *unsupported*, to request *any* aid was to admit failure. At the time of writing, in the summer of 1992, no man has yet reached the North Pole without support, although a number of teams, all of whom received air contact *en route*, have made false claims to the achievement.

At the time Mike Stroud arrived in Ward Hunt Island the world record for human travel without support stood at ninety-eight nautical miles following the near-fatal journey of the Simpsons and Roger Tufft in 1968. Subsequent attempts, such as those of David Hempleman-Adams and Clive Johnson in the 1980s, had ended in failure and frostbite less than fifty miles from the Arctic coast.

An exact physical parallel of the task involved would be to drag two heavy six-foot-tall men, tied together, through sand dunes for four hundred and twenty-five nautical miles. The terrain includes some two thousand walls of ice rubble up to twenty-five feet high, regions of rotten ice that break up and overturn as you try to negotiate them with your hefty sledge and zones of open water, sometimes as far as the eye can see, which are often laden with treacherous *shuga* ice of porridge-like consistency. Add to these obstacles a temperature that is often lower than a deep freeze and a northerly wind that cuts into exposed skin like a bayonet and it is no wonder that, despite intense international competition, the challenge has yet to be met.

Some seventy miles from the coastline, the highest mountains of which had long since faded from view, we encountered dangerous conditions caused by strong winds to our east. Strange sounds akin to thunder and gunfire wracked the ice and distant daubs of black and brown sky patched the horizon, where newly formed lagoons released warm air into the supercool atmosphere.

Struggling to force the sledges over a field of broken ice blocks, I misjudged the colour of the surface below. My sledge cannoned off a twelve-foot-high mound and knocked me from my hauling position. I hit the ice hard and was instantly immersed. Mike was close at hand and dragged me out, but the damage was done.

'We must get the tent up at once,' Mike shouted above the din of the moving pack. 'At this temperature, your wet clothes will freeze and frostbite will set in quickly.'

He was right, but I knew it would be suicidal to try to camp in a fracturing zone. The chances were too high of instant immersion and sea burial under tons of rolling ice. A lone piece of ham in a saucepan of stirred scrambled egg would have as much chance of remaining on the surface. So we continued to head north in a crazy series of tacks wherever the floating floes provided a route.

Four unpleasant hours later the scenery ahead changed abruptly from blue-white to yellow-white, as wonderful a sight to us as an oasis to a thirsty desert traveller.

Once on firm 'land' Mike erected the tent, since by then my hands were lumps without feeling and useless for such tasks. He helped me into the tent, lit the petrol cooker and unpacked my sledge as well as his. Because mine had fallen into the sea beside me, the lashing straps had been coated in brine, which then froze around them, causing delay.

Inside the tent I struggled to remove my sledge jacket, but since both it and my clumsy mitts were encased in a thick film of frozen sea ice, I had no success. All the while I battered my two boots together in an attempt to force blood to flow, but there was no feeling in either foot.

Mike at last appeared through the tent's tunnel entrance with some four inches of frozen nose-dribble stuck to the chin of his Balaclava like a gnome's jagged beard.

Unlashing the sledge had quickly made Mike cold. *Any* pause from the exhausting action of manhauling soon results in a lowered heart rate, so that the blood flow rapidly retreats from the extremities and shivering begins. Sweat caught between layers of clothing turns to ice and there is an urgent need to do one of two things. You can either return to the treadmill of manhauling or, if too tired, erect the tent and eat into the sternly rationed daily quota of fuel to provide life-giving heat.

So as to cut down cargo weight, our fuel ration allowed only for cooking, not for clothes drying or tent heating, so an immersion like mine caused major problems with the vital fuel supply. This in turn could lead to bitterness between team members, since to fall in was, or could be, considered to be the result of stupidity.

On all previous expeditions I had gone to considerable lengths to carefully vet every team member but through force of circumstance had accepted Mike sight unseen. That we proved to be totally compatible was remarkably lucky. There was no strained atmosphere, no recrimination, no hint of tension, not even the occasional heated exchange.

Mike managed to remove my mitts and I shoved my hands inside the ski jacket and under my armpits. There was a chance they might return to life, according to Mike's practised eye. My boots would not come off, however hard Mike struggled with them. The obvious answer, since it was vital we extricated my toes from their immediate frozen environment with minimal delay, was to cut through the frozen bootlaces with our pin-nosed pliers. Since the laces were completely encrusted, the actual boot canvas would need cutting too.

'If we cut up the boots,' Mike said, looking at me from beneath a fringe of iced-up eyebrow, 'it will mean the end of the expedition: failure.'

I nodded. We carried no spares. To save weight, every item not vital to progress had been jettisoned: no toothbrush, no personal mementoes, and none of those 'spares' normally considered indispensable such as extra mitts or goggles.

Since we carried no spare laces or replacement boots, we faced the choice between delaying resuscitation of my feet for at least a quarter of an hour while thawing the laces out, and cutting through the obstacles at once to give my feet a better chance.

Ruefully I remembered a day eight years before when I had fallen through Arctic ice and Ollie Shepard had saved my feet by cutting my boots off with an axe. That had been a normal *supported* expedition and an hour of rubbing my feet immediately after their immersion had saved them from frostbite, gangrene and amputation. But now we were faced with the full meaning of our self-imposed puritan regime. 'How stupid!' the armchair traveller might exclaim, or, 'Sheer masochism.' But we were no more masochists than the Everest mountaineer who refuses to use oxygen or the marathon runner who does not use a bicycle. All sports are hedged about by rules and some forms of sport involve sterner parameters than others. If all competitive sportsmen are stupid or masochistic, then so were we.

The decision was not easy. If I responded to the strong desire to ask Mike to cut off the boots, I knew we would be back again the following year, which would mean a further postponement of the Ubar expedition. The two guests had become inextricably entwined and, on a more mundane level, Ginnie and I needed a successful expedition in order to maintain a presence on the highly competitive international lecture circuit, our only source of income should the eighty-nine-year-old Dr Hammer sack me or die.

Reluctantly I asked Mike, by now shivering with cold himself, to thaw the boots out as quickly as he could. I could feel no sensation at all in either foot.

CHAPTER NINE

Mike thawed out my boots and eventually the laces. He quickly declared my left foot was redeemable, since it had remained miraculously dry except for the toes and the sole.

'Not so good,' he said, shaking his head, as he examined my other foot. Three of the toes and an adjoining area of skin were parchment-white and devoid of any feeling. Slowly he warmed up both my feet, expending valuable fuel, before applying dry dressings. Breaking the normal rule against using the cooker merely for damp clothes, he dried out my socks and slipped them over the bandages.

Next day we set out on time. I felt no pain throughout the day and was surprised when, back in the tent, Mike swore aloud on removing the dressing. What appeared to be the outer half of my little toe and a segment of flesh had come away with the bandage. A large area of raw flesh and bone was left exposed which, as soon as my foot warmed up in the tent and blood returned to the nerve ends, felt like it was on fire.

For the rest of the journey I dreaded the mornings until, after an hour or so of travel, the foot grew cold enough to deaden the nerves. Likewise the evenings, when the reverse process took place. Nevertheless, despite our heavy loads and my early-morning limp, our progress continued to outpace that of the two supported expeditions to our north. After fifteen days we passed the ninety-eight nautical miles point, the existing world record, and celebrated with an extra cup of tea.

Some days the wind blew from the north, making conditions doubly uncomfortable. Our normal schedule involved ten to eleven hours of manhauling with two breaks of four or five minutes each. When the wind was about twenty knots we often hauled for eight hours without a break, to avoid the likelihood of getting frostbitten fingers from trying to drink tea from the two vacuum flasks. These were standard titanium models, to save the extra weight of steel flasks.

In bad conditions we craved for each tea break, yet at the same time we feared the intense cold that accompanied each halt. It could take up to an hour to force the blood back into toes and fingers afterwards, so the halts were a mixed blessing.

One evening Mike announced that he had broken one of the very fragile vacuum flasks. Since this cut us down to a single intake of hot liquid each day, I felt distinctly hostile towards him, although I made no comment.

'We have a choice from now on,' Mike said. 'We can use the remaining flask either for tea or for Pre-stress.'

Pre-stress was a specially prepared quick-energy drink that helped to stave off hypothermia and which we normally alternated with tea.

'As a doctor, what do you advise?' I asked Mike.

'We'd better stick to Pre-stress, despite the taste,' he said, giving the reply I had expected.

Two days later Mike was unusually quiet in the tent and after a while broke the news that he had somehow managed to break the second and last vacuum flask. This was a major blow since the conditions were still extremely severe and, after five or six hours of maximum effort, the body cried out for an energy source to stimulate dangerously flagging metabolic rates.

Because we had to manhaul in only two thin layers of clothing in order to minimize body sweat, we were often on the fine edge of hypoglycaemia, a lethal condition in such circumstances. A single energizing hot drink often kept us from suffering exposure, especially towards the end of the sledging day. Now, this would be impossible.

I silently swore at Mike's carelessness but managed to refrain from an outburst. He had obviously thought through the results of the breakage before admitting to it, for he immediately followed the news with his plan to make amends. 'It's not the end of the world,' he assured me. 'We still have the pee bottle.'

In the extreme cold the bladder very sensibly constricts and causes frequent stops both *en route* and in the tent. To avoid going outside the tent six or seven times and allowing precious warmth from inside to escape, we used a one-pint noduline bottle with a plastic rim to which a shrunken member could not stick.

'You must be joking, Mike,' I replied. 'Are you suggesting peeing into it each night and drinking Pre-stress out of it each day?'

'Why not? We can call it Pee-stress. Urine will do you no harm, after all.'

'*Mine* won't,' I retorted. 'But I can't say I fancy the idea of drinking from a container with *your* frozen pee stuck to the outside.'

'I never thought of you as fastidious. But I'm quite happy if you don't wish to share the contents.'

'It's one short step from cannibalism,' I muttered. But the following day I noticed no change in the taste of the Pre-stress.

Only two days later, as Mike changed the bandage on my foot in the morning, the tent was filled with a foul smell which Mike recognized as gangrene. Three days earlier I had finished the last of the penicillin tablets and he had warned me then that only luck could keep the bacteria at bay. The foot was only slightly swollen – and, if anything, hurt less than normal when I forced my boot over the wound – but the writing was on the wall.

Since there are no weather stations on the Arctic Ocean, the Resolute Bay bush pilots have to rely on the often amateurish summary of expedition personnel. They must be sure of ideal conditions in Resolute Bay, at halfway Eureka and at the pick-up site. It is common enough for seven days to pass by without such a weather front. Knowing this and fully aware of the speedy progress of gangrene, Mike advised an immediate radio signal to Resolute Bay once we could find an area suitable for an airstrip amid the many miles of chaotic broken ice.

The next day we found four hundred yards of comparatively flat surface on a well-weathered floe and marked out an airstrip with coloured ration bags. I tuned in our HF radio, after laying out the dipole antenna to face south, and made instant contact with the ever alert Laurence at Ward Hunt Island. By coincidence, one of the Steger expedition, an Alaskan dog-sledder named Bob Mantell, had serious frostbite in his hands and feet. Laurence managed to contact the Twin Otter pilot as he circled above Steger's camp two hundred miles to our north. Four hours later the Twin Otter reached us, bumped perilously over our 'strip' and we said goodbye to our dreams of the Pole.

Another of Steger's men, a hefty New Zealander with two broken ribs, met us back at the base. Disappointment showed on his face and in his slumped shoulders.

We had passed the previous best northing by only nine miles and yet were still over three hundred miles short of the Pole. We had learned a number of key lessons which neither of us intended to waste. We agreed to try again as soon as the money could be raised and providing others did not pre-empt us.

The day after our return to Ward Hunt Island my foot and leg swelled alarmingly and a smell of rotten flesh pervaded the hut. Laurence had given Mike all our penicillin supply, the Twin Otter was busy removing excess husky dogs from the Steger team and my foot's predicament looked as unsettled as before.

Laurence performed miracles with his antenna systems and, after a long correspondence with the bush-pilot base, announced that, weather permitting, we could expect evacuation with a maximum of fifteen hundred pounds of cargo the following morning. Working without a break through the night, we packed up the valuable communications and scientific gear along with the ice-core samples from the previous winter. Everything else, including the wind generator system, we left in place for other teams and in the hope that we would soon return.

In Resolute Bay an Inuit nurse did her best, under Mike's supervision, to clean the open wound and I began a new course of penicillin. Two days later we were back in London and Mike contacted the Burns Unit at Roehampton Hospital, where he had once worked. A friendly surgeon agreed to operate immediately and grafted a two-inch-square swatch of skin from my thigh on to the remains of the toe and the outer side of my foot. Later that week, along with Paul McCartney for music and Billie-Jean King for sporting prowess, I was nominated for the *Guinness Book of Records*' World Hall of Fame, and described by the book as the 'World's Greatest Living Explorer'. This was especially embarrassing in the light of our recent failure to reach the Pole and I hobbled on to the BBC stage to receive my award from David Frost and Ross McWhirter wearing a black sock over the bandages and feeling very fraudulent.

- - - - - - - - - - - - - - - - -

I needed to reach the Pole and to find Ubar, but in the short term I would have to work hard to keep my job with Dr Hammer and that meant at least a year without further absenteeism. The Doctor's first major task for me was to represent him and his wife at a Moscow reception. A famous American porcelain company had produced hefty replicas of the Russian bear and American eagle which, through Dr Hammer's introductions, the formidable lady owner of the company was to present to Mrs Raisa Gorbachev in front of the Soviet press, as a symbolic gesture of peace. Business in China precluded Dr Hammer's presence in Moscow but he was anxious not to allow the porcelain lady to upstage his involvement, and I received the strictest instructions to this end.

Ginnie and I donned ball gown and black tie respectively and met up with the porcelain personage at the Great Hall of Culture. Of Italian ancestry and graced with a fine Jewish nose, the lady was upholstered with a mesmerizing supercargo that literally brushed people aside as she turned around. A thrusting crowd of

Soviet and other photographers jostled to get shots of Raisa Gorbachev talking to the foreigners and, remembering Dr Hammer's exhortations, Ginnie and I attempted to push our way into the picture.

A solid mass of bust clad in sequinned white slammed into my shoulder and forced me backwards. The strident voice behind the bust rose above the general clamour to proclaim the wonders of Mrs Gorbachev and her husband, Moscow and the entire Soviet Union.

The Soviet flashbulbs popped and, holding tight to the busty madame's elbow, I forced my way between her and Raisa Gorbachev. We had briefed Dr Hammer's Moscow representative, the delightful Nina Vlassova, to hire a photographer so that, whether or not the Soviet press announced the Doctor's involvement, we would at least have photographic evidence of our attempts to share the limelight.

I made a gushing Hammer-style speech about the great strides of the Gorbachevs. This was translated and followed by our opponent, who cradled the microphone between resonant breasts and included in her rousing oration the information that Raisa had confided in her that she had just become a grandmother. The Russian First Lady, standing beside me, whispered in English, 'How very bad. That is a secret . . . my secret.'

I later told the story to Dr Hammer, who chuckled delightedly and sent me off to Swaziland to represent him at the Prince of Wales's visit to a mixed-race college which they both supported. This was followed by missions to Rome with confidential correspondence to the ex-King of Afghanistan.

As part of his determination to bring about peace between the USA and USSR, Dr Hammer flew constantly between the two countries, then on to General Zia of Pakistan and the *mujahadeen* leaders. His proposal was based on the return of the Afghan king and the removal of the Soviets.

For me, life at this time consisted of wearing a grey pin-striped suit and shiny black shoes – a format I had avoided all my life. However, apart from a few office-bound days every month, Dr Hammer's multifaceted interests were never boring.

Ginnie and I were given the Polar Medal by the Queen, with unique bars for Antarctica and the Arctic. Ginnie was the first woman to receive the medal and later that year became the first female member permitted to join the hallowed male portals of the Antarctic Club. At the Club's black-tie Annual Dinner, where our places had been reserved next to the President, Ginnie's acceptance was to be honoured. However, somehow or other I managed to make a dreadful mix-up in my diary and we failed to attend.

Now on the wrong side of forty, I was aware that I must maintain the impetus of the expeditions and my lectures about them without a break since I could not rely on continuing employment with Dr Hammer, who consistently refused to give me a consultancy contract of more than one year's duration. There was nothing personal about this, he said; it was just the way he preferred to operate.

His Majesty the Sultan of Oman came to London and paid a visit to his old friend Tom Greening, who had been my Intelligence officer in Dhofar. Tom, by then a retired brigadier, lived in a secluded manor in Berkshire. I went there with an updated proposal for the Ubar expedition and His Majesty reminded me that he was not keen on people descending on Oman, especially the southern part, with picks and shovels. However, he had been pleased with the Omani involvement throughout the circumpolar project and would be prepared to allow me to take an expedition to the south, provided any digging was carefully controlled.

At that time I could not clearly state where I wanted to excavate but showed His Majesty a LANDSAT space image I had received from Nick Clapp that summer. This showed amid the dunes thin white lines which could perhaps be old roads.

I assured Sultan Qaboos that I would revert to him as soon as the polar expedition was out of the way and I could draw up a more detailed plan for the Ubar project. I also checked up on the Ubar balloonist, Charles Weston-Baker, fearful lest he was on the verge of discovering the lost city. From the Royal Geographical Society I learnt that in the region of 18° 45' North, 52° 45' East, and close to the Sands of Mudhaghadan, he had found pottery remains and shaped stones probably used as hitching posts for beasts of burden. Doubtless spurred on by his well-earned finds but having to leave the Sultan's Armed Forces, he organized a civilian expedition under the umbrella of Operation Raleigh, but this had collapsed for reasons I could not ascertain. The Ubar field was, it seemed, still clear.

British Aerospace agreed to provide £40,000 to fund a further polar event and one of their apprentices redesigned our sledges on the computer system they were using for their space satellite programme.

Many weekends were spent working full time for Dr Hammer, trying to cope with projects which were usually utterly disconnected with one another and a world away from the affairs of Occidental Petroleum. A black-tie dinner at the Royal Academy to hand over a £100,000 cheque would precede a flight to the Orkneys with a recently appointed British Secretary of State for Energy, merely to get to know him in case quick contact might suddenly be needed.

The Doctor was conceited in a frank and amicable sort of way and liked me to carry copies of his biography to give to the many potentates and leaders of industry who punctuated the itinerary of all his London visits. Recently he had produced, through a ghost writer, a fat and glowing autobiography, which I had then been tasked to promote in Europe. My own publisher had commissioned an autobiography which amounted to a compendium of expedition stories and my book and the Doctor's were published in London at roughly the same time.

Driving past a large bookshop in Victoria, the Doctor bade Bob stop. 'That's my book!' he exclaimed, as pleased as any author to see his handiwork prominently on view. I helped him out of the car, for he was a touch wobbly on his legs. By chance the bookshop's window-dresser had filled the window with copies of my book on the upper shelves and Dr Hammer's below. The Doctor turned and looked at me.

'Tell 'em to rearrange it,' he said with a straight face. 'They should learn to get their priorities right.'

Although Prince Charles had been Patron of my polar projects for the past ten years I knew little about him. My work for the Doctor at this time often involved decisions to be made by the Prince. At the time the Prince's image, as portrayed with monotonous regularity by the media, especially the television programme *Spitting Image*, was one of a vacillating, weak-willed princeling inspired mainly by conversations with trees. On two occasions I had found that this was far from the truth.

The United World Colleges was an educational enterprise set up under the aegis of Lord Mountbatten, the uncle and early hero of Prince Charles. I spent a great deal of time on projects devised by the Doctor to raise funds for the UWC and in attending meetings all over the world between UWC trustees and headmasters. After ten years as President of the UWC the Prince had grown somewhat tired of the factionalism in the higher echelons and did not tend to mince words at meetings. At a private dinner given by the Prince at Highgrove for thirty of the senior UWC trustees, the subject of Bulgaria was brought up by the Canadian delegation, who, with the approval of the London headquarters, had been especially keen to encourage the founding of a UWC college in the communist sector.

Privy to Foreign Office briefings and reports of atrocities that never make public reading, the Prince was opposed to dealing with tyrannical regimes. He had made this clear before and now boiled over. Why, if these people asked for his advice, did they fail to listen when he gave it?

'No, no, no.' He thumped the table and the glassware and silver clattered in response. 'If you wish to deal with those people then you must do so under another President.'

Sonny Ramphal, the Secretary General of the Commonwealth, tried to remonstrate on behalf of the Bulgarian scheme but the Prince was not to be budged.

On a windy morning in a less than salubrious district of London's Finsbury, so called after the burial site of my ancestor's heart was given to the nation, I sat outside a shabby prefabricated hut waiting for the Prince to finish his business so that I could hand him a large charity cheque from Dr Hammer.

The Prince was on a visit organized by Business in the Community to help find employment for the out of work and often disillusioned youth of the area. Disregarding anxious advisers, he said he wanted a face-to-face meeting *alone* with a representative body of the community. This had led to his entering the hut, which was crammed with angry young Londoners, most of them Rastafarians in torn jeans and berets. There were no police, officials or Royal bodyguards in earshot – merely a clutch of official photographers, the Prince's equerry Rupert Fairfax and me with my white envelope.

Inside the hut, from which I had earlier picked up a strong whiff of beer, wet cigarettes and unwashed socks, we heard a surge of fractious argument and I saw that Rupert looked extremely anxious. 'Had you better not go out and see if everything is okay?' I asked him. 'It only needs one of those guys with a skinful of cocaine, resentful as hell and a Stanley knife . . .'

'I know,' he said, gritting his teeth. 'But he specifically said he should not be interrupted and I don't want to upset him.'

Twenty minutes later the noisy meeting ended and the Prince emerged among a bundle of Rastas, one patting his shoulder, another giving a clenched-fist salute and all looking happy, especially the Prince.

Rupert Fairfax was one of fourteen successive aides that I grew to know. Dr Hammer would often call me a day or two before a London visit to say he wished to meet Prince Charles or Mrs Thatcher, the Soviet Ambassador, Earl Spencer, Robert Maxwell, Edward Heath or, even worse, some unknown with an unpronounceable name whose address he had lost but whom he had met before the war. Ginnie would set to work on the latter type of problem since she had an excellent nose for ferreting and research work, while I would rush to London from our Exmoor home and beg the most influential aide of Mrs Thatcher, HRH, or whoever, to grant the Doctor a last-minute appointment in their normally hermetically sealed programmes. To do this meant maintaining a friendly relationship with the aides and we made an annual habit of inviting one or other of the current incumbents to Glyndebourne or some such event.

Wherever the Hammer work took me I needed at all times to keep fit for the expeditions, so my Reeboks and running shorts travelled everywhere. When in the London office, I would join Ollie Shepard at lunchtimes and we would jog for an hour from Buckingham Palace to the Serpentine, twice around the lakes and back. At times of hectic schedules, I needed to remain within Occidental's headquarters. Then I would don a thirty-pound rucksack and run up and down the emergency stairs from the entry hall to the rooftop, eleven floors up.

For two weeks I went with Ginnie and a group of friends to the wildest corner of Britain, the mostly uninhabited peninsula of Knoydart, in Scotland, to fish, climb and windsurf. Dr Hammer was inclined to blow a gasket if I was not instantly available on the end of a telephone at any time of day or night, so he sent Tony Childs, the head of Occidental's London communications department, to set up a telephone system at our remote Highlands croft. Tony hired a fishing boat, since the croft can only be reached by sea, and also installed a fax machine at a tiny inn seventeen miles inland.

A letter reached us on return from Scotland with a summons to the High Court for our long awaited libel case against the Canadian magazine *Macleans* and the journalist Alan Fotheringham. Our barrister had asked the famous polar explorer Sir Vivian Fuchs and my colleague Dr Mike Stroud to appear as witnesses. The jury glowered at Ginnie and me as if they held us personally responsible for interrupting their normal routines. Not one of the twelve gave the glimmer of a smile throughout the two-day hearing.

The article had painted me as a highly unsavoury character on numerous counts and the effect on potential sponsors, for the Arctic or Ubar expeditions, was likely to be disastrous. We needed an outright apology from the magazine. The only demonstrably inaccurate statement that stood any chance of being nailed as libel was the statement that no expedition of mine was of scientific value. Our barrister showed the jury the scientific report of the Transglobe

Expedition, Sir Vivian and Mike Stroud gave evidence of their involvement in our scientific research over the years and the jury unanimously awarded us damages of £100,000 and a full apology. I could not believe my ears.

A week later the Canadians appealed and the damages were reduced to £10,000 despite the jury's decision. We wondered what was the point of having a jury award at all if it could crumble on the very first appeal. Nevertheless the Canadians did print an apology, which meant our main problem was alleviated, and they did pay all the very considerable court costs, which would have broken us for good had we lost.

I mailed copies of the apology to Nordair and other major Canadian and UK sponsors, and all the necessary equipment, transport and insurance came through. This enabled Ollie, Mike and I to try again early in 1988 for the unsupported Pole journey. Laurence Howell was again base leader, this time together with his wife Morag, who was a radio technician in her own right although her accent was initially difficult to interpret even when conversing face to face since she hailed from the Outer Orkneys.

The 1988 attempt was beset with appalling terrain and weather and we hardly managed sixty miles before time overtook us. By the end of spring the rumours of coming attempts by Norwegians, Americans and others convinced us that we must not give up and all agreed to return the next year.

- - - - - - - - - - - - - - - - -

In the summer of 1988 Nick Clapp came to London to give me the latest photographs from NASA. There had been a change in the sourcing of these photographs. In 1984 the Jet Propulsion Laboratory had installed SIR-B on the space shuttle *Challenger*. The ability of this twenty-three-centimetre-wavelength radar to image features *underneath* the Earth's surface, as long as the ground is arid, as in the Sahara or Arabian deserts, was what made it uniquely appealing in the hunt for Ubar. But, because the radar was still being developed it seldom flew on shuttle missions. One of *Challenger*'s 1984 flights first picked up intriguing fragments of desert tracks but then it had tragically exploded in 1986 and in the 1989 photographs were no longer shuttle-sourced.

Our chief helpers at JPL, Charles Elachi, Ron Blom and Robert Crippen, turned to images received from another US satellite, the LANDSAT Thematic Mapper, a source they frequently used to image the Mojave Desert, on their own doorstep, where they could as geologists easily verify on the ground the data they were given by their LANDSAT pictures. Each pixel or picture element in a LANDSAT image represented 28.5 by 28.5 metres on the ground and recorded reflected light in six waveband lengths, including those longer than the visible which are the near-infrared portion of the electromagnetic spectrum. Many features in a landscape, such as old desert tracks, are more distinct at these longer wavelengths.

Ron, Charles and Bob also studied images from the French SPOT satellites, which have a pixel size of 10 by 10 metres. This is a very high spatial resolution but is acquired in the visible wavelength region and not as useful for their interpretation methods. By combining the high-resolution SPOT images with LANDSAT, they were able to detect and map a number of ancient tracks deep within the dunes of the present-day Empty Quarter.

Whereas the SIR-B data showed only a few isolated fragments of tracks, our space detectives processed a number of LANDSAT and SPOT images using the Thomas road as their prime target area because none of the other many historical references that Nick Clapp had traced provided so accurately recorded a reference. After extensive processing of the combined satellite data, the three scientists managed to detect traces of the Thomas road at the correct location and a good number of other ancient tracks in various parts of the desert. Nick Clapp plotted every point of potential interest and asked me if I could get the Sultan's permission to visit them all.

We had been hoping, of course, for a miracle, thinking that JPL wizardry might locate the image of the city itself under the surface of the sand. This had not happened. If it had, we would have focused all our attention on that spot. As it was, all I could do was to make a brief proposal to His Majesty the Sultan, asking for permission to continue my earlier searches but concentrating on the Thomas road and the L-site.

Another difficulty that Nick revealed during his London visit was that his many attempts to raise funds in the USA had to date failed to raise a cent. An old Los Angeles friend of his, George Hedges, had been recruited with the sole and specific aim of 'helping to raise money'. George was a lawyer and a part-time country-and-western singer and guitarist. The band to which he was attached was, I gathered, called Lush Pile and the Carpettes (or perhaps it was Lush Carpet and the Piles).

Nick and George had travelled together to San Francisco, New York and Washington DC in their monetary quest, but all to no avail. On another front to launch the Saudi Arabian theme of the TransArabia film of Nick's dreams, they had seen various Saudi Arabian ministers with their proposals and had been turned down at every turn. All that was left was the Omani side of the project and that depended entirely on my own ongoing approaches to the Sultan. Nick knew and accepted that I needed to complete the polar journey before I could concentrate fully on Ubar.

Now that I knew there was no hope of a high-tech instant solution to the problem of finding Ubar, I contacted an old friend who worked in an unspecified military department in Dhofar. Major Trevor Henry, a tough and enigmatic Scotsman, had been my sergeant instructor on a long jungle-warfare course in Brunei in the early 1970s. He had fought for the Sultan during the Dhofar War and stayed there ever since. He knew more than any man alive about the country and its people and I was lucky that he agreed to do what he could to help my Ubar search. He had heard of a number of sightings of ruins or old pottery deep within the Sands, and where permitted by his Omani superiors, he agreed to check them out.

Trevor warned me that delicate negotiations were in progress between the governments of Oman, Saudi Arabia and Yemen over the exact position of their mutual boundaries in the Sands and it was important that no archaeological expedition unintentionally caused a border incursion before agreements were reached. He was well aware of my slightly dubious past within the SAS and I remembered the critical report he had sent my 21 SAS CO some fifteen years before.

There had been four other 'students' in Trevor's Brunei patrol but they were all regular SAS men. As a mere Territorial I kept my mouth shut and carefully observed how the others operated. After a few weeks one of them was evacuated with dengue fever, one received a bad insect bite on his neck following the blowing up of trees to make a helicopter pad and a third cut his head open crossing a slippery stream. The latter, an officer, was shortly afterwards killed in Dhofar. Trevor had taken everything with complete equanimity and, though a strict disciplinarian, was always fair. With him as the expedition's Dhofar representative, we were off to a good start.

Through the spring and summer of 1988 I worked for Dr Hammer without a break and found little time to follow up either expedition.

Following a visit to Highgrove to discuss charity work with the Prince of Wales, Dr Hammer was due to go direct to Heathrow, where his Boeing 474 was waiting. About thirty minutes into the flight, the four-seater Bell helicopter which I had hired in Surrey began to smell of burning electrics. I was very keen that the Doctor should reach Heathrow quickly or he would miss the strict departure time limit and have to stay another night in London. I had an expedition meeting that night and I realized, if I brought the smell to our pilot's attention, that there was likely to be a delay.

Neither the pilot nor Dr Hammer noticed the acrid fumes but after a while, remembering a crash landing in Arabia, my nerve broke and I mentioned the smell to the pilot. Quickly he checked his instruments and, with a curt warning on the intercom, he dropped the helicopter in quick spirals to the nearest green field. This was a parking lot in a caravan site beside the Thames.

The helicopter was soon surrounded by chattering locals with cameras. The pilot and I went off to find a telephone and in due course another helicopter arrived and took us to Heathrow just in time.

A week later the drama-loving Doctor wrote to Prince Charles saying that I had abandoned him in the smoke-filled helicopter to near-fatal asphyxiation.

We spent a good deal of time in Paris, where the Doctor was arranging various fund-raising events for humanitarian causes espoused by Madame Mitterand as well as trying to arrange a car deal involving a Far East manufacturer and Renault.

My work for the United World Colleges involved meetings with King Constantine, and the Queen of Greece asked us to dinner at their north London home. Apart from Lord King of British Airways, the guests were all royal and included the King and Queen of Bulgaria, King Hussein of Jordan, Princess Alexandra and her husband and a very pretty American girl next to whom I was seated and who I discovered, halfway through dinner, was the Queen of Jordan. My mind was concentrated throughout the evening on how best to make a full-frontal attack on Lord King to obtain sponsorship for the next expedition.

By autumn, after a heavy round of black-tie dinners and speeches for Dr Hammer, I had put on a good deal of weight and become disgracefully unfit. The next North Pole attempt was due in a few months, so Ollie and I did a crash fitness course, designed by him, which began with a marathon. Neither of us had ever run for more than an hour or so at a time and we completed the twenty-six miles in a sorry four hours and forty minutes. Later, with a couple of friends, I climbed the Matterhorn, Mont Blanc, the Jungfrau and Muncke, all by the easy tourist routes – not that this saved me from several attacks of vertigo. The Mont Blanc climb showed up my lack of fitness to the extent that I vowed to take jogging shoes everywhere I went. One lecture circuit of ten days saw me jogging in or near Melbourne and Perth, Singapore, Bangkok, Hong Kong, Dubai and Amman.

Luckily I was back in London when an emergency call from Occidental's headquarters announced an explosion on our North Sea oil rig, *Piper Alpha*. Over a hundred of the inhabitants perished by fire or water and Dr Hammer, against the advice of his American colleagues, flew to Britain without delay. Again, against their advice, he gave an impromptu press conference at which he took all the blame upon himself. 'The buck stops here,' he said, and added that he would donate £1 million to the *Piper Alpha* survivors' and dependants' fund. Mrs Thatcher immediately made a similar announcement.

I had ordered Dr Hammer's usual hired Rolls-Royce and his driver Bob Raynor to drive overnight to Aberdeen to take the Doctor around to thank rescuers, see survivors and generally do the best he could. Two newspapers harshly criticized the expense.

I tried to protect the Doctor from the ferreting of the British press but twice risked potential 'revelations' of the sort Fleet Street loved to manufacture. The Doctor had long been scheduled to attend London meetings a week or so after *Piper Alpha*'s sad end. Since he had done his level best for the survivors he could see no reason to cancel any of his existing schedule. To do so would benefit neither the dead nor the bereaved.

As part of the visit, eight of the Doctor's colleagues were due to join him for a theatre evening. I had asked the booking agent to reserve seats at the play or musical currently most popular with Americans. The day before, I was sent the tickets, and to my horror I noticed that the play was called *The Deep Blue Sea*. Shuddering at the thought of the play on words the tabloid editors might produce, I cancelled the tickets.

The following week the Doctor was due to attend a major auction of English paintings at Christie's, so on the Saturday a private preview was arranged. 'Doctor,' I told him, 'a photograph of you entering Christie's at this time would be a boon to the nastier news hacks.' He refused to cancel the preview but consented to Bob taking the Rolls from Claridge's on such a labyrinthine route to Christie's that even the KGB would have lost us.

The lengths to which the British press would go for some VIP scandal was finally made clear to Dr Hammer that autumn. The occasion was the fortieth birthday party of Prince Charles, given by his parents at Buckingham Palace.

Dr and Mrs Hammer were lucky to be included on the tightly controlled guest list of close friends and relatives totalling no more than three hundred. I dropped them off in the forecourt of the Palace and pointed to the red-carpeted entrance.

'Over there, Doctor,' I said. 'Bob and I will be back here in two hours.'

'Whaddya mean?' the Doctor's voice raised ominously. 'You're coming with us.'

'I can't,' I assured him. 'I'm not on the guest list.'

Dr Hammer made a noise signifying disgust and finality which I recognized as a danger signal. I decided, since I was in a dinner jacket, that the best course was to escort the Hammers into the reception lounge, introduce them to someone who would keep an eye on them and then disappear smartly. In the great hallway I noticed a queue of finely attired guests and many a well-known face slowly ascending the long, curved stairway towards the royal reception upstairs. Dr and Mrs Hammer, both frail and in their late eighties, must not join the queue: they would never make it up the stairs.

I noticed Harold Brown, the Prince's butler, and begged him to look after the Hammers.

'No problem,' he said, and led them by a back way to a small lift.

'Goodbye, Doctor,' I muttered, but he gripped me by the sleeve and I found myself heading upwards.

'Here we are,' said Harold as he slid the lift door across, immediately opposite the Queen. Dr Hammer introduced himself with his broadest grin and the Queen was her usual charming self, while the Princess of Wales looked radiant and patted the Doctor's shoulder. In fact all went well up to the point where Prince Charles saw me. He knew precisely who was and who was not on the guest list and must naturally have assumed I was a gatecrasher. If looks could have killed, I would have disappeared through the floor.

Two hours later, after an evening hobnobbing with the great and good, the euphoric Hammers retired to the Rolls.

'Spaghetti,' exclaimed the Doctor. 'Ran, you must know a good place for pasta.'

'Everywhere is closed,' Bob muttered to me. 'It's gone eleven p.m.'

'Armand, you've been eating all evening,' said Frances, his wife. 'Surely you can't want more.'

'Those bits and pieces at the Palace were all that *nouvelle* stuff. No body to it. Come on, Ran, spaghetti.'

I knew the chef at the nearby Langans Brasserie in Piccadilly and we went there at once. I rushed out of the Rolls but was too late: the wrong chef was on duty and last orders had been taken. I returned to the car to find it surrounded by the restaurant's habitual *paparazzi*. It was obviously a poor night for visiting film stars.

We returned to Claridge's and the following morning I took the Hammers to Heathrow. In the afternoon Ginnie and I flew to Barbados, where we were to join a ten-day cruise along the Orinoco as paid lecturers for a British Wildlife Society outing. The trip was also doubling as a holiday since the first three days involved no lectures while the cruise guests assembled in Barbados.

Not long after we had settled down on the beach with a thankful sigh, a hotel porter arrived with a fax from Dr Hammer. I was to contact his London solicitor at once and begin proceedings against a London newspaper. Attached was a copy of an article in that tabloid including a photograph of the Doctor in the back seat of the Rolls outside Langans. His left arm was draped around a young brunette whose real name was given. The script left no doubt in the reader's mind that, after the Palace party, the good Doctor had picked the girl up for obvious purposes.

I thanked God that, by chance, Frances Hammer had been present, for she often was not, and so would know there was no truth to the allegation.

By dint of many calls I persuaded the Doctor that I could as easily deal with the guilty party from the cruise ship's signals room as I could by returning to London. A full apology was shortly thereafter printed in the tabloid, but many who read the first piece never saw the retraction. The KGB Disinformation Department would have been proud of the newspaper.

- - - - - - - - - - - - - - - - -

In 1988 Tom Greening asked me to a lunch he held in London for Sultan Qaboos and I asked the Sultan about Ubar. His eyes lit up and he quoted me the full Quranic reference to the lost city.

'When,' he asked, 'will your expedition be ready?'

I explained that we were having problems with a polar journey. He laughed. 'Never mind, Ubar will doubtless survive the delay.'

The following spring Mike Stroud and I again tried for the North Pole from Ward Hunt Island. The conditions were average but we fell short of the record that we had ourselves set in 1986. I decided to call it a day from the Canadian side of the Arctic. Certainly the journey was possible; our 1986 timings, despite our impossibly late start that year, showed that it could be done given good surface conditions. The problem would remain the impossibility of predicting when a 'good year' would be.

Halfway during our 1989 attempt I bruised my foot in a fall from a pressure ridge and soon afterwards the skin graft of three years earlier came away altogether, leaving a wound very similar to the initial one. This time Mike had ample penicillin tablets, which staved off the onset of gangrene. As we left Ward Hunt Island for the last time I asked Mike, who nursed nine frost-damaged fingers, if he would like to try once more, next time from the Siberian side of the Pole. 'Glasnost permitting,' he replied with a grin.

CHAPTER TEN

In the spring of 1990 an elite of the world's polar travellers was ready to tackle the first journey to the North Pole without outside assistance. Russians, Canadians and Norwegians made announcements that they would commence their various attempts at the first appearance of the sun along the rim of the polar sea.

In Moscow I met Dr Dmitri Shparo, a Hero of the Soviet Union and the proud possessor of the Order of Lenin. His Arctic exploits are revered throughout the former Soviet Union and I was delighted when he agreed to become the organizer of our North Pole attempt that year. He warned me of stiff competition from Colonel Vladimir Chukov of the Soviet Special Forces, who was also about to attempt the Pole unsupported at the head of an eight-man team.

According to Dmitri, Chukov had led a strong polar assault two years earlier. Two of his men had died in the attempt and two had become so weak that a helicopter had evacuated them along with the corpses. Chukov had later reached the Pole but accepted that air contact had compromised his claim. In 1990 he was entirely confident of success, as were three Norwegian ski champions and four Canadians, all intending to set out from the Canadian side of the Arctic.

The Canadian team was led by Jackie McConnell. Twenty-five years before Jackie had been a trooper in my tank squadron in Germany and I had taught him cross-country skiing. In 1971 we had together completed a five-month wild-river journey in British Columbia and become good friends. He so loved British Columbia that he left the British Army and emigrated to Canada, where, in 1981, he had joined our circumpolar journey for the Yukon sector. Jackie's hobby was the annual international 'Iron Man' competition and he visited us in London early in 1990 on his way to one of them. At the time the police had removed my driving licence and Jackie agreed to drive my Occidental-supplied Rover to a nearby car wash for me. Approaching Hammersmith bridge at thirty miles per hour he noticed a steel bollard set in the middle of the road to separate buses from cars. His judgement was poor and he collided with the bollard. The impact was such that one wheel was ripped off its axle and the entire car forced out of alignment.

As Jackie explained to the policeman, he lived in Moose Jaw, where there were few cars, only one set of traffic lights and no bollards. The next I heard from Jackie was the news that he was to lead a North Pole attempt of his own in the spring.

Mike and I trained hard in the winter of 1989 and, before our departure, passed through numerous body analysis tests in the experimental chamber at the RAF Institute of Aviation Medicine in Farnborough, Hampshire. Our bodies proved to be remarkably resistant to cooling. A two-hour immersion in a cool tank designed to lower the core temperature of most men of normal build produced a report that my 'resistance was extreme with core temperature actually *rising* slightly during the course of the immersion'. The fitness report stated that I was twice as fit as a normal serviceman ten years my junior. Mike, who was eleven years younger, was stronger and fitter but much lighter than me.

From Moscow a Soviet Air Force cargo aircraft flew us for many hours over Siberia until bad weather forced us to land at the Siberian mining town of Vorkuta. At Shredniy in Novaya Zemlya we stayed in a scientific camp with eighty or ninety contractors. This was a highly classified part of the then USSR where only a year earlier, before Gorbachev's advances towards democracy, we would never have been allowed. The station was the Soviet equivalent of a Defence Early Warning (DEW) base in Canada.

Two heavy lorries drove us for three hours along a snow track to the remote five-man station of Galyameni. One of the five inmates had been killed and partially eaten by a bear and the cook at the base showed us photographs of the poor fellow's mauled body lying in the snow outside the main hut. One of the four camp huskies had a long, livid scar along her back, inflicted during her brave but futile fight to ward off the bear.

None of the four staff spoke English but they explained through our interpreter that we were to be their guests that night at a dinner they wished to hold for us, for we were the very first foreigners to visit Galyameni 'since the days of the Czar'.

Two days later an ex-Afghan gunship helicopter flew us the hundred miles to Cape Arktikiski, the most northern point of land in Novaya Zemlya.

After photographs taken with Dmitri and holding our respective national flags, we moved off into broken pack towing three hundred pounds each. Ahead lay nine hundred and sixty kilometres of highly mobile pack ice, a journey some one hundred and sixty kilometres further than the Canadian route to the Pole and beset with far stronger sea currents.

There would be a great deal more open water than we had experienced on earlier attempts but our sledges were lined with buoyant foam. Mike Stroud wrote the following account of our journey:

'The terrain consisted of broken, moving ice, a fragile skin on an ocean more than three thousand metres deep. On the seventh day my ski binding broke and I was condemned to wade through knee or thigh-high snow. We carried no spare bindings for every extra pound was at the expense of fuel or food for a journey that would entail cold and hunger.

'Despite my handicap we made good progress for a week and even when a three-day blizzard broke up the pack with winds in excess of ninety-five kilometres per hour we continued to travel, stumbling through the white-out and cursing the horizontally flung pellets of ice that filled our hoods and stung our eyes. We knew that if we became separated we would never find each other again. The man without the tent would die. Visibility was down to a couple of metres, footsteps were covered up as soon as they were made and shouts were immediately lost in the storm.

'After three weeks we were hindered by numerous areas of open water. It was slow work to lash our sledges together since our hands were clumsy in their frozen mitts. Any time lost through water-crossing delays was made up at the end of the day but the resulting thirteen or fourteen hour shifts took their toll and we began to have a serious weight problem.

'We each consumed five thousand calories daily, yet, after fifty days, we looked emaciated, having lost some thirty pounds each. Our resistance to cold had fallen away. Earlier, at $-50°C$, we had easily erected the tent poles by slipping off our mitts for brief periods. Now, even in the relative warmth of $-20°$, our hands were intensely painful following even the briefest loss of circulation.'

One day I noticed that Mike had dropped a long way back. I grew extremely cold waiting for him and, as he staggered up, he mouthed, 'Hot tea.' He was in the early stages of hypothermia and we stopped at once.

The next day we came across the fresh prints of a polar bear. I automatically felt for my revolver, only to realize we no longer had any form of defence. For the first time on the Arctic pack ice I began to feel distinctly ill at ease. But exhaustion and hunger soon drove away fear. A large blister on the Achilles tendon had turned into a deep ulcer that was eating into my heel. Even on skis I needed to limp to favour the wound. My eyesight had begun to blur and my eyes increasingly refused to focus. After a previous expedition five years before, an eye surgeon had warned me to stay clear of bright sunshine but, because of the unavoidable fogging of goggles, I always navigated without eye protection. Now I remembered his advice on my condition: 'Always wear ultraviolet light protection or you may well lose the sight of both eyes.'

I looked back on one occasion and there was no sign of Mike in all the dazzling white expanse of moving ice. Something made me take the unusual step of retracing my tracks. I heard him calling and went faster. I found him struggling in a narrow canal with sheer, five-foot-high ice banks. Only his head was above water and the air temperature was −42°. He wore a heavy backpack and his mitts were encumbered by the frozen leather straps of his ski sticks. I managed to pull him out, but only just. Somehow we put the tent up and fired the cooker.

Over the following weeks we each fell in six or seven times, sometimes because of weak canal banks but also through misjudging weak ice. Had we both fallen in at the same time the outcome would have been quick and fatal.

Around 88° North with seven hundred and twenty kilometres behind us, our strength quite suddenly disappeared as the extreme loss of body weight reached the point where we became debilitated. Cold began to pervade our bodies and sleep, always difficult on ice that shrieks and shudders, became impossible lying on thinly padded bones. In addition my eyesight became too poor to navigate, so I took to following close behind the vague outline of Mike's body, cursing each time I tripped over unseen ice blocks.

On the forty-eighth day, by which time we were within a tantalizing eighty-nine miles of the Pole, I began to feel the icy north wind blowing on to my right ear rather than my nose. After an hour of this I tapped my stick against Mike's back. He was dazed and could hardly speak. With no idea of direction and suffering from hypoglycaemia, Mike was in a vulnerable state.

We were ten days away from the Pole, having lost twelve or fourteen days through the contrary drift and the broken ski binding. The surface conditions in the Arctic that year were as good as or better than in 1986, so we would have been better off on the Ward Hunt route. But this we could not have known in advance.

We activated a miniature radio beacon as arranged with Dmitri and within twenty-four hours a Soviet gunship helicopter took off from the Soviet ice island three hundred miles to the north-east. The biscuits and tea they gave us tasted like nectar. The next eight days we remained on their ice floe during a major break-up which split their airstrip into seven floes and their hut camp into two.

Because my feet were very swollen, Mike gave me desiccation tablets, which had the unforeseen result of shifting a kidney stone into my urinary tract. I was violently sick and contorted with stomach pains.

A week later we returned to Moscow, where the Soviet Komsomol President gave us medals and Dmitri Shparo confirmed that we had made the longest and fastest journey in the Arctic to date. The Canadian team of Jackie McConnell had retired with frostbite problems after two weeks. The Norwegian and Soviet teams both received air contact and lost members of their teams *en route*, thus compromising their claims.

The North Pole remains a fascinating challenge that, as this book goes to press, has yet to be successfully met by a group without air contact or other outside support.

Back in London I went without delay to an eye surgeon of high repute. He diagnosed retinopathy, a legacy of prolonged exposure to high levels of blue light over years of polar expeditions. He gave me a clear warning for the future which put further Arctic travels out of the question – at least until the advent of fog-free goggles.

There being no point in crying over spilt milk, I turned immediately to the Ubar expedition. Nick admitted that neither he nor his fund-raiser friend George Hedges had been able to raise a cent either to fund the film, the making of which was Nick's main aim, or indeed moneys to help underwrite the expedition itself.

I asked David Douglas-Home, the banker son of Lord Home, if he could advise me of possible British sources of funding. Since he was a confidant of many influential Omanis and of the company directors with whom they did business, I rated his advice as the best. Nevertheless I enjoyed as little success as had the Americans in raising UK-based funds. So I visited Muscat and called on a number of old friends. The response was cautious but never negative, which in itself was a massive improvement on London. However, since Dr Hammer was not well at the time I was able to devote much of my time to seeking backers in Britain as well. So, when Edward Heath asked us to lunch at his Salisbury home, I approached him for help. His response was to introduce me to the paraplegic son of the Chinese President with a request for help to establish a hospital for paraplegics in Peking.

'Why not try Mr Heath's great friend, Maggie Thatcher?' Ginnie suggested. That month she asked me to dinner at 10 Downing Street in honour of the Crown Prince of Morocco, and it was my good fortune to find myself sitting at her table with Prince Andrew, Lord Jellicoe, the Crown Prince and Angus Ogilvie. Twice I tried to broach the topic and each time the conversation veered to rumours of strange goings-on in Iraq. As things turned out, I raised every penny in Muscat itself.

Dr Omar Al Zawawi, who had helped sponsor the polar expeditions over a period of sixteen years, kindly made it possible for the Omani International Bank, of which he was the most influential director, to become our holding sponsor. The bank agreed to coordinate all fund-raising activities from Muscat and said it would consider making a cash donation.

In the summer of 1990 I spent a hectic four days visiting twenty-two Omani company executives and sixteen expatriates. The result was immediate success. Gene Grogan of Occidental Oman, with whom I had previously worked on Occidental UK affairs, agreed to provide twenty thousand dollars' worth of help, plus whatever field survey and camping gear we might need.

I checked out various food companies and received a generous offer from Matrah Cold Stores of food and cooks for the expedition. BP of Oman promised us unlimited fuel anywhere in Oman and Land Rover's local distributor, Sheikh Mohamed Haider Darwish, promised me three free Land Rover Discovery vehicles, which are unquestionably better for long periods in soft sand than any of their competitors.

For transport of personnel and cargo, insurance and a thousand and one other necessities, I made agreements with other local companies and as for accommodation, free living in great luxury was assured by the Al Bustan Palace Hotel of Muscat and the Holiday Inn in Salalah. The former magnificent structure had just been voted the best hotel in the world by a European travel magazine, so the Ubar project was showing distinct signs of becoming an excursion rather than an expedition.

Prince Charles had set up an appeal to raise funds for Europe's first and only Multiple Sclerosis Research Centre by raising one penny per mile during our Pole journey.

Now the Society informed us that we had raised £2 million as a result of the Siberian North Pole Expedition. The Prince, who was delighted, gave a reception at Kensington Palace for all those involved. Unfortunately, since we did not reach the Pole, the funds were not as much as they would have been. The suggestion that we try again did not appeal to me after the eye surgeon's warning about the risk of going blind. However, I knew that in Antarctica, unlike the Arctic, we had always been able to wear dark goggles without misting-up problems. Mike Stroud soon agreed to join me in Antarctica to complete his physiological studies on body stress and to try to raise a further £4 million to complete the funding of the Multiple Sclerosis Research Centre in Cambridge.

I wrote to Chris Brasher, the one-time breaker of the four-minute-mile barrier and now the organizer of the London Marathon and the Chairman of Reebok UK. Would Reebok sponsor an expedition to cross Antarctica without support; the longest such polar journey ever undertaken? I also wrote to His Majesty Sultan Qaboos to say the Ubar expedition was now financed and to ask if we could complete a reconnaissance as soon as possible. He agreed and told me to arrange it through his Minister of Palace Office Affairs, General Ali Majid.

The General had served in the Dhofar War and I remembered him well as an outstandingly brave officer. I visited him in Medina Qaboos and asked if the Army would help the reconnaissance with an escort, vehicles and a helicopter. After making enquiries he decided that the Royal Oman Police were better placed to help and he gave orders accordingly. I thanked him and left. The arrangement would have been excellent but for an unforeseen development back in England a few months later. I signalled Nick Clapp in Los Angeles; he was still working on the complex arrangements needed to make his documentary film of our search. I told him that everything was now in place and the reconnaissance must begin in midsummer.

I had hoped by now, somewhat naïvely, that the NASA space images might have come up with an outline, revealed from under the sand, of some form of ruins for us to excavate. But they had not, so all we had to go on were the vague appearances of an old camel trail in the same region as the original Thomas road and the L-site not far away from it.

The reconnaissance hopefully would enable us to visit one or two sites such as Andhur, Fasad and Hanun, all places noted by previous archaeologists, then to search other regions of Dhofar for historical clues and finally to go into the Sands by helicopter to examine the only two clues provided by space imaging.

The archaeologist who had volunteered to join us, Dr Juris Zarins, worked at the Southwest Missouri State University and the love of his life was Arabian archaeology. Any excuse for fieldwork in Oman was manna from heaven to Juris.

He was well aware that all classical work by archaeologists in southern Oman had come to an abrupt stop in 1972, when the Oxford archaeologist Andrew Williamson was killed near Sumhuram. His Land Rover was blown up by a landmine.

In selecting an archaeologist to join a lengthy expedition it is tempting to go for the person with the most resounding reputation for previous discoveries in the relevant region or period of history. This is likely to produce a mad professor or an embittered genius, someone perhaps who creates a feisty atmosphere that is likely to affect the rest of the team.

My own reading on the subject of archaeologists, mainly written by the archaeologist Paul Bahn, had given me a jaundiced view of what to expect. Some typical observations by Bahn:

Never let the fact that nothing is really known about past events stand in your way: instead, use it to your advantage.

Eccentricity is a hallmark of the profession. So is an addiction to alcohol (in fact archaeology could be a synonym for alcoholism). You can wryly attribute this fact either to the need to drown one's sorrows in the face of unattainable solutions, or simply to acute embarrassment at practicing an inherently ridiculous and often futile profession.

Field archaeologists undergo long periods of nothing much happening but there are compensations. Few other occupations enable you to go off into the wilds at regular intervals with a bunch of nubile youngsters who are eager to have fun and obtain good grades.

Juris Zarins was a pleasant surprise and, apart from a vague similarity to Indiana Jones, complete with a battered brown trilby, there was nothing traditionally professional about him. He was not stuffy, narrow-minded, humourless or susceptible to the attractions of his students. Born in Europe, Juris attended high school in Lincoln, Nebraska, and began archaeological work in the holidays, preserving Sioux sites at $1.65 per hour. More fieldwork followed, in Apache reservations, Viking villages in Sweden and palaeolithic sites in the Dordogne.

After serving in Vietnam and then completing his doctorate at the Oriental Institute of the University of Chicago, Juris worked in southern Iraq before moving on to eastern Saudi Arabia. There he worked for the Ministry of Cultural Affairs with Dr Abdulla Masriy, who had been a fellow student in Chicago. Juris's title was Archaeological Adviser to the Kingdom of Saudi Arabia. He lived with his wife and five children in Riyadh on a five-year survey programme until 1975, when, as an Assistant Professor of Archeology at Southwest Missouri State University, he began to alternate between university work and fieldwork in Saudi Arabia. During the next seven years his digs included Jabreen, Hasa, Abqaiq and Thaj. He traced the old incense routes from Najran in Yemen via Jebel Tuwayq to Saudi Yamama and specialized in the study of pastoral nomadism, the origins of animal herders in the Arabian Peninsula. This work took him three times into Egypt's Eastern Desert and aroused his interests in the Dhofari nomads.

When the chance to join the Ubar search came his way, Juris saw it as a wonderful chance to visit Oman. He knew well that no new excavation work had been permitted in Dhofar for eighteen years and that prime sites existed that were almost certainly ripe for plucking. He gave little credence to the tales of Ubar and he did not like the thought that a high degree of interference with his work was likely from Nick's film team but, for the opportunity to work in Dhofar, he was prepared to put up with a lot.

The reconnaissance journey was to take place in July 1990, at the time Saddam Hussein was about to invade Kuwait. Luckily nobody knew of Saddam's intentions, so the Sultan's Office stamped all the visas. The team would consist of Nick and me, Juris, Ron Blom from the Jet Propulsion Laboratory, Nick's wife Kay, and George Hedges, the fund-raiser for Nick's film. Once we reached Dhofar our main guide and adviser would be Major Trevor Henry. Our archaeological director, I was informed by the Palace Office, would be Dr Al Shanfari, the Director of Archaeology at the Ministry of National Heritage and Culture. A scion of a leading Salalah family, Dr Shanfari was married to a Hungarian and their daughters were at school in Scotland.

The last two weeks before our departure included a busy visit to London by Dr Hammer, who was building up his art collection for a museum he was about to open in Los Angeles. A major sale at Sotheby's included fourteen masterpieces favoured by the Doctor. Whenever I bid for paintings at auctions on his behalf, I did so under my wife's name. Since none of the auctioneers knew my identity or could recognize me, there was no risk of a painting being 'bid up' by any third party simply because Dr Hammer appeared to be in the race.

Five days before the auction the Doctor came to London with one bodyguard and his private doctor, a charming Mexican lady. He insisted that I accompany him to the preview, and this resulted in a number of Sotheby's staff connecting my face with Dr Hammer. I am not suggesting that Sotheby's operated a 'bid up' system – merely that we thought that they might. I stress this point as I have no wish to be on the wrong end of a libel suit.

The Doctor left London with the words: 'Make sure you get those paintings well below my maximums.' To ensure that our bids were not recognizable as Hammer-instigated, Ginnie drove up from Somerset and handled the bidding herself. Watching from the rear, I became aware that I ought to be seen to be bidding for some of the pictures in which the Doctor, at the preview stage, had shown an interest. I knew I could easily drop out well before other bidders began to go cool.

A sombre oil of a naval engagement, giant black waves and valiant men-of-war in flames, was advancing slowly but surely between four bidders when, at a point where my last intended false bid had just been accepted, all other bidders went silent. I had become the not-so-proud owner of a painting the size of a dining-room table, costing £12,000 plus VAT. I sweated profusely. Ginnie had done very well with all the items the Doctor had ordered, some £2 million worth, but she was flabbergasted when I admitted to my dreadful error. We prayed that the Doctor, due back from a one-day visit that week, might decide that he actually liked the gloomy sea battle.

'Doctor,' I told him, on the way from Heathrow to Claridge's, 'we have all your paintings at excellent prices as marked in this catalogue and we also obtained the naval painting for £12,000.'

'But,' my employer immediately observed, 'I told you to forget about the naval painting.'

'No problem,' I said and, swallowing hard, I left it at that.

At two a.m. in his suite the following morning, Dr Hammer was dictating various memos for me to send to Chinese coalminers, Washington powerbrokers and far-flung oil minions when he began to doze off. As he was ninety-two and had just had a week of jet-setting around the globe, this was excusable. I helped him to bed and will long remember his words as he lay back:

'What a damn pity it is to grow old. I've so much to do but my body's just letting me down.'

'I'll be back at six,' I told him. 'The plane leaves at nine-thirty a.m.'

'Goodnight, Ran,' he said, and I left the room. As I closed the door I heard him shout, 'You can put that horrible naval picture down on my list.'

Enormously relieved, I phoned Ginnie, waking her up with the joyful news.

'I like his sense of humour,' she laughed. 'He kept you sweating long enough to teach you a lesson.'

CHAPTER ELEVEN

The American members of the Ubar team arrived in London in mid-July and we flew into Muscat on one of the hottest days of the Omani summer.

My polar expeditions normally start in dark, freezing shacks with a handful of comrades who know each other well and understand the minutiae of the straightforward aim to get to the Pole. The Ubar reconnaissance expedition began in Muscat's plush Al Bustan Palace Hotel and involved a group who were mostly strangers to each other, none of whom knew how best to set about searching for their goal, and each of whom had a different motive for being there.

Juris Zarins, the archaeologist, was not particularly interested in the concept of the lost city of Ubar, nor did he feel that we stood a cat's chance in hell of finding it – if indeed such a city ever existed. He was extremely keen to conduct archaeological work in southern Oman and if searching for Ubar provided a pretext, fair enough.

Nick Clapp, a maker of documentary films for thirty years, had known since his three-day visit to Oman in 1980 that he must find a reason to come back and make a film here. He had rifled through the history and the folklore of Oman until Bertram Thomas's Ubar story had come his way, providing him with an appealing 'search story' with all the ingredients for a magnificent documentary whether or not the search were to strike metaphorical gold in the shape of a lost city. Nick was in Oman to make a film of that search.

Ron Blom, a geologist and interpreter of satellite images of Earth's geology, lived his work and was fascinated to think that his ultramodern techniques might be applied to search for ruins two thousand years old. He hoped to learn a great deal about the effectiveness of these techniques by matching up his satellite pictures with actual ground features such as the L-site. To find the city would be a nice bonus, but he would lose no sleep if we failed.

George Hedges, the Los Angeles lawyer and Nick's fund-raiser for the documentary, had no skill remotely useful to the expedition but I gathered from Nick that he had personally risked funds towards the making of the film so he deserved to be present.

Kay Clapp, Nick's wife, was a charming lady from Jackson, Texas, with long, blonde hair and the key ability to look after and account for the sponsored funds I had raised in Oman. She had accompanied Nick on many film-making projects as his producer and, as a federal probation officer in Los Angeles of twenty years' standing, was unlikely to be fazed by the occasional scorpion or snake.

The fact that nobody but myself had staked his or her reputation on locating the lost city made for a loose and easy atmosphere from the start. Juris was an affable bear of a professor with a gentle sense of humour, eyes that really did twinkle behind his thick spectacles with every awful pun that he produced, and an affinity with deserts that came of two decades grubbing about in them.

After thirty years of marriage, the Clapps were still touchingly tender towards each other. Kay, aware that Nick's focus was seldom on the real world except where it merged with his vision of how it should look through a camera lens, was ever ready to cover for him and ensure that his personal welfare was not neglected. This was important, since Nick was often simply not there to look after himself: his physical being was present but his imagination was busy being a fly on the wall, looking down at us all and deciding how we ought to be going about the business of his unwritten, perpetually evolving film script.

Ron was a quiet and genial scientist, naturally honest and without an ounce of nastiness towards his fellow men. When I reflected on the time and effort I had spent before so many polar endeavours in selecting the right characters to form the teams, I was amazed at my good luck in having with me this merry bunch of Americans, who, for all their unusual skills and intelligence, were a pleasure to be with on a day-to-day basis. Perhaps, if they had been asked to manhaul heavy loads at deep-freeze temperatures for hundreds of miles, their very niceness would have gone hand in hand with a lack of that aggressive mettle needed to challenge the elements.

The elements in this case consisted initially of the spectacular Al Bustan Palace Hotel. (The name means 'the garden'.) The Omanis have carefully kept all but the richest and, by association, the most conservatively behaved tourists at bay. No shirtless, vomiting, foul-mouthed, package-tour yobbo is likely to get a No Objection Certificate, as Omanis call their visas, and the special feeling of remoteness that most of Oman still retains will continue all the while this policy is followed.

Green lawns, fragrant flowers and white, if lightly oiled, sands fringe the hotel in its mountain-girt bay. The rich and the famous come here and the staff were even then preparing for a visit by President Mitterand with an entourage of two hundred.

Leaving Nick and Kay to explore the beach, I went to the Ministry of Palace Office Affairs, where a succession of smart soldiers and robed acolytes led me to the sumptuous office of General Ali Majid. I thanked him for his support and promise of police escorts. He bade me call at the headquarters of the Special Task Force (STF), an elite police unit entrusted with unusual tasks inside Oman.

Humaid Khaleefa, the STF colonel assigned to our care for the next two weeks, was a slightly podgy, carefree Omani who spoke good English but freely admitted to a limited knowledge of Dhofar. This made it especially fortunate that Major Trevor Henry took us under his wing as soon as we reached Salalah, a ninety-minute flight by Oman Aviation Services jet to the south of Muscat. Despite the time of year the heat was bearable, and since we were based in the air-conditioned comfort of the Salalah Holiday Inn with a palm-fringed Indian Ocean beach attached, there were no complaints.

Trevor had completed land patrols to, or flights over, all the desert sites that I had queried on account of unusual features on satellite photographs or rumours of artefacts found by *bedu*. He showed us his map and told us in his concise, measured way that, were there to be any surface ruins in Dhofar, they would have been seen by oil prospectors, talkative *bedu* or patrols by land or air from the Sultan's Armed Forces.

'If the city is out there at all,' he murmured 'then, in my opinion, it has to be sub-surface.'

Together we planned a tight schedule which, in eight days, would take us to every worthwhile archaeological site in southern Oman. With Juris's practised eyes as our antennae, we should pick up any clues that existed by visiting every site thought to have been involved with the frankincense trade. Since Ubar's *raison d'être* could only have been the servicing of incense caravans, such clues could lead us to Ubar through step-by-step detective work.

Before this sleuthing process began, we intended to fly by police helicopter to the northern deserts to inspect the twin results of all Nick's research and Ron's

A net fisherman at Salalah.

An Omani fisherman.

An Omani dhow-builder.

An Omani fisherman with a shark.

A jebali *mountain house.*

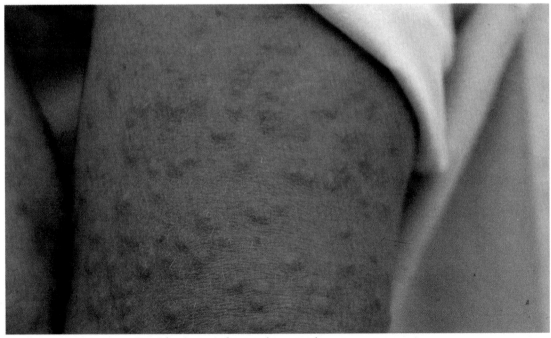

Ron Blom's arm after two hours in the monsoon mountains.

The escarpment of Jebel Samhan above Mirbat.

Lake Darbat during the monsoon.

The map of Arabia based on the coordinates of Ptolemy, the Greek-Egyptian mathematician, geographer and astronomer of the second century.

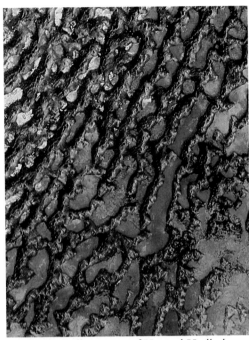

A SPOT satellite image of Uruq al Hadh dunes.

A LANDSAT 5 satellite image of the south-east sands and Shis'r.

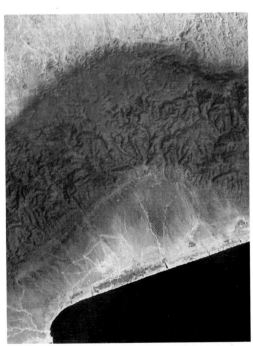

A LANDSAT 5 satellite image of the Dhofar mountains and the Plain.

The eighty-foot-long grave of Nabi Umran in Salalah in 1968.

Nabi Umran's grave (beautified) in Salalah in 1992.

Triliths in the nej'd.

Nick and Kay Clapp at the ruins of Sumhuram.

Islamic graves in Dhofar.

Pre-Islamic graves on Salalah Plain.

Terry Lloyd of ITN by myhrr tree in the Dhofar mountains.

Kay Clapp by frankincense tree near Kanoon.

Thread from this desert plant is used to sew up jebalis' leather waterbags.

Frankincense gum recently tapped.

Desert fruits are particularly good to eat.

Desert cactus found in the Jebel Samhan.

This parasite, which grows on the roots of acacia for only twenty-four hours a year, makes a delicious meal.

Hydnora Africana, *a desert parasite.*

A cactus typical of the nej'd *region.*

Camels in the Wadi Darbat.

A camel of the nej'd.

A camel with its young.

Rock graffiti.

Unknown hieroglyphics on a polished rock found in Dhehaban.

Pecked rock drawings.

A pecked rock depiction of a camel.

Ali Ahmed Ali Mahash al Shahri with his cave paints experiment.

A pecked rock cave drawing of camels.

Cave graffiti.

space imagery, the ancient camel trail and the mysterious L-site – our great white hopes for a quick and easy discovery.

We strapped ourselves into a Bell 205 helicopter at Salalah airbase and flew north over the monsoon clouds of the Qara hills. An English-loaned pilot with an Omani co-pilot chatted together over the intercom and pointed out the features of the *nej'd* once the monsoon zone had passed away below us. Then followed mile upon mile of level gravel plain veined by long-gone water channels and seemingly as devoid of all life as the surface of the moon.

Black dots appeared below, spurting light dust spumes and the pilot veered towards them: four heavily armed Land Cruisers of a Frontier Regiment patrol. The Baluchi commander of the little force greeted us without enthusiasm. He clearly resented time spent helping civilians search for useless lost cities.

Spreading my map out on his vehicle's bonnet, we noted the exact bearing and distance of the Thomas road. This was merely a matter of switching on Ron's Magellan Global Position System and, in seconds, our position to within a few metres clicked on to the screen, the result of a backbearing from three satellites. Ron quickly pressed a number of buttons, then read off the data necessary for the next leg of our flight.

Plus ça change, I thought, watching with a tinge of envy as the bright young men of the desert patrol climbed back on to their battle wagons, their *shemaghs* wrapped about their heads and their water bags a-swing, just as ours had been some twenty-two years before.

An hour or so later we entered dune country, at first mere yellow pimples but then strips, and, finally, widening bands of sand that rolled from horizon to horizon and made me think of those awesome ocean rollers that power around the roaring seas of the South Atlantic, tamed by no land mass and fuelled by the spin of the world.

We stopped once more for Ron to check his GPS away from the electronics of the helicopter.

'Three miles to go,' he shouted in my ear.

Then we arrived. With no fuss and as little old-style romance, we had reached the Thomas road. We could not *see* it, but technology indicated that we were in the correct place, so we all piled out and headed for the nearest high ground in an attempt to spot camel trails. There was no wind and an egg would have fried quickly on any rock. Everyone drank Coca-Cola thirstily.

'There is no trail round here,' Juris shouted, squinting into the heat shimmer.

He then turned his attention to the ground and his expertise was quickly apparent. Within minutes his pockets were filled with neolithic remains, arrowheads, axe-heads and flint cores. It was not safe to stand behind him, for a stream of rejected stones flew over his shoulder as he worked.

I found a promising item with a distinctly man-made look about it. 'This,' he announced, looking over the top of his spectacles, 'is a fine example of an AFR.'

'Arab flint remains?' I ventured.

'Nope. An AFR is what I get given by ignorami such as yourself and a proportion of my dimmer students. The letters stand for Another F . . . ing Rock. From now on you buy me a Guinness for every AFR you produce.'

The helicopter took us to a thousand feet above the supposed Thomas road and then circled slowly. With the sun behind us it was just possible to make out two or three distinct and perfectly straight tracks heading north-north-west or thereabouts over a low gravel plain and straight into the heart of a sand dune over two hundred feet in height. Some of our group later increased their estimation of the dune's height to six hundred feet. The accuracy of dune descriptions does tend to suffer with the passage of time, as with fishermen's tales.

Nick and Ron both seemed as happy as cats with cream. The satellite imagery had proved itself. Man-made tracks did indeed exist in the inhospitable furnace of the Sands and since they were in part covered by thousands of tons of sand they could fairly be assumed to be ancient.

Next stop the L-site. In twenty minutes we again landed in the desert and this time the landscape feature that we sought was immediately as apparent on the ground as in the picture taken from two hundred and sixty kilometres in space.

Different surface patterns and the movement of the sand had shaped a letter L between two separate dune formations. Ron and Juris quickly agreed that, sadly, mankind had taken no part in forming the L-site. It was merely an ancient lake bed and our only excitement was the discovery by Juris of a pre-Islamic site with artefacts testifying to ties with the Qara hills, three hundred miles away. He later found ruins, of enigmatic date, half a kilometre from the L-site and close to a sandy pass between two great dunes. Stone patterns of ancient dwellings and hearths, and even an intermittent connecting wall, became clear with prompting from the eagle-eyed Juris.

In order to refuel and save valuable flying hours, the helicopter pilot told me he would leave us with a cold-box of Cola tins and return in an hour or so, by which time our appraisal of the area should be complete.

An hour passed by and, the inspection completed, we sat or squatted on a mesa top, high enough to catch any breeze to alleviate the oven-like heat of midsummer. But there was no breeze, not even the slightest of zephyrs, to cool our sweat-soaked shirts. The cold-box was soon empty.

I walked around the rim of the mesa and, peering over the western side, spotted an aperture, more a slit in the rock than a cave. There was enough room for all of us and an aperture in the ceiling caused a slight through draught. After an hour and a half I noticed a certain apprehension. Even Juris was not his usual talkative self. The thought was slowly dawning that, if the wheel of fortune were to cause the helicopter to crash, we could moulder here on the mesa until the end of time.

'Ssh!' Kay whispered. 'Listen.' She thought she had heard the distant beat of the helicopter. There is nothing easier than to hear the vibration of imagined sounds when hoping for a rescue. Many a time in deserts and polar wastes I have distinctly caught the approaching beat of an aircraft engine, expected to bring vital supplies or to remove an injured colleague. But the sound was as often as not merely my imagination.

Two anxious hours passed by before our pilot returned. We flew to Thamrait base and then to the little-known ruins of Andhur. On the journey I reflected how, in some ways, I was now back at square one. By hoping for space-age technology to identify the actual site of Ubar, I had fallen into the trap of suggesting as much to the sponsors. I had known that the glamorous mix of satellites and buried cities would excite even the most reluctant sponsor. Now, with all our space cards a busted flush, I still had to convince His Majesty and our sponsors to back the main expedition.

Over the seven days that remained of our reconnaissance we must come up with something new, some rationale to keep our search on the rails with our backers. Trevor had arranged a schedule that would cover visits to every known archaeological site that might have a bearing on the frankincense trade with relevance to Ubar. From Thamrait to Andhur, four hours by four-wheel-drive vehicle, we sped in thirty breathtaking minutes.

The pilot needed to keep his hand in at low-level approaches and the result rivalled any fairground rollercoaster. Banking, twisting and side-slipping between the rock walls of narrow canyons, dodging sudden pinnacles and, with rotor blades never more than a few metres from contact and immediate destruction, we were totally in the thrall of the pilot's second-by-second coordination. One slip on his part and we were all destined for incineration in the same ball of fire. Juris, remembering some awesome helicopter pilot in Vietnam, grunted in my headset, 'He was so young and flew so frightful that they called him the Flying Foetus.'

The ruins of Andhur visited by both Thomas and Thesiger, were superficially excavated by Wendell Phillips in 1952. Phillips noted that the ruins represented a pre-Islamic fort built to guard and control the collection of frankincense from the surrounding area, which housed the best incense trees in the world. It was, he opined: 'a highly important stopping place on the old caravan route leading northward to the Persian Gulf and westward to Hadhramaut . . . Even today camel tracks can be seen leading out to the north-west in the direction of Shis'r.'

I dared to look out of a porthole when I felt the helicopter slow and the palm trees of Andhur were all about us. High, crumbling crags looked down on the oasis. Hundreds of goats stampeded below us and I glimpsed the furious features of a Mahra herdsman waving an automatic rifle. Perhaps the pilot saw the Mahra too. Whatever his reasons, he decided to land us on a ridge above the trees and close to the excavated fort. The helicopter skids settled uncertainly, with no room for error, on a narrow parapet of rock. A vertical drop behind and a scree run falling away a few metres to our front called for a cautious exit with our gear. Colonel Humaid and his four men were armed and they quickly dispersed along the ridgeline. The rotor blades, I noticed as the unladen helicopter rose into the air, slushed by within a metre of a ridge-top boulder.

We set up camp as dusk fell. I went with Juris to inspect the ruins, no bigger than the smallest of English cottages and squeezed on to the widest section of the ridgeline. Inside the walls of the main room was a smaller, secondary sanctuary and outside this double chamber was an almost whole storage tank of cut stone. The inside of this trough had been lined with mortar and further broken masonry lay all about.

Juris was as thorough as any detective searching for clues. Angry shouting drew me back to our camp-site. Three Mahra, all armed with Kalashnikov rifles, were gesticulating at Humaid, whose soldiers had unslung their own weapons. The tribesmen disappeared after much unintelligible chit-chat.

'I don't trust them,' Humaid told me. 'I will keep two men on guard all night. They say we owe them a great deal of money because the helicopter caused six of their goats to be crushed. Also that this is a holy area and we should not camp or light fires here.'

'Are their tribal dead here?' I asked.

'Maybe. Maybe not. But they have no right to tell us where to go or where to sleep. We are here now and tomorrow we will go. There is no problem. Thanks be to God.'

The moon and the stars caressed our high eyrie that night and I thought of many such times in the days of strife. The soldiers and the armed Mahra would have shot each other on sight in my day. The reign of Sultan Qaboos had worked wonders but even now the *bedu* flashpoint was low enough to be easily sparked. In the morning I walked down to the oasis with my rucksack and was bidden to take coffee by the oldest of the Mahra goatherds.

After hospitality had been coldly but sufficiently acknowledged two of my hosts simultaneously launched their attack. Why had we come without permission? This was Mahra territory. We should not be here without the agreement of their *firquat* (a group of former communists). Did we not know it was wrong to sleep in a holy place? We had caused great injury to the goats, their only livelihood. They would tell the Wali of Dhofar about our behaviour unless I immediately paid twelve hundred rials to their leader by way of compensation.

'But I have only limited money,' I protested. 'We are a small expedition, not a government-supported project. You ask for twelve hundred rials. We can give you only two hundred. This is all we possess.'

Four of the Mahra shouted at once. I understood very little but their argument sounded very reasonable. We had lost them the results of six goat sales. The goat price in Salalah was one hundred and fifty rials, or so they said, so we must compensate their loss of livelihood.

'Where are the goats now?' I countered. This received no response. I had no wish for any complaint to reach the Governor of Dhofar. Anything that might endanger Omani permission for the main expedition must be avoided. Even punitive prices for goats that may have broken a toenail or two were preferable. 'As I have little money will you accept two hundred rials and some gifts of clothing?' There was silence.

I emptied my rucksack on the sand beside the coals of their fire. One man immediately picked up my birdwatchers' binoculars. In fact they were Ginnie's.

'Those belong to a friend. I cannot give them to you.'

'They would suffice . . . *Haadha kafee.*'

I shook my head and indicated my army camouflage jacket. This they accepted, along with two Marks & Spencer cotton shirts. 'Good,' I said. 'Thank you and again my apologies for the behaviour of our *Abu Garaat*. I used the old army expression 'father of locusts' for helicopter.

'We need another shirt,' the Mahra leader insisted. I groaned inwardly as he fingered my oldest and best Hawaiian batik sweatshirt. I protested that it was not worthy of him. Surely he would prefer these tracksuit trousers of one hundred per cent cotton?

The batik shirt left the pile and the deal was done. I shook their hands. There were no smiles but they would not make an official complaint.

We spent the rest of the morning watched by the Mahra in a painstaking search for pottery shards. Juris divided us into groups, with one soldier staying behind to guard the camp. He pointed out different areas of high ground and caves for each party to cover and I ended up with Major Humaid on a mile-long mesa. We found nothing and the only excitement of the day was when Humaid slipped and fell down the side of a rocky outcrop, cutting his legs and arms and twisting an ankle.

Back in Salalah we patrolled many areas of the *Jarbaib* or coastal plain; wherever Trevor knew of ruins.

At Ain Humran, Taqa, Mirbat, Sumhuram and other, nameless places of interest Juris made copious notes. He was at his happiest moving from site to site and theorizing on the past. 'There is endless work here,' he enthused. 'We must definitely dig at Humran and the Oracle well in the Wadi Naheez. There are great opportunities at Raysut and, hell, at Kohr Sawli. Trevor and I have traced what looks like a mile-long jetty or harbour wall. We have seen only the tip of the iceberg.'

I could see that he was in paradise, with mouth-watering possibilities wherever he looked. For Juris, all archaeology here would be rewarding and informative. Ubar was almost irrelevant – simply the icing on an already magnificent cake.

Trevor took us into the Wadi Naheez, the most heavily wooded valley in the Qara hills, and picked up two Bait Qatan guides: one a fat and talkative fellow, the other a young aspiring geologist. The humidity was high and monsoon flies were about, raising red pimples that itched for days. Ron nearly trod on a viper but Trevor spotted the snake and before he could stop them the Bait Qatan killed it.

Centipedes, scorpions and spiders added interest to our trek, up a side valley to a wonderful cave that, in the past, I had only visited by night, for purposes of ambush. We slithered on the orange mud and avoided the dripping lianas with their colonies of stinging ants. The cave was wide and as high as a church, with a floor deep in the animal dung of centuries. Bats chirped from the dark recesses of the rock roof and Trevor led us to the mouth of an interior passage.

'Leopards live in here,' he told us, indicating the outline of feline spoor. The portly Bait Qatan, Amr bin Said, moved ahead and knelt down at the very mouth of the lair. At that moment Trevor emitted a spine-chilling scream with a fair attempt at ventriloquism. The Bait Qatan leapt higher than I would have believed possible. He and his fellow tribesman soon saw the joke and joined in the general mirth.

With the help of a powerful torch we inspected painted figures high on the inner cave walls, symbols that seemed to include laden camels but interpretation varied to reflect the individual aspirations of the viewers. Nick, for instance, was keen on camels since from an editorial point of view he could the better splice this cave sequence into a desert scene filmed a week before.

Sweat glued our shirts to our backs and our socks to our ankles, bites itched maddeningly and I marvelled yet again how local mountain folk can survive such a hell on earth for the three monsoon months every year of their lives.

We searched other caves and jungle-clad ravines. In one sunny nook below the village of Shair Trevor pointed out aloe trees – 'very good for curing wounds', castor-oil trees – 'you know what that's good for', and three deadly poisonous but pretty plants: euphorbia, the Sodom apple and datura. We tramped through dry bushveld that looked for all the world like the Kenyan outback without the monkeys. Trevor led us to the Jebel Kasbah (or Kaysh), a lofty crag two thousand feet above the spring of Tobruk. Hidden by thorn and mimosa, a tangle of ruined, half-buried walls puzzled Juris, who had for once no ready solution to explain or date the site. A large rectangular room, well plastered and hardly damaged over the centuries, still stood in the centre of the hill-top ruins where once, perhaps, it had served as a reservoir for trapped monsoon water.

Since any occupants of this place could observe much of the Plain of Salalah, including the pre-Islamic ruins of Taqa and other coastal landing points, it was reasonable to deduce that this was a mountain garrison from which the incense trade was policed. If so, and should these ruins tie in time-wise with the pre-Islamic city of Sumhuram, then we could draw a theoretical line over the mountains towards Andhur and the only other known frankincense storage centre, Hanun. No invaders from the sea could head inland for either of these key storage sites without being spotted from this key vantage point. It was an interesting fragment of our jigsaw puzzle but not a clue to Ubar.

Forays with Trevor and other guides took us out to Ayun and the ruins at Hanun and Mudayy. Juris was fascinated but found nothing that directly helped our search. For him a dozen new areas of interest were revealed every day. The country brimmed with archaeological potential and sites that were crying out to be investigated by Juris's trowel. Such places needed no vague and endless searching: unlike Ubar, they were right here, ripe for plucking.

Poor Juris had to exercise great patience, for I had little immediate interest in anywhere without Ubar connections. Thus it was onwards to ever-new nooks and crannies that might or might not hold a key to our grail, dragging with us the drooling Juris, since none of us but he could read portents in the strange relics that we were daily shown.

When our whirlwind tour of the Plain, the mountains and the *nej'd* was done, we moved back to the edge of the Sands, this time without a helicopter and, in two Land Cruisers, drove west from Thamrait to my old Ubar hunting-grounds of Shis'r and Fasad. Both places had undergone considerable change. Where, in 1968, there was only barren desert, now there flourished cultivated plots of palms, fruit and vegetable. Houses too had sprung up around the water sources. At Fasad these were mostly wood and tin shacks, but at Shis'r there was a modern, Arab-style housing development designed to catch the breeze and to attract the few remaining nomads in from the nearby Sands to a stable existence and planned crop rotation to feed their goats and camels.

Fasad was now the local headquarters of the civilian 'frontier patrol force', a *firqat* with a difference, made up of young Dhofaris with desert skills whose duty was to know everything that happened along the sensitive borders with Yemen and Saudi Arabia. They greeted us with warmth, curiosity and varying degrees of credulity or scepticism regarding Ubar. I spoke to their leader, a Rashidi with a cruel hawk-face that transformed, when he smiled, into open friendliness. He spoke of Ubar's fate as though it were an integral part of his people's history.

'Maybe Irem lies in Yemen, or Saudi, or Oman. In those days there were no such borders, so, no matter. Allah was good to the people of Ad who built the city, a paradise on earth. But *they* were bad and forsook Him for other gods, so He destroyed Irem.'

The Rashidi made a pile of sand between us and then, scooping up another handful, dashed it down violently on to his makeshift city.

'Like this,' he said, 'so did Allah treat the people of Ad.'

'Is Irem of the Qur'an the same place as Ubar?' I asked him.

'Maybe,' he said with a shrug. 'Who knows?'

Juris spoke the Arabic of the Saudi *bedu* and, as long as he kept to the field topics that he had for so many years discussed at desert digs, he could converse well enough with Omanis. He learnt from our hosts that the Fasad region was barren of artefacts other than neolithic flints. The arrowhead, some eight thousand years old, known to archaeology as the Fasad Point, which has one fluted side only and includes a stubby shaft extension, was first found close to the village. However, Juris was interested in pottery of a more recent age and of that there were no traces.

Later he struck lucky at the village of Heilat Araka, a hundred kilometres east of Fasad, where he found fragments lying about on the gravel plain and a football-sized stone graven by the repeated friction of ropes. This was our first find of significance, but it was well to the south-east of the Sands, where Ubar was meant to be.

From Fasad we returned to Shis'r. Previous visitors told of tracks running west to the Sands from Shis'r and others heading *to* Shis'r from Andhur. Its very location, so close to the edge of the Sands and astride the best aquifer in the steppe region, indicated that the ancient camel trains must have watered here *en route* for Yemen with their cargo of incense. Our satellite photographs had confirmed that these old trails were still visible in fragmented sections but so were many others elsewhere, so at the time we read nothing of import into them.

Nevertheless Shis'r was worth a visit along with all the other main watering points at key geographical locations. Especially since the ruins, where I had twice camped before Ubar searches in the 1960s, were of unknown age and might be of some interest to Juris.

Although the local *bedu* had always told me that the rubbish pile, for such was the most apt description of the ruins, was no more than a hundred years old, others had different ideas. Wendell Phillips, possibly using Bertram Thomas for source material, wrote: 'Legend attributed the construction of this stone fort to the early-sixteenth-century Hadhraumi ruler Badr bin Tuwairiq.'

Juris had told me at Sumhuram that successive civilizations built on top of each other's ruins, so perhaps Tuwairiq's fort was sited on an earlier Adite fort. My erstwhile boss, Sultan Said bin Taimur, had built his own tiny fort close to the Tuwairiq ruins and obtained most of his building materials from them.

Even in 1950, only eighteen years before my first visit to Shis'r, the water-hole had a notorious reputation. Thesiger wrote of it:

The ruins of a crude stone fort on a rocky mound mark the position of this famous well, the only permanent water in the central steppes. Shis'r was a necessary watering-place for raiders and had been the scene of many fierce fights.

Bertram Thomas approached Shis'r in 1931. He wrote:

Shis'r's loneliness makes it an inevitable place of call for raiders and it is a proper practice to fill in a waterhole when leaving to delay possible pursuers. At Shis'r nature does the work, sand filtering in and filling it up in a day or two . . . Approach to a waterhole is made with much caution, for if an enemy is already in possession, there is a choice between hasty retreat tormented by thirst and fear of pursuit, or a fight for possession.

A kindly Bait Masan inhabitant invited us to share coffee and dates in the Shis'r *majlis*, the communal hospitality room, and although the village head, the *naib wali*, was away he felt sure nobody would mind our looking around the locality for artefacts.

We spent three hours wandering about the heap of rubble above the thirty-foot-high cliff overhang that protected the well. Juris was delighted for he found fragments of pottery and various ambiguous mounds, which he called tufa, evidence of former springs. He felt sure that sedentary people had used the place for longer than the three hundred years theorized by the only explorers to have previously visited Shis'r. We did not entertain visions of Ubar at Shis'r or Fasad, Heilat Araka or Andhur, but at least there was potential at these places for excavation work and the finding of clues. By contrast, out in the Sands, since our space technology had unearthed no outlines of man-made dwellings, there was *no* tangible starting-point for our search.

- - - - - - - - - - - - - - - - -

Having taken leave of our Omani and expatriate friends, we left Arabia and began to attack the many problems to be solved if the main expedition was to begin, as I had indicated to the Sultan of Oman, in the following spring, April 1991.

A fortnight after I left Muscat, Saddam Hussein pushed his troops into Kuwait and Oman joined the other Gulf States in condemning this aggressive move against an Islamic country. At this point our chances of keeping to our schedule looked poor, but I was expected by the relevant Omani Ministries, as well as our sponsors, to send them a concise report summarizing the results of the reconnaissance and plans for the main project. I needed first and foremost to have the considered opinion of Juris.

He was nothing if not frank. 'Didn't see any real places,' he said. 'Just some pottery at Shis'r. I didn't think anything about any of the sites. Nick kept asking me and I kept saying, "I don't know." They just looked like interesting sites. I do *know* there is *nothing* in the Rub al Khali. We have done the reconnaissance and have *nothing* to show for it.'

This was all very well but, were I admit it to His Majesty or the sponsors, I feared the main expedition would not be allowed to take place.

Some extra time was gained by the worsening situation in Kuwait. On 7 February 1991 I was forced to write to the Americans to tell them we should postpone the main phase until November. I laid out a suggested schedule that involved archaeology on the Plain of Salalah, with Salalah as our base, then moving north to excavate at Shis'r, Heilat Araka, Andhur and elsewhere, using Shis'r as our base.

Nick wrote back on 31 July: 'The schedule you propose is excellent.' He sent a number of desert grid references to check out in the meanwhile, culled from further studies of JPL satellite images and documentary research. I passed all these immediately to Trevor Henry, who in due course managed to visit them all and one or two of his own besides. At one of the latter he came across an interesting collection of artefacts and some fine neolithic flints well into the Sands and dangerously close to one of the borders. This he reported to his senior officer and was forbidden to divulge his information outside the country. The report, which we sent to the Omani Ministries and to all our sponsors, made the best of a bad job by stating the obvious, making a good deal out of little and concentrating on the few positive clues that our brief reconnaissance had genuinely unearthed.

We stressed that there were 'previously unsupported major settlements' at three of the sites Trevor had shown us, Raysut Hemara, Kohr Sawli and Ain Ḥumran. We further elevated the bits of pottery Juris had picked up at Shis'r by calling that village 'a far more ancient and significant site than previously suspected where we will excavate the water-hole area.'

In an attached report, Juris stressed some minor triumphs:

Above the spring of Hanun, we recorded for the first time the presence of Acheulean hand axes and thus the unique presence, so far as is known, of a Lower Palaeolithic site in southern Arabia.

(This was the result of a side trip Juris had made at the suggestion of an officer of the Omani Air Force, Colonel Ian Ord, who knew of the site.)

At Mudayy we located an unreported Neolithic site characterized by the presence of bifacial arrowheads and rods. Neolithic materials were also found at Shis'r but the most intriguing site of this period is Andhur, where neolithic peoples used to mine the flint nodules, breaking them up into smaller cores for further transport and reduction. Such a site is hitherto unknown in the Arabian peninsula.

Post-neolithic sites in the region are rare. Our focus will be on Shis'r, where early surface pick-ups suggest that some of the burnished ceramics may date to the Bronze Age. It is not impossible that Shis'r may turn out to be mythical Ubar . . .

The rationale for this last hypothesis was given as Shis'r's commanding position on ancient frankincense trails and the likelihood that the water supply had once been greater, as evidenced by the tufa mounds of defunct artesian springs. It would have been extremely useful to state that satellite imagery had indicated further evidence pointing to Shis'r. But this would have been untrue, so Juris left it at that and we all hoped the report looked strong enough to impress all that read it with our progress and our chances of eventual success.

The reconnaissance finding that we did not stress in our report was the uniform conviction that the Thomas road did not lead *to* the city of Ubar. How could it be when the Sands were so hopelessly dry and wells so scarce that even a *bedu* family, travelling between them, knew they could never count on finding water? The ancient incense caravans of many hundreds of camels and cameleers would have needed far stronger and more predictable water supplies.

Since the Thomas road definitely existed and headed along a known azimuth, why, we mused, should it not lead *from* Ubar? The lost city then must lie in the *nej'd* (where there was ample water) and not in the Sands, where every *bedu* and almost every historical reference clearly put it.

One complication to all this was that the theme of Nick's film was the search for Ubar, which, from a scenic and logical point of view, needed to start in the desert. The most appealing conclusion for such a film would obviously have been the discovery of Ubar from space. This was no longer possible but at least he could re-enact our negative journey into the Sands and record in retrospect our conclusions, namely that we must thenceforward look to the east in defiance of all folklore and all previous theories.

Since Nick had an alarming part of his personal finances tied up in the film, I was happy to go along with a scenario that appeared to lead us from the JPL images to the Thomas road, but beyond that I would not cooperate, since the space help had clearly ended there. As Juris later commented about the film theme: 'Nick was in a quandary wondering where Ubar was. As far as I was concerned, at the *end* of the reconnaissance they were going to have to do some spectacular punting to find anything. And that was exactly where we stood when we came back later to Dhofar. He had really banked his hopes on that L-shaped thing and this ancient caravan road and that they could see underneath the road and all that kind of crap.'

In Juris's view, we had done the reconnaissance and had nothing to show for it. However, from Nick's point of view with regard to the documentary film, this was quite wrong, since he had been able to travel around much of Dhofar and was now in a perfect position to plan the shape of the film.

As with all media reportage, in retrospect the facts can be put over in a hundred subtle ways that do not actually constitute distortions of the truth but merely selective exaggerations. With the writing of a book such as this it is, of course, also possible to remember only certain salient points and forget or ignore others. But no author will last long if he strays from the historical truth of actual events unless he writes of a solo unwitnessed endeavour that cannot be checked. If only one companion is present, an author can be sure his exaggerations or distortions will be noised abroad to the detriment of his future reputation.

By contrast, in a film the voice-over of an unseen narrator is more anonymous. Additionally, the subliminal effect of, say, the facial expressions of an expedition team on the minds of documentary viewers can lead to their assumption of mutinous feelings against an expedition leader. In reality those same grimaces may have been filmed in reaction to bad food or bad news but edited into an unconnected episode under a misleading narrative.

While it is undeniably easier to shape the viewer's perception of a film in this way, I had at that time no reason to suspect Nick of doctoring his analysis of the events. Therefore we were all in agreement to spend time, during the main expedition, re-enacting our reconnaissance into the Sands the previous summer. Since there would be a limited work period of three months, the time Juris could be spared by his university, I could foresee conflicting interests between archaeological and film-documentary requirements.

I had promoted the project to His Majesty Sultan Qaboos, the Ministries and the sponsors as an archaeological search that would be recorded on film, not as the making of a beautiful documentary about Dhofar with the central theme of a search for Ubar. This was a subtle difference which it was important for all parties on our team to remember and not to abuse.

For me, the latter half of 1990 was fraught with a good deal of work for Dr Hammer. He had so many irons in the fire I sometimes did not know whether I was coming or going. That September I lunched with him and Robert Maxwell at the alcove table at Claridge's. Together they were involved with the Soviets and a major US aircraft manufacturer to set up a joint production company. My own overtures to British Aerospace, whom Dr Hammer wished to include in the project, eventually came to nought. I was also involved in a United World Colleges' fundraising effort at the time and, after two years' hard work, had raised £1.5 million with a great deal of help and advice from Prince Charles.

The last time I saw Dr Hammer was in October and he seemed well enough. 'You can count on my being around, Ran,' he had chuckled, 'for at least another eight years. This new pacemaker they've just installed is guaranteed that long.' His recovery from a heart operation in his early nineties was in itself a comment on his robust nature. It came as a shock and a personal sadness to me when a month later he died of 'old age'.

I had been fortunate to get to know a unique individual who helped to shape the course of the twentieth century as much as many a president or prime minister, perhaps more so. I arranged the Doctor's Memorial Service in London, and it was attended by Prince Charles, Mrs Thatcher and a great many people, rich and poor, from the many walks of life that his business and his charities had touched.

One evening that October I had an unpleasant, near fatal, experience at my

Exmoor home that was to have serious consequences for the Ubar expedition. As a result of this event I came across a London-based group who asked me to write their biography. This I eventually did and the resulting book, *The Feather Men*, became number one best-seller in the United Kingdom. It also sparked a good deal of controversy with ex-SAS members and with certain past and present expatriate members of the Sultan's Armed Forces. In particular one of the Royal Oman Police Air Wing officers felt that the book smeared the good name of his unit and of its former chief.

Not long before the expedition was due to depart I was contacted by an Omani friend, who warned me that senior elements in the ROP had suggested to the Ministry of Palace Office Affairs and the Ministry of Information that the entire Ubar project should be quashed because of the revelations made in *The Feather Men*.

I telephoned the Ministry of Information in Muscat, to whom I had sent a copy of the book some weeks before. I was told that since there was nothing in the book that was even slightly offensive to Oman there could be no reason for interfering with the expedition. My contact in the Palace Office echoed this. Nevertheless, the force upon whose help we would need to survive in Dhofar was to be the Royal Oman Police, especially their Air Wing. So I contacted the complainant in the hope of making peace.

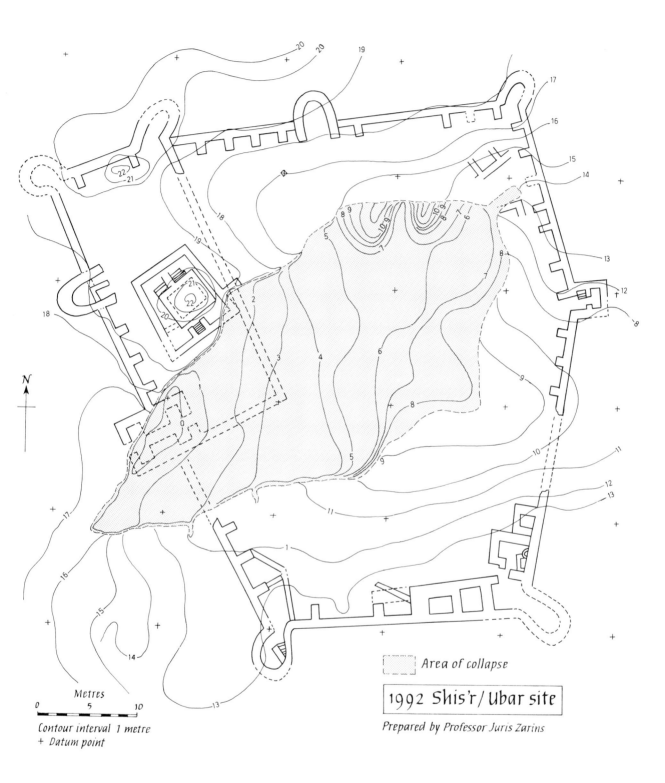

N

Metres
0   5   10

Contour interval 1 metre
+ Datum point

Area of collapse

1992 Shis'r / Ubar site

Prepared by Professor Juris Zarins

CHAPTER TWELVE

On the day we set out for the Ubar expedition, I left Ginnie at home and drove to London by dawn for an early-morning meeting at the Polar Desk of the Foreign Office in Whitehall.

The news was bad. There would be but a few months, after our return from Oman, in which I could organize a thousand things for the longest unsupported polar journey in history, a crossing of Antarctica on foot. I had hoped for American approval but the Polar Desk officer, an old friend from previous struggles with the international polar establishment, now warned me that my arch-enemy from Washington's National Science Foundation, the most powerful single body in the frozen continent, was the new boss there. Since there was no time to begin plotting the strategies necessary to counter such an enemy, I decided to take one step at a time: first try to locate Ubar, then tackle the Antarctic problem.

I met Nick and Kay Clapp at Heathrow shortly after the annoying discovery that, in my rush, I had collected the wrong travel bag from our London store. Instead of tropical shirts, suncream and malaria tablets, I had a duffle bag with snow goggles, Balaclava, mitts and the like. I decided not to mention this to the Clapps in case it alarmed them. They had never been to Dhofar and the entire responsibility for our well-being out there was in my hands. They might lose confidence in my preparations if they knew the contents of my travel bag.

For twelve years Nick made films for David Wolper, the king of documentaries in the US, then served as executive producer of National Geographic films in Los Angeles. He had worked for Disney, MGM and Columbia and met just about every VIP you could name. Always a freelance, Nick was able to indulge in specialist topics every now and again. Underwater wildlife films followed adventure, history and Indian tribal movies. Many a time he had tramped the Mojave and other Californian deserts capturing the last nostalgic remnants of the Wild West.

In the early 1980s, Nick took on the mammoth task of editing my Transglobe Expedition film which, in turn, led him to employment with the late Dr Hammer and cooperation with me to find the lost city. Some months after our rival Ubar-searcher, Charles Weston-Baker, had written to JPL asking for help from satellite images, Nick had done likewise and had cultivated a lasting relationship with the organization.

For co-leaders to react happily to one another on a fraught expedition is abnormal from all I have heard of previous such arrangements, especially when the two 'chiefs' are from different cultures and share no background interests. I had never before tried sharing leadership, since I find it difficult to head in a different route to my chosen path. There were two things that I think kept Nick and I the best of friends, with never a heated word between us. First, I had undisputed command of the expedition itself in Oman and Nick had total control of the film, including my own compliance as an 'extra'. But, more importantly, neither of us was an extrovert and neither tried to score over the other. Only when the expedition was done did differences of opinion arise and these were merely a question of differing memories, as with two witnesses describing the same murder.

Anglo-American relations in Arabia have not always been cosy. The Ubar-searcher Wendell Phillips in *Unknown Oman* quoted an Englishman's directly expressed opinion as:

Why don't you trouble-making Americans remain at home where you belong? Isn't your United States big enough for you? Why did you have to encroach where you have no right to be? We British have always ruled the Persian Gulf and if it had not been for you meddlesome Americans we would still manage the affairs of the Middle East as in the past . . . You dollar-loving Americans know nothing really about Arabia, you learn two or three words of Arabic which you can't pronounce, wear an Arab handkerchief on your heads and think you are all Lawrences of Arabia.

Again:

Actually, if the truth was told, England's real enemy in the Arab world is America . . . It was different when we ruled the world. We all know this archaeology business of yours is just a front to cover up your other activities.

What do you know about archaeology? We British are the leaders in this regard. You should restrict yourself to digging up Red Indian mounds where you can't do any harm.

Over a great many expeditions to remote spots, often subjected to close confinement with others of different backgrounds and race, I have never found any particular ethnic group especially difficult, except perhaps Yorkshiremen, who have honed to a fine art the dour habit of finding fault.

The day after our arrival in Muscat I introduced Kay, who was to look after all culinary aspects of the venture, to the ex-military gentleman Mike Curtis, whose company, Matrah Cold Stores, was providing all our sponsored food. He was wont to chide me on the lack of good old-fashioned 'suffering' which the Ubar expedition would experience. 'Not really an *expedition* at all,' he rumbled, 'what with all these delicatessen items.'

Kay unknowingly played into his hands. Thumbing through the supplies list, she requested the addition of napkins. Mike's eyebrows shot skywards. 'Napkins?' he cried.

'Yes.' Kay was serious. 'We must conserve paper whenever possible and if we all use paper napkins for four months, what a waste. No, we must have cloth napkins. It makes sound ecological sense.'

Mike chuckled like a hen, shook his head bemusedly, then shrugged.

'Oh, well. If it's napkins you want . . .'

'And, of course, rings,' Kay interjected. 'Napkin rings, so we can tape our names on. Otherwise there may be cross-infection of germs.' At this Mike exploded with mirth.

'You shall have them,' he roared. 'Napkins with rings all round.'

As Mike amended his list, he gave me an evil sideways leer. I knew what was coming. It would, in no time, be all over Muscat and unlikely to stop there: 'Ran Fiennes takes silver napkin rings on desert expedition.'

I left Kay with Mike enquiring as to the identity of menu item *foul medames* and took a taxi to the nearby headquarters of the police Mutahariqa or Special Task Force, where I was introduced to our new escort commander. Major Humaid Khaleefa, who had so ably looked after us on the previous year's reconnaissance, was on other duties and his subaltern, Lieutenant Gumma Rashid al Mushayki, a fine-featured Jaalaani from the Sharqeeya, was appointed to escort us with three other officers in a well-appointed Toyota wagon. They helped us load tons of sponsored goods on to a heavy lorry that the police loaned us for the journey.

Thompson CSF (Communications) fitted HF and VHF radio sets to our three loaned Land Rover Discovery vehicles, and their Corsican technician gave us largely unintelligible instruction in radio usage but none of us assimilated his warning about the 'kill button'. This was a green knob that looked harmless but, when pressed, destroyed the programmed contents of the machines' memory, rendering them quite useless. One of us managed to select and press this evil button within twenty-four hours and even Ron Blom of JPL was unable to resuscitate communications for many days thereafter.

The young Omani, Malik al Hinai, who had masterminded our preparations from his Oman International Bank office in Muscat, came to see us off on our thousand-kilometre overnight drive to Salalah. He handed me a portable telephone on loan.

'This will get you anywhere anytime, no problem,' he said.

'Anywhere at all?' I asked.

'Absolutely. The Kremlin or Buckingham Palace . . . We can try now if you'd like.'

'Go ahead, Malik.' I gave him a London number I knew by heart as a result of work with Dr Hammer. 'That's Buckingham Palace.'

Malike laughed, clearly disbelieving me, but dialled the number. The team were grouped about and we heard the East London accent of the palace telephone operator. 'Buckingham Palace,' she grunted. Malik's mouth opened wide and he held the telephone well away as though it would bite him.

Fourteen hours later, not far from Thamrait, a police patrol car stopped us. I had no official papers but our own Special Task Force escort arrived and Lieutenant Gumma saw the traffic police off in seconds.

Nick's camera team used one of the three Discovery vehicles so that they could film wherever we went. I was relieved to find both men were strong characters, and not 'whingers', which I had previously found to be the case with some BBC camera teams. Kevin O'Brien the cameraman, like Nick and I, had worked for Dr Hammer for a number of years. From Los Angeles, Kevin had travelled the world in style, filming the multimillionaire Malcolm Forbes on his motorcycle-and-balloon expeditions to China and elsewhere.

George Ollen, the sound man, was forty years old and unmarried. Too restless by nature to settle for a single woman or job, he had forsaken a planned career in the US Marines to become a professional nomad. One night a garage attendant shot him in the shoulder for no particular reason, which led in a roundabout way to a three-year session selling video tapes – his first profitable activity – until, in October 1991, Nick had lured him into joining our team.

In Salalah, Trevor Henry, so indispensable to our reconnaissance the previous year, warned me that, as part of the ongoing removal of all expatriates from the Omani Armed Forces, he was due to leave Dhofar in the near future and we could no longer count on his assistance.

He had earlier referred me to another Scotsman, named Andy Dunsire, who had lived in Dhofar for some eighteen years and knew the country almost as well as Trevor. 'Andy works for Airwork, the aircraft engineers in Thamrait. He will give you any help you need,' he assured me.

One problem I foresaw was a lack of labour to excavate any ruins that we might locate. Juris Zarins was expecting two staff and four students from his university but we might need six times that number of diggers. Andy saw no problems, especially when I mentioned that the American archaeologist students were mostly nubile young blondes. 'Just clear it with our boss and I'll get you the volunteers.'

I picked up an unemployed Indian hitchhiker in the mountains. He agreed to help dig with two strong friends for a modest wage and gave me his Salalah address.

I unpacked my smartest trousers and, donning a tie, went to see the Governor of Dhofar. I had requested this meeting many months previously by mail and even detailed the matters I needed to discuss. The majority of Omanis in all walks of life are the most charming and yet sincere of Arabs. The Governor, His Excellency Said Musallim Abu Saidi was too cold of manner to be charming but he was sincere in the extreme and I gained the impression that he neither approved of the project nor believed in our chances of success. Nevertheless he said nothing to discourage my proposed schedule and gave his permission for excavation at the eleven possible sites I had listed for him.

Our first task involved a thorough search of the Plain and the mountains. For this work we would be comfortably based in Salalah. To the north of the mountains, the best location from which to operate in the Sands and the central steppes was Shis'r, for there were modern buildings and fresh water in this *bedu* village.

'That I cannot sanction,' the Governor told me. 'I have no objection to your working from Shis'r, but the houses belong to the *bedu* there. If they agree to rent you their houses, so be it.'

I drove to a wild and remote part of the *jebel* where, after many enquiries, I found my old friend Hamed al Khalas staying with a wealthy camel-herder. The quarter century that had passed since we had worked together under Sultan Said bin Taimur had been kind to Hamed. We talked for two hours over a bowl of foaming camel's milk and I told him of our plans. He promised to guide me to any of the 'old places'. There was nowhere in Dhofar that Hamed could not find.

Nashran bin Sultan was also in good health and living in Salalah, for he had long since retired from government Intelligence. His memories of our long patrols in the *nej'd* were undimmed but he was as adamant as ever that Ubar lay to the west of the Wadi Mitan.

All the camping and excavation materials loaned by Occidental Petroleum of Oman and an oil supplies company called Desert Line arrived in Salalah on time, so we moved to the first work site on the Plain. This was a long-abandoned well some seventy feet deep which Ptolemy had described as the Oracle of Diana. Juris wanted to excavate the shaft itself and the ruined village around the well's mouth so I borrowed a mobile crane from BP of Oman in Salalah.

Nick and I were lowered into the shaft inside the crane's bucket. The smell of rotting flesh was overpowering and emanated from the bloated bodies of dead foxes. I manoeuvred the corpses in polythene bags and swatted at the fat flies that settled on my arms. I tried to keep my thoughts off the glistening carpet of insect life that crawled, leapt and slithered in that foul-smelling hole.

Even inside the swinging iron bucket we were attended by a host of flying, biting insects, but the stench lessened once the foxes' bodies were gone. Subsequent lowerings took us back with shovels and we began the task of hoisting debris into the buckets. Each time we raised a new item, be it a tattered tent canvas or a stinking mattress, hundreds of disturbed spiders, cockroaches, scorpions and unidentifiable creatures of all imaginable shapes and sizes scuttled in all directions.

One night I drove out over the darkening Plain to take a food parcel to Lieutenant Gumma's police, who were guarding the shaft site. They were greatly excited, for one had narrowly avoided treading on a carpet viper inside their tent. Since this particular snake can and often does cause immediate death to humans they had good reason to feel uneasy.

The well shaft was some sixty feet in diameter and Juris assumed that Ptolemy,

Ibn Batuta and others had noted the site as an oracle because, in ancient times, some local priest had hidden down the shaft and shouted up oracular responses to questions from paying visitors. This being so, we should find traces of a cave or crevice halfway down the shaft.

Andy Dunsire, an experienced caver, fixed two harnesses to one of the Discoveries parked above and, braced against the upper neck of the shaft, we attacked a suspect protuberance with pickaxes and brushes. In a while four well-cut, plastered stone slabs were clearly delineated but further work began to dislodge them, so we never discovered if they led into a horizontal passageway, long since choked with dirt, which might have hidden some trickster and acted as an echo chamber to his platitudes.

The deep stratum of modern garbage and animal bones that formed the floor of the shaft defeated our attempts to reach detritus from earlier times, so we left the Naheez valley and headed north, via Shis'r and Fasad, with eight days' supply of food, fuel and water. Andy Dunsire came as our guide but, in Fasad, I asked the Imam, a gentle Rashidi named Mohamed Mabhowt, if he would take us to a nameless spot out in the Sands.

Ron Blom produced one of his satellite pictures, taken from two hundred and sixty kilometres above Earth and clearly delineating each and every sand dune. Mohamed made various grunting sounds that indicated comprehension if not recognition and agreed to accompany us. One thing he could promise us: *wherever* we ended up, he would be sure to find the quickest route back out again. Just as no man could, for many centuries, travel the Sands by camel better than the Rashidis, so nowadays they were accepted as the master rally drivers of the great dunes.

This was no idle boast. Mohamed drove our lead Discovery, travelling over the softest sand and mounting the most severe of slopes where none of us could follow without embarrassing results.

Somewhere well within the eastern furrows of the Uruq al Hadh, with high dunes on all sides, we camped and Ron extricated his Magellan GPS satellite navigator in order to locate our position to within one hundred metres. We eagerly awaited the results of this high-tech magic, the box of tricks which rendered any city-dweller a capable navigator overnight. Ron appeared nonplussed. 'Odd,' he muttered. 'Very unusual . . . They certainly never gave any warning of this.'

Magellan had decided, for unstated reasons, to make their navigation services unavailable to ground users for twenty-four hours. So much for reliance on state-of-the-art boffinry, I mused, but said nothing, not wishing to upset Ron.

The next day we reverted to old-style position-line navigation, using the satellite pictures as though they were maps. This was a slow process involving many stops and interesting debates between the film director, the explorer, the space scientist and the Imam of Fasad, through whose familiar home terrain we were hesitantly creeping. If only we could have given him a familiar name as our desired goal he would quickly have taken us there by the best available route. But the faded tracks of the Thomas road had no name and their grid reference could not be speedily inferred from our own, until the latter was indisputably revealed at such a time as Ron's Magellan condescended to supply the relevant data.

There was even now no way of knowing that the elusive Ubar did not lie beneath the very sand that we trod in our wanderings that days.

When, sixty years ago, Philby had vainly sought Wabar in this same great desert, one of his guides had sung him the age old ballad of the lost city:

'From Qariya strike the sun upon the town
Blame not the guide that vainly seeks it now
Since the Destroying Power laid it low
Sparing not cotton smock nor silken gown.

Hear the words of Ad, Kin'ad his son
Behold my castled town Aubar y'clept,
Full ninety studs within its stalls I kept
To hunt the quarry, small and great, upon . . .'

When Philby had asked the famous Saudi governor, Ibn Jiluwi, where was Ubar, the reply had been: 'Somewhere in the Rub al Khali.'

Sadly, the satellite photographs had not provided any more specific information than Ibn Jiluwi. They had shown up the Thomas road but Thomas had already established this feature and its location without the help of the space shuttle *Challenger*.

Towards noon on the following day we found the correct valley, having negotiated various sand bridges across the serried ranks of dunes thanks to Mohamed and his impressive dune-driving techniques.

The Americans slept on all sides of the vehicles, the Clapps in a small tent.

Ron, Juris and the camera team were scattered about on portable canvas 'beds' lent by the police. Gumma's three men, wrapped in blankets from which only the barrels of their rifles emerged, patrolled the camp perimeter in watches through the night.

Andy and I, keen to savour the still beauty of the desert nights, found dune folds behind the circle of sleepers. The night skies were wild and clean, evoking all the limitless chances of life, of a future still worthy of dreams; a fine if brief antidote to the narrowing outlook of middle age.

Sirius, the Dog Star, crept, brilliantly glinting, into the lacuna of pre-dawn luminosity between two crested ergs. Desert dew settled and tiny grains of sand whispered in their millions as they trickled down the face of their mother dunes. Allah was close by on such a night. It is written in the Qur'an's Chapter of the Star that:

It is He who makes men laugh and weep, it is He who kills and makes alive . . . He is the Lord of the Dog Star, He who destroyed Ad of yore, and Thamud, and left none of them, and the people of Noah before them. Their cities, he threw them down and there covered them what did cover them.

The Dog Star, if I could only speak with him, could tell me every secret of the Sands and where to find Ubar.

At the break of day the clear and mellow voice of Mohomed, Imam of Fasad, sounded the morning incantation to God. The soul of Arabia, the thunder of the Saracens and the air of the desert came together in the passion of the mullah's voice. No God could ignore such a sound:

'*Allahu Akbar, Allahu Akbar . . .*'

Soon after dawn, and carrying all the filming gear, we plodded to the ridge of the highest dune, filling our shoes with sand and exposing the unfit to the less unfit. The view made the effort worthwhile: mile upon mile of crests and peaks, battlements and moving shadows. To capture the colouring, wonderfully soft and diffuse, would have taxed the most subtle of artists.

The Thomas road at this point was clearly shown by satellite image to disappear underneath the sand dune to our immediate east. We searched with binoculars, but not until late afternoon, when the harshness began to fade from the desert light, could we distinguish the tracks. There were two main trails, which, as they became easier to see with the naked eye, did indeed appear to vanish beneath a three-hundred-foot mountain of sand. This certainly seemed to provide an argument that the track had been in use many centuries ago. Exactly how old? This is difficult to say, but camels were not used as load-carrying beasts before 2500 BC, and so, if the track is older, then only humans, mules and horses can have used it.

An expedition by the Smithsonian Institute to a Baluchistan desert monitored twenty-foot-high dunes that moved six inches a day, but only in the windy season. Juris scoffed at the idea of major sand advances in the Rub al Khali. 'The mass of these dunes,' he told me, 'haven't moved their butts since the Ice Age.'

Nick directed the camera team to cover our negative discoveries out by the Thomas road and the nearby L-site. This recaptured on celluloid our reaction to the disappointment suffered on our reconnaissance here the previous year and our subsequent deduction that Ubar must lie to the east of the dunes rather than within them, as was generally believed.

Where Nick and I suffer a radical divergence of opinion is as to the nature of our reasoning at that point. He believes that series of JPL-produced images showing a network of tracks converging on the region of Shis'r led us to the assumption that Ubar must be somewhere along an arc of tracks which included those at Shis'r and stretched all the way, albeit at sporadic intervals, to the Thomas road and beyond.

Juris, on the other hand, agrees that our only reason for basing ourselves at Shis'r was its excellent position as a base from which to work the region to the north of the mountains. This had always been the plan and no JPL data amended it. Shis'r was one of a dozen places of potential interest both for clue searching and for film-making. Our brief 1990 visit there made Juris reflect: 'Sure, Shis'r had a bit of pottery . . . You can always find something to do archaeologically but it had nothing to do with Ubar.' Later, in 1992, he told me: 'I didn't think Shis'r was Ubar even when we started digging there.'

From the early days I knew there were three main aquifers running north into Dhofar's southern fringe of the Empty Quarter. The existing water sources at Fasad, Shis'r and Mugshin all lay at a latitude through which the Thomas road may easily have passed. The water at Fasad is very sulphurous, and at Mugshin highly salty, but Shis'r's water, that of the Wadi Ghadun aquifer, is famous for its sweetness.

Since water availability is an obvious key to the siting of cities, one did not need to be an archaeologist or a student of satellite maps to deduce that Shis'r could itself be a candidate for Ubar. As recently as 1972 Harvard archaeologist Judith Pullar had found neolithic flints here. Nevertheless we had all, including Juris, no idea that we might find the city at Shis'r any more than at a great number of other sites which our original space images showed as interesting blips, such as the L-site (the most promising), or Heilat Araka, or merely places reported by Trevor and *bedu* informants. We intended to dig and film at them all. The only reason Shis'r stood out was its suitability as a base camp. Militating against Shis'r was the fact that Thomas, Thesiger, Phillips, later archaeologists and every Omani we spoke to, all wrote off the Shis'r ruins as a mere three hundred years old or less.

The Naib Wali of Shis'r and seven of his tribe, the Bait Masan, received us graciously and, when I told them I had spoken to the Governor of Dhofar about possible rental of their houses, showed immediate enthusiasm for the idea.

One of the younger Bait Masan, Marbruk bin Ahmed, took us around three empty houses in the village. None was more than two years old nor had been previously lived in for any length of time. His cousin Said, the businessman of the tribe, eyed me shrewdly and, after a conversation with the others, speaking too quickly for me to comprehend, he made an offer that would have been admired by the sharpest of New York property dealers. I knew I had no choice, so I did not haggle, and settled for prices equivalent to renting de luxe beach houses on the Muscat seafront. There was a basic water system in Shis'r but it did not reach our bungalows. Andy Dunsire told me not to worry. His Airwork lads would fix up pipes for water and a generator for electricity.

CHAPTER THIRTEEN

I grew to like Juris and gradually became fascinated with the complex world of conflicting theories and missing jigsaw pieces that were both his work and his hobby. A major theory of his was the site of the Garden of Eden.

'From 8000 to 6000 BC,' he told me, 'south Arabia was too arid for human habitation. Around 5000 BC things improved and some folk from Syria moved south and all over the Peninsula. They built stone hearths and houses such as we have seen traces of at Shis'r, Ayun, Heilat Araka and elsewhere. Two or three people to a hut.

'At that time there was a flood plain around Shis'r, a wide, slow-moving river. Foliage and game to hunt. Even then these early neolithic people traded in incense. They moved south and north on foot or with mules and horses. Only in 2500 BC did they themselves domesticate camels to bear loads. By AD 79, at the time of the eruption of Vesuvius, which destroyed Pompeii, some three thousand tons of incense was traded north from south Arabia.

'The folk who controlled all this trade are known as the people of Ad,' Juris speculated. 'These same people lived at the oracle in the Naheez, they lived in the Dhofar mountains and their children's children still do. The modern *jebali* in Dhofar is of the same race as the People of Ad. Now they are the last of the cattle herders but we know from archaeology that cattle were prevalent throughout Arabia between 5000 and 6000 BC.

'The Old Testament is an allegory which gives clues to history. When Adam and Eve arrived in the Garden everything was good. When Adam sinned he was cursed by being made to work. Later he was forced out of the Garden. All this was roughly taking place around 5000 BC, which has been thought to be the beginning of agriculture. In 6000 BC there was no agriculture in the Garden of Eden. By 4000 BC nearly all that region was farmed.

'What area?' I asked him. 'Where is Eden?'

'That deserves a reasoned reply, not a quick one,' Juris laughed. 'Remember Genesis?' he wagged a finger in his preacher mode. '"And the Lord God planted a garden eastward in Eden . . . And a river went out of Eden to water the garden and from thence it parted and became into four heads. The name of the first of Pishon in the land of Havilah where there is gold. The name of the second is Gihon in the land of Ethiopia. The third is Hiddekel [Tigris] and the fourth is Euphrates."'

'Where now are Pishon and Gihon?' I asked.

Juris paused. 'For centuries scientists have asked this question and many thought the Nile and the Ganges were the missing rivers. But satellite pictures show the Wadis Rimah and Batin in Saudi were once a great river that met up with the Tigris, the Euphrates and the Karun [Gihon] rivers at the head of the Persian Gulf. The Garden, the fertile regions, had to be close to this great riverine confluence.'

Juris's research had moved from the allegories of Genesis to the unfolding archaeology of Saudi Arabia and his decade of fieldwork there. He consulted the sciences of geology, hydrology and linguistics and then added LANDSAT satellite-image information.

Around 30000 BC, probably in the eastern Mediterranean and in Iraq, Neanderthals developed into modern Man. As a result of the Great Ice Age, the Persian Gulf was then land, well watered by the four great rivers and a natural paradise for the humans that lived and hunted there. Ships have recently used sonar equipment to discover deep river beds and evidence of once-great sand dunes on the sea floor of the Gulf, which is up to one hundred and fifty feet deep.

Around 6000 BC this area witnessed the stresses of hunter-gatherer tribes flooding into a region settled by the new agriculturists. Juris believes that, about 5000 BC, these pioneer farmers settled along the then fertile Kuwaiti and Saudi coasts. Their legends and mythology passed into the world's first written language, Sumerian, in 3000 BC. At this point words such as Eden and Adam, with their attendant myths, entered history. During the period that the compilers of Genesis, the Israelites, were forming as a nation, between 1500 and 900 BC, Mesopotamia was conquered by the Kashshites. The Israelites could not help but read and learn the legends of Mesopotamia, which, in Hebrew, were then recorded in highly condensed form in Genesis.

'The whole Garden of Eden story,' Juris added, 'when finally written down, could be seen to represent the point of view of the hunter-gatherers, not the farmers. It was the collision of two ways of life. Adam and Eve were heirs to natural beauty, with everything they needed. But they sinned and were expelled because they challenged God's omnipotence. In so doing they represented the agriculturalists, who took matters into their own hands and tamed nature. They relied on their own skills and knowledge instead of God's bounty.'

One further considerable complication enters Juris's theories. It concerns a worldwide phenomenon, called the Flandrian Transgression, which caused a sudden rise in sea level. The whole Gulf was flooded and by 4000 BC Eden was buried under up to two hundred and fifty feet of sea water and the contemporary Sumerians retreated north into Mesopotamia.

By 3000 BC the original Eden was, Juris believed, replaced by a district of the eastern Saudi coast, which at that time was joined to and included Bahrain. This was called Dilmun not Eden. The concept and the name of Eden originated very early, with the Sumerians, and was transmitted from them into Akkadian, from which the Hebrews derived their own version of the story.

'Although the Hebrews had close associations with Egypt,' Juris explained, 'their earliest spiritual roots were in Mesopotamia. Abraham travelled to Egypt, Joseph did likewise and the Exodus story is concerned with Egypt, but there is nothing whatever Egyptian about the early chapters of Genesis. All these early accounts are linked to Mesopotamia. Abraham probably came from Ur and the writers of Genesis needed to link up with his history. Therefore they drew from the literary sources of the greatest civilization that had ever existed, that of Mesopotamia. In doing so they turned Eden (Sumerian for fertile plain) into the Garden, Adam ('settlement') into a man, and a compacted history of things that occurred millennia before was compressed into a few chapters.'

If Juris is correct and his theories take advantage of the very latest information revealed by several fields of scientific research, then there is embedded in the Old Testament a very ancient folk memory, not only the story of Creation but also the story of Man's emergence, around eight thousand years ago, from total dependence to perilous self-reliance.

When first I planned which areas were most suitable for Juris to visit, the key person who judged the value of each site (whether a suspect JPL blip in the Sands, an old village in the steppes, or a nest of ruins on the Plain) was Trevor Henry. But in the mountains, where our clues would mostly consist of cave drawings, and in the maze of *nej'd* wadis running north from the mountains (where the pecked rock, graves and triliths mostly lay), our chief guide and adviser would be a remarkable Dhofari of the Shahra tribe named Ali Ahmed Ali Mahash.

Back in the 1960s Ali had, like many Dhofaris, joined the British-trained Trucial Oman Scouts. His outstanding qualities of leadership soon saw his promotion to lieutenant and he was sent to Mons Officer Cadet School in England two years after I graduated from there.

In the late 1960s we both worked at the Army School of Languages in Beaconsfield, where I was a student of Arabic and he was a teacher. He was recalled to the Gulf States as a captain and, the best young officer of his generation, was selected for a three-year posting to a British regiment. Unfortunately the Gulf intelligence services discovered that Ali was promulgating revolutionary ideas and he was jailed in Muscat for seven years.

On his release he obtained a government job in Salalah but remained restless until, in March 1988, a fellow Shahri showed Ali some cave writings in the Wadi Naheez. Ali was fascinated. He knew that the history of his country, of his people the Shahra and the lost people of Ad, was locked within a pre-Islamic language that existed only in southern Arabia and especially in Dhofar. Modern progress, especially the proliferation of four-wheel-drive jeeps all over the country, was already defacing many rock drawings on valley floors.

Ali told me: 'The Phillips expeditions of 1952 and 1953 represent the only archaeological work carried out in Dhofar and the only inscriptions so far published are written in the language of the Hadhraumi coastal settlers of AD 100. There is nothing in any local language and a remarkable dearth of information about our ancient history.'

Ali decided, without official prompting or support, to make a systematic survey of all the caves in Dhofar. Since there are many thousands of caves, often deep and inaccessible, in the *nej'd*, the mountains and along the coast, Ali's intentions were enormously ambitious. He had no formal training in data recording and could only use his spare time for the project. He took many photographs of each new discovery and attended photography courses at London's Institute of Archaeology. Over the months he drew up individual groupings of different symbols that formed the cave writing at various sites. He intended to decipher the unknown early alphabet of his ancestors. To find out how the writings and the pictures were painted, he mixed dyes from over one hundred and thirty different sources, vegetable and mineral, in a backroom at his Salalah home.

Ali was enthusiastic about our work and agreed to take us to his discoveries.

Whether or not the paintings or graffiti would provide us with clues, we would only know when Juris could see the sites for himself. Over a three-week period Ali took us by vehicle and on foot to remote and wonderful places all over Dhofar.

Ginnie came out to establish a proper HF communications network with radios based in Shis'r, Thamrait and with each vehicle. When the archaeologists arrived and we separated into groups, good long-distance communications would speed up the search and help in an emergency. Ali went with the two of us east to Mirbat, west to Rakhyut and just about everywhere in between. We drove the track east from Sudh to Hadbin until it tapered out on a precipitous coastal track in the mountains west of Hasik.

Although Ali and I had been trained at the same British institutions, there was a good deal of heated discussion, since we had ended up fighting on opposite sides. When, in remote villages he introduced me as an ex-officer of Sultan Said bin Taimur, I sensed a certain coolness from time to time. Under the benevolent rule of Sultan Qaboos all the old enmities have been buried but memories of powerful events and emotions do not disappear in Arabia any more than elsewhere.

The caves of the eastern *jebel* wadis were rich in paintings, especially those used by goatherds. These were sometimes high up cliffs of the wadis and difficult to reach. Writings and drawings, Ali had found, were best preserved in these high caves, for they were often above the mist line, better protected from seasonal rainstorms and floods and, unlike the larger cattle or camel caves, they were not subjected to the dense smoke of the dung fires lit through the monsoon periods to keep away insects and provide warmth. The heat of the fires splits the stone of the cave walls and covers them with a thick deposit of soot which has obscured many of the paintings.

Ali took us to the homesteads of his people, the Shahra, high on the grassland downs of Kizit, where they are cattleherders, and deep in the Wadi Darbat, where they keep large herds of camel. The caves near each settlement reflected in their paintings the business of the region. Camels were everywhere, depicted walking, trotting, emaciated, fat with large lumps, couched in pairs or in long caravan lines, suckling babies or being milked by herders. Pictures of camels being ridden immediately told those of us who had previously listened to Juris that the paintings must be later than 2500 BC, when camels were first domesticated. We were fast becoming amateur archaeologists.

The author at Shis'r.

Nick Clapp, who carried out painstaking research into Ubar before filming the expedition, in Uruq al Hadh.

The Ubar Expedition team in Uruq al Hadh.

Dr Juris Zarins, the expedition's archaeologist, in Salalah.

Jana Owen, Dr Zarins's senior assistant, and Rick Breitenstein.

Amy Hirschfeld, who handled filing, registration and computer work.

*Bakheit bin Abdulla bin Salim Bait Masan,
along with Marbruk bin Ahmed bin Saarleh
Bait Masan, helped with the dig at Shis'r.*

Bakheit's father Abdulla bin Salim.

Marbruk bin Ahmed bin Saarleh, like Bakheit a member of the Bait Masan tribe.

Julie Knight and Rick Breitenstein work at Shis'r.

Neil Barnes and Airwork's volunteer man the 'Sieve'.

The main north-west tower at Shis'r.

Shis'r by night.

The south-east wall partially revealed.

Marbruk in the south-west rooms section.

The team at work on the north-east wall.

Shis'r from the air. MAIN PICTURE: *Shis'r.*

The north-east circular tower.

The author with Bakheit bin Abdulla and Said bin Musallim.

Omani Ministers at the site with Juris Zarins in the foreground. General Ali Majid is in uniform.

Artefacts discovered at Shis'r.

Neolithic flints found at the site.

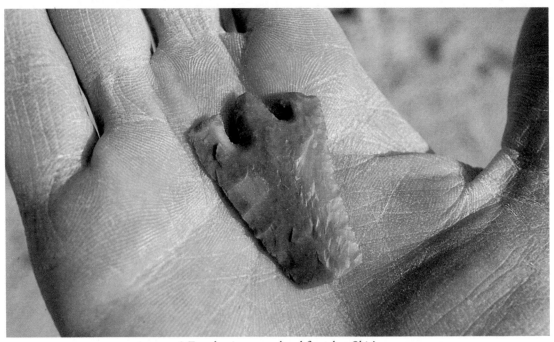

A Fasad point arrowhead found at Shis'r.

LEFT: The key Jemdet Nasir pottery from satellite site 18: the rim of a clay jar dating from about 2800 BC. It was discovered in an old fireplace in the Heilat Shis'r area. RIGHT: A piece of wall plaster showing graffiti in an unknown script.

The woven-reed pattern of a builder's hod from three thousand years ago is still visible on the wall plaster.

A frankincense burner from southern Arabia, probably made between 500 BC and 300 AD.

Imitation Greek or Roman pottery with impressed rope pattern, from around 500 BC.

A dot and circle design not previously known on pottery, seen here on burnished brown ware dating from 2000 BC and later.

The first chess set found in southern Arabia, made of soapstone and dating from around 1000 AD. The pieces are a soldier, a king, a castle, an elephant, a bishop, a knight and a rook.

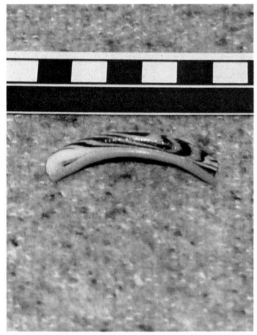

An early Islamic glass bracelet piece from around 700 AD, probably made in Aden.

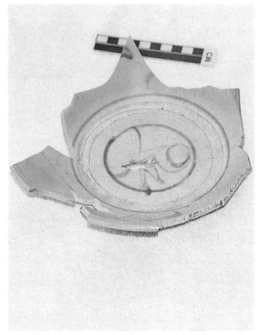

A Celadon porcelain plate from Canton, made between the tenth and twelfth centuries AD.

In the cave system of Tawi Ateer.

The author at the hand-over of 13,000 artefacts to Ali Ahmed Ali Mahash.

There were also goats, cattle, horses, foxes, snakes, wolves, ibexes and leopards. Less frequent were palm trees and plants, crude maps, planets, especially the sun and moon, and various types of sailing ship.

Ali took us to many of the northern wadis in the *nej'd* to inspect graves, tombs and different types of burial ground. We never tampered with Islamic graves and only checked the human remains of sites already open to the air. Some graves are up to thirty metres in length, which reflected, Ali assured us, the great wealth, not length, of the inmate. Many Dhofaris still go to these tombs to make vows and to pray. Oaths are sworn and those accused of crime will swear their innocence there. Agreements and truces are legitimized when made at such places.

He also showed us weird groups of standing stones; often three uprights capped by a fourth flat stone. These Ali described as tetraliths. Many of the cap-stones were inscribed with the symbols of the mysterious alphabet which so excited Ali. Thesiger and Thomas came to no conclusion as to the meaning of these stones, but thought they were monuments rather than graves.

Thesiger summarized his thoughts with these words:

> . . . whatever may have been their purpose, these piles of uncut stones are among the tangible monuments which the Arabs of the past have left behind them in Arabia. They seem to me a fitting memorial to the ancestors of a people who, at their best, have cared little for material things.

Sadly for us, this lack of egoism left few or no positive leads towards Ubar or any other citadel of the *jebalis*, our lost People of Ad. One day I witnessed an act of innocent vandalism that encapsulated the fate of tangible history in this part of the world. Ali led is to the little known Mahra water-hole of Leeat, an hour or so east of Hanun and tucked into the base of the mountain cliffs. Years ago I had twice been ambushed by communist forces at this place and the memories flooded back.

Although nobody lived at Ain Leeat, or Wobet as it used to be called, there were a dozen or more tribesmen of the eastern Mahra close by the spring at a burial ground. Their dead cousin was, they all agreed, one hundred and nine years of age. Ali seemed to find this acceptable and joked, as was his way, with the Mahra. He thought of them and the remnants of the Botahari as distant relations to the Shahra. The Qara and Kathiri tribes were later arrivals who had for many years enslaved the Shahra.

'Was it not the Mahra,' Ali loved to ask men of that tribe, 'who killed the camel of the Prophet?'

'No, no,' they would always respond. 'The Shahra did that thing.'

As I watched the last of the Mahra depart in their battered Toyotas, Ali pointed to the newly fashioned pile of gravestones. He shook his head and clacked his teeth. 'We must educate them *not* to do this,' he muttered. He showed me a heavy squared stone which had quite clearly been taken from one of the more ancient tombs close by. 'This is their practice and it will be most difficult to eradicate. Building materials are expensive and difficult to come by. Since their earlier relatives died a good many years ago and are now in Paradise, why should they mind if later generations pinch a few handy stones?'

With only a few of the more inaccessible caves to explore, we thanked Ali and made our way over the mountains to Thamrait and thence to Shis'r with two lorryloads of food and equipment.

Andy's friends cobbled up a plumbing system and an ancient generator. We swept out sackloads of desert sand that past storms had blown into our three rented houses. Given another thousand years, I mused, this place will be as covered with sand as Ubar.

Juris's archaeological team arrived not long before Christmas, all in their early twenties and none with previous experience of Arabia. The five girls were blessed with long hair, pretty faces and well-rounded figures. I thanked God (and Juris) for an excellent selection process and felt confident there would be no problem in Andy Dunsire finding a great number of volunteer diggers from among his Airwork colleagues at Thamrait. If the attraction of the actual digging was not enough, this bunch of alluring American belles would surely do the trick. I nursed mental images of hundreds of randy diggers shovelling aside vast amounts of sand from our sites over the next three months.

There was one male student from the same university, Rick Breitenstein, who had never spent a day outside Missouri and had never previously travelled by air. Within twenty-four hours he had jetted to Los Angeles and London, then on to Muscat for two nights. He arrived, amiable and quite unperturbed, which greatly impressed the rest of us.

I handed out *shemagh* headcloths, sand goggles, camp-beds and water bottles to everyone, including the hitchhiker and two other Indians who arrived from Salalah. Together with the anticipated influx of Thamrait expatriates, we should total up to forty diggers on a good day.

I hoped that none of our girls would get quickly involved in emotional attractions in case this put off the majority of other diggers, who might feel their chances of romance had become too slim to warrant the boring hours of desert digging in midsummer.

Once we were established in the rented houses at Shis'r, two partly different programmes had to be followed. Juris and his diggers were to excavate all hopeful sites in the immediate area for a month and then move south to work for a further two months in the mountain and on the Plain, based in Salalah. Nick, Kay and the camera team, with both Andy and Ali Ahmed kindly ready to take them more or less anywhere they wished, would complete the documentary film.

I had received the permanent assistance, from sponsors, of a cook and helper in both our bases. Two were Goans and two Bangladeshis. The latter went by the name of Gomez. Their only intelligible comments were, when grateful, oft-repeated renditions of 'Thank you too much' or, occasionally, 'Thank you not very much.'

The Mr Gomez who looked after our welfare at Shis'r conducted a running battle with one of Lieutenant Gumma's policemen, whom he suspected of appropriating cooking brandy and cigarettes from the storeroom. He was famous among the Asian community in Thamrait for the amazing heroics in which he had indulged during the Free Bengali War. Since he was visually the nearest thing imaginable to a humanoid spider or stick insect, though his gestures were grandiose and heroic, he caused great mirth and helped create a generally jovial atmosphere about the base.

The common picture of Western archaeological students and field diggers, as defined by Bahn, was in our case short of the mark, but may well have been what our Thamrait helpers were expecting:

Diggers, undergraduates and volunteers are the cannon fodder of any dig. They normally provide all the sweaty labour and are kept in a state of blissful ignorance about what they are doing and why. Amazingly, some even pay to be treated in this way. Their basic task is to move dirt from one place to another and occasionally sieve it into different sizes before dumping it. Useful items they take on excavations include:

Scruffy old clothing including T-shirt marked 'Archaeologists do it in holes'.

A pointed trowel except in France where bent screwdrivers are preferred.

Insect repellant.
Insurance against trench collapse.
Condoms and bottle opener . . .

Bahn also warns of the qualities endemic to many modern archaeologists where their field reports are concerned:

A basic rule is to fill your reports with 'maybe', 'perhaps' and 'possibly'. This enables you to make an orderly and dignified retreat in case of attack. Another way to side-step criticism is to make your prose so obscure and tortuous that nobody is quite sure what you are saying. If later proved wrong, this smokescreen will enable you to claim you were misunderstood and that you actually said nothing of the kind.

Another ruse in print is to include lots of lists and tables which nobody will ever bother to check or read through but which serve to make your work seem scholarly and thorough. Similarly, many authors, many of them French, put a long bibliography at the end, containing numerous impressive sources – most of which are never actually referred to in the text. It is just window-dressing but very effective since it is unlikely that anyone will read the entire work and notice the absences . . .

Lawrence of Arabia became an amateur archaeologist as a teenager in Oxford and retained the interest all his life. This and his love of Arabia make feasible the rumours that before his death he had planned his own search for the city that he called Atlantis of the Sands.

Juris had selected Jana Owen as his senior assistant, a girl who had worked with him before on prehistoric American Indian sites. With a Masters Degree and experience in underwater archaeology, Jana was an ideal choice.

'American women,' she later told me, 'are very outspoken and very visible but my fear that the Omanis might not like us has thankfully proved wrong.'

In fact our Bait Masan hosts in Shis'r took to the team from the first and their two most outgoing young men, Marbruk and Bakheit, joined the dig from the first, though neither believed that Ubar was to be found in their village. Like everyone else, they knew that it lay out in the Sands to the west.

Juris and two of his teaching colleagues were given a budget by their university which allowed for a team of six. Jana called an old school friend, Amy Hirschfeld, to handle all the filing, registration and computerization work. Amy, a Bostonian, was busy completing a book on the catacombs of Rome, but she did not hesitate. She and Jana first met the rest of the field team at the airport but they were confident there would be no bad apples, since Juris had selected everyone with care from a healthy list of applicants.

CHAPTER FOURTEEN

The month of December rushed by with preparations and a good deal of filming work. Three days before Christmas I heard the two Omani students, who worked with us on loan from the Ministry of National Heritage and Culture, commenting on the fact that we had been in Shis'r for ten days, the teams were ready and yet all we seemed to do was to film each other. This seemed a fair summary and it would not sound good in the wrong quarters.

Months later Juris, laughing at the memory, told me: 'By 23 December we had done *no* archaeology in Shis'r.' But by Christmas day, with a workforce of four Omanis, three Asians and six Americans, he was looking decidedly perky. I asked what was up but he was cautious.

'It's good,' he said. 'Interesting.'

'Is it four hundred years old?' I pressed him. 'Like they say.'

'No,' he replied, winked and returned to the room where retrieved artefacts were beginning to spread all over the improvised shelves. The team were buried in site maps, lists and hushed discussions. There was an unmistakeable air of excitement.

At first Juris concentrated his small force on or close to the original rubble pile. Within a week the outline of the rock heap had taken on the clear-cut silhouette of a ruined tower connected by low battlements to a second round tower and a beautifully built horseshoe tower to its east. Pottery and flints were hourly unearthed, including, to Juris's great pleasure, both Roman and Greek-style urns from the period that would have been Ubar's heyday.

'You ask me when I began to think Shis'r was Ubar,' Juris objected, 'but there was *no* one single day that I said, 'Oh, my God, this is Ubar or this is Omanum Emporium.' Until we find an inscription we can *never* one hundred per cent say that!'

Days later a piece of red pottery was found identical to the pottery style of the

Jemdet Nassir period in Uruq, Mesopotamia. If carbon dating proves this to be so it will predate previous thinking as to the commencement of trade between Mesopotamia and south Arabia from 5000 to 4000 BC. That in turn will effect many other evolving theories about our human history.

'I am not going out on a limb,' Juris told me, 'and saying this is or isn't Ubar. I will go back to the university to check out all our findings: then I can make some statement. But I can already say this is a very important Roman site. It probably goes back at least four thousand years.'

Why, I asked him, had the middle of the walled citadel (a more appropriate word than 'city' since the whole walled area was not much bigger than a football field) collapsed? It was as though a bomb had blown out a crater, leaving only the outer walls and towers with a few rooms and hearths on the inside of the walls. How many other internal structures there might have been before the collapse, may never be known.

'As with many well-built, walled caravanserai,' Juris said, 'this was built around a strategically sited water-hole – and what could be more of a controlling site than this?'

He paused, looking down into the sandy pit below the cliff. 'I suspect that as they used up more and more water during a dry period, the water table lowered and the immediate surrounds fell in to form a typical doline or karst collapse. An earthquake may have even assisted by undermining the solutional cavity.

Charles Elachi and Ron Blom, before returning to JPL, set up a mobile EM31 sensitivity unit and ran a scanner, mounted on tiny sledge runners, over the surface of the collapsed area. At a depth of twenty-eight feet beneath the sand they detected the outline of a four-metre-square well-head. Juris decided we had too little manpower to attempt to excavate this feature. At a later date we could perhaps use sand-suction gear to reach the well-head and the buried remains of the citadel's heart.

On a particularly hot day, with Andy Dunsire and an English climber named Peter Eades roped to the top of the cliff, where they worked at the remains of the north-east tower, a rock fall rumbled down from the overhang and landed on the sink-hole floor. Luckily no diggers were hurt, but, to minimize future hazards, I knocked steel poles across the face of the overhang and joined them with a heavy red rope. Juris forbade any of his diggers to work beneath the cliff wall.

When free time was available, I took a shovel and pickaxe to the site and attacked any area that did not require more delicate attention using trowel and handbrush. Jana, however, allergic to shovels, would scream and chase me away, so I spent more time plodding about in the desert six or seven miles east of the site searching for subsidiary camps rich in axe-heads and arrowheads. Once these were located, I would fetch Amy or Juris with their position-locating gear to plot each new satellite site.

In the days when the area was verdant, travellers would have camped within sight of the many-towered citadel but far enough away to settle their camels and sort out their loads. Altogether we found thirty-five such camp-sites to the north, west and east of the citadel and up to eight miles away from it.

The central site would have appeared majestic and without equal in the land to the *bedu* cameleers. For nine hundred kilometres of desert in any direction there was no edifice even a quarter the size of Shis'r, or Ubar as I by now described it. The walls and towers would have stood out to the weary and thirsty traveller from up to twenty miles away – to them indeed a city of the desert.

Nigel Groome, once Aden's Director of Antiquities, writes of south Arabia:

The general impression gleaned from a survey of the archaeological remains that have come down from the tenth century – and they are considerable – is that cities were built on a small scale, that buildings were simple and modestly constructed from materials locally available and that the standard of living was far from luxurious when compared to that prevailing in other parts of the ancient Near Eastern world.

Of our site Juris told me, 'So far we have walls and towers that are square and round and horseshoe-shaped. There was clearly a central tower, an inner sanctum and an outer wall which had a minimum height of between ten and fifteen feet and a consistent thickness of eighty centimetres. Some of the original rooms, complete with hearths, did not collapse into the sink-hole and these have already yielded rich finds for the key periods between the second millennium BC and around AD 300, when trading activities seem to have dropped off.'

In the northern corner, the site of the main structure, a great deal of stone was missing as a result of appropriation by Sultan Said bin Taimur's workforce to build his own small fort fifty yards away in 1955. The original building work of the Ubarites was excellent, consisting of semi-dressed stones cemented with a white plaster similar to that used in the north of the peninsula by contemporary peoples such as the Nabataeans.

Rick showed me four chunks of this plaster that still clearly bore the woven-reed pattern of the plasterer's hod basket of over three thousand years ago. One bore a clear inscription in unrecognizable glyphics.

Jana, almost purring with pleasure, showed me the only ancient chess set ever to be found in south Arabia. The six soapstone pieces, each two or three inches high and well polished by the fingers of the players, had lain buried for over a thousand years. Shutrinj, the forerunner of modern chess, was a Persian war game and the king was *shah*. The word for dead is *ma'at* and a victorious player, cornering his opponent's monarch would shout '*Shah ma'at*' – not so different from 'checkmate'.

After a month the diggers were three feet down in places and pottery from Rome, Greece and Syria joined Celadon and Ming plates from China, glass bracelets of bright, clear colours from Aden and neolithic flint weapons from 5000 BC.

Juris often appointed a digger to a three-metre-square patch and roped it off on a grid system. If the relevant person did not turn up from Thamrait for a week that patch might well be left empty until his return. This encouraged a certain proprietorial pride and increased care unless it proved to be a 'bad' patch with little or no yield for days of painstaking work.

The three Indians and a rota of others removed spoil buckets and sieved them with three-foot-square shaker-mesh, through which fine sand and grit passed, leaving larger bits for inspection.

Juris, Jana and Amy logged every item as to its precise location, numbered each fragment and entered all data on their computers. Everyone was hot, dusty and tired by dusk. Kay and the Gomez cooking team then came into their own. They catered for the curry tastes of the Omanis and Asians, the red meat and veg needs of the British and the pizza, spaghetti, jelly and peanut-butter requirements of the Americans. At Christmas Kay produced an ingeniously festive tree fashioned from a spiky desert bush with winking lights. There was no snow but plenty of Christmas fare was produced from personal luggage.

Kay's shopping centre was the sprawling market village to the south of our Thamrait base only an hour's drive to the east. The graded gravel track was excellent but sudden camel wallows of soft sand and sharp switchbacks hiding double bends made fast driving hazardous. Our two Omani graduate archaeologists unfortunately lost concentration momentarily while driving a brand-new Toyota four-wheel-drive jeep in broad daylight. Fifteen miles east of

Shis'r they overturned, the roof concertinaed and both were injured, one breaking a leg. They were hospitalized in Salalah and we never saw them again.

- - - - - - - - - - - - - - - -

Word of our discovery soon reached the Omani and Gulf press and tourists in Land Rovers began to arrive from Salalah. Was this Ubar? Was it Irem? If so, where were the golden pillars and the whole fabulous city? The fantasies of the *Arabian Nights* had a lot to answer for.

By the end of January we had found no major inscription but nine towers were unearthed, some sixty per cent of the main outer wall and over six thousand individual artefacts.

Nick's documentary film had progressed well with the help of Ali Ahmed and Trevor. Dr Ali Shanfari, our appointed director from the Ministry of National Heritage and Culture, sounded happy with progress when I called him in Muscat and so did our Omani sponsors.

Andy Dunsire had told me of a cave system six hundred feet down at the base of a giant sink-hole called Tawi Ateer, the Well of the Birds. He had promised to show me a great cavern which I hoped might contain wall writings or at least paintings, for it was known, certainly until the advent of recent rockfalls, that Dhofaris used to descend into the hole by way of vertiginous pathways.

Andy drove me with a Range Rover full of his friends to the village of Tawi Ateer on the high plateau of the *jebel* and a mile to the north, and we trekked into the dry bush with rucksacks and ropes. His three friends were to camp at the edge of the six-hundred-foot deep crater to ensure that our descent ropes were not removed during the night.

Because I was inept with the special rope techniques Andy used, he took an hour to make everything ready. I felt a touch giddy, for the cry of pigeons and the starling-like Tristram's grackle echoing around the vast natural chamber kept reminding me of the long drop down to the cave system.

By the time we were ready, dusk had filled the huge, perfectly rounded cauldron and, as Andy encouraged me to let go of the safety rope by the crater lip, stars were already appearing in a sky of midnight blue. I could not see below me and my helmet torch, striking a rock, went dead. This had the advantage of making it impossible to see the six hundred feet of thin rope dangling down into the void between my swinging feet.

After many minutes of painfully slow descent the two-inch-long alloy crocodile clasp, which slid down the rope at a speed I could control with a lever, suddenly came up sharp against a knot of rope coils. I winced as the rope elasticated. I imagined the feel of it breaking and the sudden rush of air. Panic was not far off. Sweat stung my eyes. Because all my body weight rested on the point where the metal teeth grasped the knot and since there could be no upward impetus from my dangling legs, it took me many long minutes to free the impediment without disentangling my lifeline by mistake. For a while I despaired, then a lucky tug freed the coil, and ten minutes later I arrived shaky kneed at the floor of the great shaft.

The foul stench of civet dung hung about in the warm air and I heard the scrabble of the striped cats in the darkness. Andy arrived after twenty minutes and I followed him via boulders and sloping ledges, past stalactites and a descending series of passages, to the edge of a scum-laden lake. The beam of his head torch disturbed a cloud of flying creepy-crawlies.

On a previous visit Andy had secreted two Land Rover inner tubes close by, and stripping down to our pants and desert boots, we slipped into the evil-smelling waters.

Andy beckoned me away from one side wall where a swarm of giant mosquito-like insects rose in anger from their nest.

'There are blind fish in the caves.' Andy pointed downwards and added: 'Keep close.' I nodded, needing no second warning.

For fifty minutes I swam on my black tube and soon gave up any attempt to memorize our tortuous route. Sometimes the ceiling on the tunnel approached within inches of the water and, copying Andy, I turned over and swam on my back. There was just enough room to breathe and then, when the gap improved slightly, to haul on a long cord attached to my tube to pull it under the obstacle.

I kept a nagging claustrophobic fear at bay through total trust in Andy's cavemanship, if that is the right term. But it came to me how easily he might suffer a sudden heart attack, for he was well into his fifties. How then would I find my way out of these evil waterways? Certainly not by memory.

My faith in Andy collapsed and my inner fears surged when his white beard lifted from the oily surface and he spluttered, 'Which way did we enter this chamber?'

I told him and he disagreed. We bobbed under an even lower ledge with no more than three inches of clearance and I smelled putrefied flesh close at hand. An animal skull with wet, green flesh attached in floating ribbons nodded against my shoulder – some civet or goat lured to its death by thirst.

After an hour and a half Andy shook his head, dislodging all manner of flying insects.

'I can't understand it,' he grunted. 'The main passageway must be underwater. I just can't locate it.'

So we gave up and, to my considerable relief, Andy found no difficulty in retracing his route to the entry point.

We slept on a ledge free of civet dung until dawn when, back at the base of the crater and the single length of rope, Andy attached two special grips to my foot and shoulder.

'You go first. If you get into trouble, shout, but do not look down.'

After about four hundred feet the tautly stretched rope felt as thin as string. The swish and shriek of disturbed grackles and my empty stomach combined to make the climb unenjoyable, but I managed to force from my mind the tiniest thought about the ever-increasing drop below.

When Andy joined me at the upper rim of the crater, he looked disappointed. 'Never mind,' he said, 'we'll come back when the water-level drops.' My enthusiasm to find the cave graffiti had lessened but I took care not to show it.

Juris needed an aerial view of the site and the surrounding area. The Government kindly sent down a Bell helicopter from Muscat. The crew included an Englishman named Mike Crumbie.

The aerial photography work went well and the crew were highly efficient. That night they slept in our houses at Shis'r and, at dinner, the conversation veered to *The Feather Men*.

'It is definitely fiction,' Mike Crumbie volunteered.

'Why should you think that?' I asked him.

'There is one excellent reason,' he replied. 'The helicopter outside this building, exactly the same model as that which crashed and you referred to, is proof positive that no saboteur could have entered its "hell-hole" while a cargo hook was in position.'

The Feather Men had clearly stated that the doomed Augusta Bell 205 A-1 was indeed sabotaged by way of its hell-hole. Mike Crumbie had shown me proof that the helicopter *did* have a cargo hook in place on the fatal day.

There was little I could say. I had been told the full details and had recorded them in the book. However wrong my informants may have been, I was, as the author, to blame. The following morning Mike Crumbie took me to the Bell shortly before they took off.

'See for yourself,' he said. 'Nobody could get through there.'

I squeezed between the helicopter's belly and the ground and knew there was no way I could enter the narrow work-shaft. Nevertheless, back in 1976 somebody had done so. I remembered Andy's torch-lit, helmeted face down in the cave system: he had made me squirm beneath ledges that looked equally impassable. Removing my shirt, I struggled upwards between the steel hook and the rim of the circular shaft. Suddenly my rib cage seemed to deflate and I popped past the bottleneck. The rest of my body followed with ease and there was ample room to work on the gearings above my head. Extrication took rather longer as now my ribs faced the wrong way but, somewhat bruised, I eventually emerged.

- - - - - - - - - - - - - - - - -

Some five weeks after the first key finds at Shis'r, a police van with four armed officers arrived around midnight with a summons for me to go at once to the Palace in Muscat. The police drove me to Salalah and, by ROP flight, I reached Muscat the next morning. A Royal limousine took me to Seeb Palace, where various new Ambassadors were being accredited. After an hour's wait in what must rank among the most splendid palaces in the world, I was shown in to His Majesty Sultan Qaboos's *majlis*. He was delighted with the success of the expedition and keen to ensure continued excavation at Shis'r until the ruins were fully revealed. He asked me to give him a list of actions I thought might best be taken to follow up the discovery.

'Is it definitely Ubar?' he asked me.

'I believe so, Your Majesty. It is difficult to know what else it could be.'

The warmth of his smile and the strength of his handshake reminded me of my meeting with his father twenty-four years before. I felt then that the long years of hoping, the set-backs and the false trails had all been worthwhile.

POSTSCRIPT: THE LOST CITY

I asked in my report to Sultan Qaboos that Ali Ahmed be appointed Field Director for Archaeology in Dhofar, that Juris be contracted to continue excavations and that the Shis'r site be protected against damage by visitors.

Back in Salalah I handed over all the equipment and organizational details to Juris. Apart from the archaeologists, all the team left Oman early in February. The search for Ubar was over. A few weeks later I returned to report to the Minister of Information, His Excellency Abdul Aziz bin Mohomed Al Rowas, who had been appointed by the Sultan to chair a ministerial committee to oversee all aspects of archaeology in southern Oman.

To my delight, Ali Ahmed Ali Mahash had been appointed as director, with responsibility for all future work in Dhofar. I was to ensure that all artefacts were handed over to him before Juris and the team left Oman. Since I had personally given Dr Ali Shanfari a document taking full responsibility for all such items, I was keen to comply.

I sat on the floor of Ali Ahmed's new office in the Ministry of Information with Jana and Amy and over a period of three hours we handed Ali more than thirteen thousand artefacts fully computerized with individual reference numbers.

Our Acheulean axe-head from Hanun was over two hundred and fifty thousand years old, arrowheads from Shis'r's thirty satellite camps were mostly seven thousand years old, pottery originated from Bronze Age Syria of 2000 BC and from the later Iron Age, Hellenistic and eastern Mediterranean Roman periods. Juris and Jana retained samples of charcoal, seashells and bones for C14 radiocarbon dating, which will eventually help establish the overall date range of the ruins.

There were Fasad Points, arrowheads from between the sixth and fourth millennia BC. The first buildings, in a Shis'r satellite camp, Bil Rizat, dated back to 2000 BC, and this was where Juris found the pottery shard likely to have come from Uruq. This single artefact, when the dating is proven, is likely to alter historians' chronology of the incense trade in south Arabia by a thousand years.

The majority of the pottery, soapstone lamps and incense burners stem from Shis'r's trading heyday, probably between 500 and 300 BC, which was the Roman, Greek and south Arabic period. This confirms Shis'r's case for identification with Ptolemy's Omanum Emporium. The Greek word *emporion* was applied to cities on or close to the coast. This is confusing until the point of view of the *bedu* who used the city is considered. After travelling nine hundred kilometres south through the Sands, Shis'r in the southern steppes would have been considered more coastal than central. The informants of Ptolemy would not have seen Shis'r for themselves, but they would have relied on information that stemmed from the *bedu* traders. For hundreds of years the precise locations of important incense sources were purposely kept hidden from the Romans and Greeks by means of secrecy and misinformation.

There was an abrupt dearth in materials between 300 BC and AD 300. This was the period when Shis'r declined and its original name is likely to have fallen into disuse. Quite when the current *bedu* name of Shis'r, or 'cleft', came into usage is not known, but by the time of the Qur'an, in the seventh century AD, the location of Ubar or Irem was no longer known.

Chinese porcelain, both Celadon and Ming, the chess set, copper needles, coins, bracelets and fine glass from Aden were plentiful and bear witness to a renewal of trade in the Arabic, early Islamic period from AD 650 to 1200. This ties in with the Islamic network of trading horses from central Arabia to the Dhofar coast.

My preconception of archaeology was born of work with ice-core drilling in polar regions. With ice, all data is stratified so that, at a certain depth, analysis will show traces in the ice of a known volcanic eruption or atomic bomb test. At Shis'r, our team located artefacts acorss the entire timespace of occupation from each level. Because each successive human occupation mixes up the detritus of previous inhabitants with their own rubbish, stratification does not often help with the dating process. 'So what?' said Juris. 'If you were an archaeologist of the twenty-ninth century AD and you dug up a 1990 Ford you would clearly differentiate it from a Fifties Chevvy . . . Well, pottery is just as stylized and has fashions that alter year by year. We know what period they represent, however shallow or deep we may locate them.'

The day we left Shalalah Jana gave me her thoughts on the dig. 'Very exciting,' she said, 'but hot, real hot. When things started to appear it was like striking gold. It was a lucky find but it is a very significant site. Now we have at least a year's work of analysis. There are the animal bones to identify, the carbon dates of items from sealed layers, including ostrich shells and seashells from which to establish trading patterns.' She paused. 'Whether or not it proves to be Ubar is irrelevant. The variety and the timespace of our findings indicate a major trade centre, an important place where people came together, where things happened, goods were exchanged and products from far-distant places were bought or exchanged for materials and goods. It was a key centre of trade and activity throughout its functional period.'

Back in 1953 Danish archaeologists told the Sultan of Oman's Intelligence officer Malcolm Dennison, now Lord Lieutenant of the Orkneys, that the discoveries they were then making in Bahrain all pointed to the Gulf States and Oman as being the region where the next great discoveries would be made.

Juris was outspoken: 'Historians and archaeologists the world over have always had the opinion that there's nothing of value in Arabia, that nothing will ever come out of Arabia and that mis-notion still persists today. So the number of people who do any work in Arabia is minimal. Only in the last twenty years have we begun to discover that Arabia is an integral part of the human experience of Mesopotamia, Palestine and Egypt. Opinions are only now being forced to change due to the new Arabian data. But you still run into resistance. Nobody's being trained to dig in Arabia in terms of its intrinsic value. Like most people, I went to school interested in Iraq not Arabia. It took me three years to figure out how to work in Arabia. You walk over sites and you misinterpret things right and left.'

Each new artefact had helped to fill in the puzzle, which Juris needed to reconstruct, that was the unknown past of Shis'r.

Between 8000 and 6000 BC the region was too arid for humans. In 5000 BC, with wetter weather, neolithic folk from Syria and further east arrived and built hearths. Even then, Juris believed, they traded in incense and travelled the then less arid interior, now the Sands, on foot and, after 4000 BC, by donkey.

'The peoples of Ubaid, of south Iraq and Sumer,' Juris stressed, 'traded in painted ceramics by 5000 to 4000 BC. I believe incense from Dhofar was traded then too. After all, their early texts of 2500 BC already talked of incense. It is a small jump back to 4000 BC, but at that time they could not write so they left no *proof*.'

All that Juris learnt from Shis'r and its related sites about the People of Ad, the descendants of the neolithics from the north, would help fill in our knowledge about the trading and life patterns of the age before that described to us by the classical writers of the first and second centuries AD. These men were not themselves able to penetrate Arabia. They were forced to report mere second-hand information so, although Shis'r probably did not decline until after the days of Strabo, Pliny and Ptolemy, none of them was able to go there.

By the seventh century AD, when the Qur'an and later Islamic writers described Irem, the site itself was gone, a place only of fanciful legend. The decline would partly have been due to the natural catastrophe that caused the town's collapse between AD 100 and 300, but Roman power faded in AD 300, Christianity spread and the demand for incense dwindled. Without the Dhofar frankincense trade, the key to Shis'r's former glories, the inhabitants of the half-ruined site returned to a *bedu* existence and for seven hundred years only squatters and nomads needing water came to Shis'r. After AD 1000, the time of the Ming china and the chess set, the horse trade brought back a second lesser glow to the wounded city and then, in 1970, Sultan Qaboos built homes, a mosque and a school there. Now the Bait Masan tribe, descendants in all likelihood of those early arrowhead makers and incense traders, have made it their permanent home. They too will leave their traces in the ground at Shis'r or Ubar, Atlantis of the Sands.

- - - - - - - - - - - - - - - - -

On 5 February 1992 an article by John Noble Wilford was splashed across the front page of the *New York Times*, giving the news of our discovery of Ubar. This article was picked up and given major coverage all across the world, for there was a shortage of hard news at the time. All major newspapers and TV networks across the USA gave the story prime rating and suggested that the project was an entirely American-inspired success.

'Guided by ancient maps and sharp-eyed surveys from space,' wrote the respected Mr Wolford, 'archaeologists and explorers have discovered a lost city deep in the sands of Arabia.'

Keen to be properly grateful to JPL, who had indeed gone out of their way over a long period to try to help us, and naturally eager to tie in the romantic idea of modern technology with ancient lost cities in the documentary film of our search, Nick himself began to see things very differently to the clear events that I remember and have described in this book. I only wish satellite photography had led us to Shis'r, for it would have made a wonderful theme for this book and for the illustrated lectures which are my bread and butter.

When in March I returned to Shalalah and told Juris that the American media were implying that we were led to the discovery by satellite imagery, he said: 'That's not entirely true, but it sounds good. It sounds like technology is at work and all that kind of rubbish. The truth is, it was found by hard work and excavation. The satellite imagery allowed us to eliminate sites so we could concentrate on the most probable areas.'

'Did all that LANDSAT/SPOT stuff about water help?' I asked him.

'No,' he was adamant. 'That's just for publicity.'

In 1992 Nick wrote in his summary of run-up events to the expedition: 'In March 1990 the LANDSAT/SPOT composite image enables us to ultimately plot approximately one hundred kilometres of the Ubar road stretching in an arc from Shis'r to the Saudi border. Somewhere along this arc should be Ubar.'

This again implies that we decided to search Shis'r as a result of logic made possible by the image data. Had this been so, we would all have attacked the Shis'r excavation with great anticipation and gusto. Juris would never have said to me, as he did in March 1992: 'I never thought Shis'r was Ubar even when we started digging.'

I have no wish to labour this point and certainly bear no ill will to Nick or to JPL. However the scientific community has already begun, in magazines, to perpetuate a myth which is a distortion of the truth. This book is the only chance I have at least to attempt to re-establish the facts about an endeavour which I led and of which I am proud. Those facts can best be summarized by openly admitting that a large slice of luck, a lot of hard work and the experience-honed instincts of Juris led us to the discovery. Good vehicles, generous sponsors, the support of the Sultan and so many Omanis, a wonderful team of volunteers, including JPL, and technological aids in many forms, all contributed to our success.

The announcements of most archaeological discoveries are tempered by a howl of dissent from not very fraternal archaeologists around the world with differing theories. Reaction to the Ubar revelation was muted. Donald Whitcomb of the University of Chicago said: 'We're talking about preliterate mythologies of Arabs. There's probably a grain of truth in them . . . I don't know whether they discovered Ubar mainly because I'm not sure whether Ubar really existed.'

The Gulf media was jubilant and the Egyptian *Al Liwa Al Islami* quoted various specialists as being certain it was the same city as that mentioned in the Quran.

The Saudi press was clearly unhappy with any suggestion that Ubar or Irem were not within the Saudi borders. *Al Majilla* reported:

Dr Abdel Al Ansari, eminent Saudi scholar and archaeologist, thinks the argument for Ubar is based on stories in the Old Testament and is designed to give Israel an excuse for its ambitions in the Arabian peninsula.

The Saudi scholar Hamed Al Jasir says there is a big element of exaggeration and there is no evidence to support Sir Ranulph's argument for Ubar . . . Dr Abdulla Al Masri, the assistant Saudi Under-Secretary for Archaeological Affairs says, 'In Saudi Arabia we have found similar sites over the past fifteen years.'

In *Ashawq al Awsat*, Dr Masri was more explicit:

The best of these sites was when, in 1975, we uncovered more than one city on the edge of the Empty Quarter, in particular the oasis of Jabreen. Also the name Ubar is similar to that of Obar, an oasis in eastern Saudi Arabia. We must await further details but so far we have more important discoveries at Jabreen or Najran.

Not all Saudis were hostile to our announcement. Professor Mohammed Bakalla of King Saud University wrote:

Your discovery is very important and I expect future discovery will unveil the extraordinary civilization of Irem-al-Imad. I will not be surprised if Ad's nation cities are underneath what has been discovered by you or in the close vicinity.

The main objections voiced in the Saudi press by non-scientific sources were that our site was small, contained Islamic (not just pre-Islamic) artefacts, did not show evidence of temples and was not found fully preserved by tons of sand.

Since we had not to date unearthed a plaque naming Shis'r as Ubar, Irem or Omanum Emporium, all our evidence was indeed circumstantial but no more so than the discovery of a body in the vicinity of where somebody has disappeared and, by certain aspects of the remains, assuming the identity of the body.

It is easy to summarize our evidence. In AD 150 Claudius Ptolemy was the only geographer to leave map coordinates of Arabia. In 1870 the German Sprenger analyzed medieval reconstructions of Ptolemy's map and found that the principal frankincense source was close to the Plain of Salalah. Just north of the Dhofar Mountains he also placed the tribe of the Oubaritae, the men of Ubar. He gave only four other place-names in south Arabia associated with incense, which was at that time the greatest of all trading commodities and one of these was Emporion Omanum (Omani market).

A century or so before Ptolemy, an unknown Greek sea captain left behind his coastal notes. This *Periplus* survived the centuries and clearly enables Moscha to be identified as the present-day ruins of Sumhuram. He too identifies the Omani market-place as a site known to seafarers of the time.

Ptolemy places this trading centre in the central steppes of Dhofar, not on the far sides of the Empty Quarter, where Jabreen and Najran are to be found.

Ptolemy, the author of the *Periplus* and other classical writers were unaware that Dhofar incense had for centuries travelled north and north-east to the coast of the Arabian Gulf. Only the 1992 discoveries in Shis'r have provided evidence of this. Five hundred years after Ptolemy, by which time our site was a long forgotten outpost, Islamic writers were unable to provide further useful clues. They spoke of the region of Wabar as containing the lost cities that are also mentioned in the Qur'an as Irem, Ad and Thamud, but any direct link between these cities and Wabar or Ubar remains hypothetical and based merely on the Quranic fate of Ad.

The Saudi suggestion that Jabreen is Ubar is sensible from the point of view that the discoveries there (for which Juris was also largely responsible) included Roman and Greek pottery of the correct period. But Jabreen, Juris was quick to point out, *already* had its name on the Ptolemaic map and that was Labrus. Likewise, Najran was known as Najran to Ptolemy.

Jabreen or Labrus, in Juris's opinion, was the northern end of the incense route from Dhofar to Al Hasa oasis. Since it is nine hundred kilometres of desert away from the source of the incense, it would take an incense-laden camel (at the accepted daily rate of twenty kilometres) some seven weeks to reach it. This alone precludes Jabreen doubling as Ubar/Omanum Emporium, since Ptolemy clearly locates the latter site on the *southern* edge of the Sands, conveniently situated near Hanun, Andhur and other frankincense collection points.

Since our learned Alexandrian Greek, Ptolemy, knew of Omanum Emporium's existence in this area in AD 150, during the height of the incense trade with Rome, any site with claims to be the Emporium *must* possess signs of Roman trade. Shis'r has great quantities of such evidence.

Juris said: 'You can go all over the Rub al Khali looking for Roman pottery and, apart from in Jabreen and Shis'r, you won't find it.'

'In between these two sites,' he added, 'there are spaced water-holes. Some, according to Philby in the 1930s, still had well-cut stone faces. But Shis'r is not just a water-hole. If it was, why all the mass of pottery? And why build a great structure like this out in the middle of nowhere only fifteen miles from the dunes? Trade is the only reason and many artefacts can only have come from the north. That,' Juris paused for emphasis, 'is the greatest result we have. Proof that this Ubar/Jabreen route is the oldest of the incense routes and connected ancient Mesopotamia with Dhofar.'

'Could there not be other Ubar sites yet to be dug up?' I asked him.

'Sure there could be, but where? I have been all over Saudi and the Empty Quarter for twenty years and nobody has come up with another site, let alone one that is both where Ptolemy put it and has Roman pottery. Something as big as Shis'r shows up on air photos. Aramco and PDO oil surveyors have tracked all over the Sands for thirty years, never mind the *bedu* and the Army. Yet nobody has reported an alternative. Perhaps it is buried in sand, but sand doesn't move that fast, as you can see at Shis'r.' Juris thumped his knees. 'Shis'r is unique. There is nowhere like it in the desert for nine hundred kilometres.'

Professor Barri Jones from Manchester University visited Shis'r at the request of Oman and drew up a report on behalf of UNESCO. He wrote:

The purely archaeological discoveries that are emerging from Shis'r are of the greatest importance for south Arabian archaeology in their own right . . . The archaeological integrity of the site should not be allowed to be affected by possible disputes regarding its name.

The world-wide attention aroused by the expedition brought tourist and television teams aplenty to Shis'r. Sultan Qaboos knows that oil revenues will diminish and a lucrative alternative source of income could be tourism once the Omani government decides the country's infrastructure is ready to accept an invasion of package tours. At present only individuals and groups likely to behave in an inoffensive manner are welcomed as tourists and these are the sort of people who are best enticed by cultural attractions. Well-organized tours of a 'frankincense trail' to Al Balid, Andhur, Hanun, Shis'r/Ubar and Sumhuram could provide a rewarding and memorable visit. But Shis'r needs several seasons of excavation and protective screening. So do other relevant sites such as Ain Humran (likely to identify with Ptolemy's Saffara Metropolis) Taqa, Rasat, Moscha and Raysut.

Sultan Qaboos, by appointing the Committee of Ubar with a membership made up of Ministers and by giving Ali Ahmed Ali Mahash responsibility for the future survey and protection of sites, has led the way to a good future for archaeology in Dhofar. Already he is discussing the possibility of museums, the training of Omani archaeologists and the encouragement of public awareness of the need for conservation.

In April 1992 I was asked by the Minister of Information to become International Adviser to the Ubar Committee, a post which I welcome, for where else is there a people and a land of such enchantment?

BIBLIOGRAPHY

Muscat and Oman, Ian Skeet, Faber.

Frankincense and Myrrh, Nigel Groom, Longman.

Arabia Felix, Bertram Thomas, Jonathan Cape.

Egypt in the Classical Geographers, Dr John Ball, Cairo Government Press.

The Koran with preliminary discourse, George Sale, Frederick Warne & Company.

The Empty Quarter, H. St J.B. Philby, Constable & Company.

Journal of the Central Asian Society, No. 20, 1933.

The Book of the Thousand and One Nights, Richard F. Burton, The Burton Club.

As the Arabs Say, Isa Khalil Sabbaqh, Sabbaqh Management Corporation.

Arabian Sands, Wilfred Thesiger, Penguin Travel Library.

Bilal Ibu Rabah, Muhammed Abdul-Rauf, American Trust Publications.

The Ruba'iyat of Omar Khayyam, trans. Peter Avery and John Heath-Stubbs. Penguin Books.

The Countries and Tribes of the Persian Gulf, S.B. Miles, Frank Cass & Co.

Unknown Oman, Wendell Phillips, Longman.

Where Soldiers Fear to Tread, Ranulph Fiennes, Hodder & Stoughton.

Warlords of Oman, P.S. Alfred, Robert Hale.

The Persian Gulf, Sir Arnold T. Wilson, George Allen & Unwin.

Islam in Focus, Hammudah Abdalati, American Trust Publications.

Oman since 1856, Robert Geran Laaden, Princeton University Press.

Nomads in the Sultanate of Oman, Jorg Janzen, Westview Special Studies on the Middle East.

The Southern Gates of Arabia, Freya Stark, John Murray.

The Adventures of Ibn Batuta, Ross E. Dunn, University of California Press.

The Periplus of the Erythraean Sea, trans. Wilfred H. Scoff, Longman.

Encyclopaedia of Islam.

Marco Polo: The Book of Marco Polo, the Venetian.

The Arabs: A Short History, P.K. Hitti.

Arabia Deserta, C.M. Doughty.

Arabia: The Cradle of Islam, S.M. Zwemer.

The Portuguese in India, Frederick Charles Danvers.

In Unknown Arabia, R.E. Cheesman.

The Marsh Arabs, Wilfred Thesiger.

Sand Fountains in Southern Arabia, R.A. Bagnold.

ACKNOWLEDGEMENTS

I would like to thank all the members of the Ubar team, our helpers, sponsors, advisers and volunteer diggers. I apologize to those whose names have been omitted or misspelt. May they rest assured that this in no way lessens my gratitude for their help. Sincere thanks are due to:

His Majesty Sultan Qaboos bin Said, Sultan of Oman
His Excellency Dr Omar Al Zawawi
Ministry of Information of Oman
Ministry of National Heritage and Culture of Oman
Ministry of Palace Office Affairs
Ministry of Housing
Royal Oman Police
Royal Oman Police Air Wing
Royal Air Force of Oman
Royal Farm, Salalah
Royal Stables, Salalah
Special Task Force, Royal Oman Police
Oman International Bank
GulfAir
Al Bustan Palace Hotel
Salalah Holiday Inn
American Airlines
BP Middle East
Desert Line
DHL
Sheikh Ahmed Farid
GTO
Genetco
IBM Oman
Kamal Ali Sultan
Land Rover UK
Mohamed Haider Darwish
Matrah Cold Stores

Nortech
Occidental Petroleum Corporation
Occidental of Oman Inc
Olympus Cameras UK
Oman Aviation Services
Oman Refinery
ONIC
OUA
PDO
Shanfari
Southwest Missouri State University
Spinneys
Suhail and Saoud Bahwain
Taylor Woodrow Towell
Thompson CSF
Anthony Ashworth
Chris Armstrong
Dr Awad Issa
(Aqeed) Abdul Wahid
Amer Tabawq
Ali Ahmed Ali Mahash al Shahri
His Excellency Lieutenant General Ali bin Majid Al Ma'amari
Amin al Riyami
(Ameed) Abdulla Ali Hamadi
Mark Albany-Ward
Ritchie Arnold
His Excellency Abdul Aziz bin Mohomed Al Rowas
Dr Ali Shanfari

His Excellency Ahmed Salim Al Rowas
Mr Jog Arrow
Achmed Maher
S.M. Ali Lamki
Abdulla Mohomed Alowi
(Arif) Ali
American Foundation for the Study of Man
Richard Byford
Bob Brown
Bruce and Valerie Blackney
David Bell
Mike and Rachael Curtis
Chris Bental-Warner
Major Bob Brown
Patrick Brook
Neil Guru Barnes
Terry Baccus
Martin Beck
Sean Bowler
Ian Brown
Dave Butler
John Blackman
Mark Bentley
Kevin Burns
Robert Bowles
Lisa M. Barge
Alan Cairnes
Roy Carter
Mr Chandran
The Clapplets
Sir Terence and Lady Clark
Graham Clark
Chris and Chris Cowdray
David Cochrane
Dr Robert E. Crippen
Major Mike Crumbie
Geordie Cunningham
Ralph Daly
Stu Danes
Dawood Khan
Richard Dawes
Brigadier Malcolm Dennison
Nick Deufel
Michael Dunn
Peter Eades

Nick Easthope
Dr Charles Elachi
(Aqeed Ruqn Tayyer) Fareed bin Ali bin
    Abdulla al Amri
Terence Fernandez
Kevin Fletcher
John and Joan Fulford
Alex and Ben Gardiner
John Geddes
Pat Gilbert
Dr Marshall Gordon
Andy Graham
Gene and Jan Grogan
Lieutenant Gumma bin Rashid al Mashayki
Mr and Mrs Hisham Al Hadi
Hamed al Khalas
Christine Hanna
Hamed al Rashid
Harvard Semitic Museum
Elizabeth Hart
John Heck
Major Trevor Henry
Rosemary Hector
(Aqeed Ruqn Gawi) Hilal bin Amr bin Hamed
    Al Hajri
(Muqadam) Humaid bin Khaleefa al
    Khanbashi
Huntington Library
Ken James
Dr Albert Jamme
Jet Propulsion Laboratory, NASA
Alan Jutze
Lalantha Katalonga
(Sqn Ldr) Kamis Ali
Khaled Salim Al Ghassani
Tim Landon
Dr Don Landon
Terry Lloyd
Ian MacLeish
Malik al Hinai
Major Madhu Sohani
Marbruk bin Mohomed Al Rowas
His Excellency Mahfudh bin Suleiman al
    Hadobi
Julie Masterson

Judie Miller
Mohamed Ahmed Fareej
Mohomed Mubhowt 'Thinaya' ar Rashid,
    Imam of Fasad
Mohamed Bakheit al Hamar Bait Kathir, Naib
    Wali of Fasad
Mohomed al Riyami
Nigel Moss
His Excellency Said Musallim al Busaidi,
    Minister of State and Governor of Dhofar
(Muqadam) Mubarak al Alowi
Mr Nass'r (BP)
Jean-Marc Naudin
Nassir bin Saoud al Ruwahi
Nooh Sabeel al Baloob
Tony Northway
Ian Ord
Oussama Massoud
Richard and Joanna Owens
William Overstreet
Sharon Patterson
David-Claude Pichavet
C.S. Ramon
Mr Rajan
Rosie Raynsford
Miles Rosedale

Bob Storer
(Aqeed) Salim Basha
(Fareeq Awaal) Said bin Rashid al Kalbani
Lieutenant Colonel Salim Ali Khaleefa Al-
    Maskiri
Said Salim Ahmed al Shanfari
Said Sabti
Saleh Al Kindy
Saleh an Naimi
Seif bin Hamood al Behlamy
Mark Selway
Sharki Sultan
M.A. de Souza
Robert and Irene Spikins
Colonel David Sutcliffe
Mr Tewary (BP)
Paul Toom
John Wright
Robert Whitcombe
Dr Bernice Warren
Dave Yourish
Yahya Abdulla
Jan R. Yoshimitzu
Yusef Ali Khan
Barry Zorthian

For their kind agreement to use their photographs in this book, I would especially like to thank:

Ali Ahmed Ali Mahash al Shahri
Abdel Adas
Neil Guru Barnes
Bruce Blackney
Olivier Blaise/GLMR
Dr Ron Blom
British Aerospace
Bryn Campbell
Nick Clapp
Dr Robert E. Crippen
Edmund Dulac (dec.)
Andy Dunsire
Earth Observation Satellite Co
Kevin Fletcher
Khamis al Muharbi

Geoffrey Gaussen
Yves Gellie
JPL/Caltech
Terry Lloyd
Ministry of Information of Oman
Nigel Moss
Sebastian Munster (dec.)
Mohomed Mustapha
Mubarak bin Obeid
Kevin O'Brien
George Ollen
Said Shanfari
Helmut R. Schultze
SPOT Image Corporation (© CNES)
Dr Mike Stroud

The Ubar Team

Dr Ali Shanfari   Director of Archaeology, Dhofar, Oman

Ranulph Fiennes   Leader, organization and field activities

Nicholas Clapp   Leader, research and documentary film

Dr Juris Zarins   Senior archaeologist

Kay Clapp   Expedition assistant

Jana Owen   Assistant archaeologist

Amy Hirschfeld   Registrar

Jean England   Archaeology student

Amy Horn   Archaeology student

Rick Breitenstein   Archaeology student

Julie Knight   Archaeology student

Lieutenant Gumma bin Rashid al Mashayki, ROP   Escort commander

Dr Ron Blom   Geologist, Jet Propulsion Laboratory

Dr Kristine Blom   Sub-surface radar, Jet Propulsion Laboratory

Kevin O'Brien   Documentary cameraman

George Ollen   Documentary sound man

Sandra Zarins   Archaeology assistant

Ginnie Fiennes   Communications

George Hedges   Fund-raiser for documentary film

Miles Rosedale   Financing for Bait Masan liaison

Ali Ahmed Ali Mahash al Shahri   Dhofar glyphics expert

Major Trevor Henry   Dhofar liaison

Andy Dunsire   Dhofar liaison

Bakheit bin Abdulla bin Salim   Bait Masan liaison

Marbruk bin Ahmed bin Saarleh   Bait Masan liaison

Mr Gomez, Mr Gomez, Mr Lawrence, Mr Jacko   Culinary services

Salim Amr Naseeb al Amri   Archaeology student (temporary assistance)

Said Mohamed al Mashayki   Archaeology student (temporary assistance)

Said Salim Ahmed al Shanfari   Archaeology assistance

Hamed al Khalas   Desert guide

Terry Lloyd   ITN

Robert Bowler   ITN

Shis'r assistance

Musallim bin Abdulla, Naib Wali of Shis'r

Salim bin Mohamed

Said bin Musallim

Marbruk bin Ahmed

Said bin Abdulla

Salim bin Abdulla

Mohamed bin Bakheit

Ahmed bin Mohamed

Musallim bin Mohamed

Salim bin Sehayl

INDEX

Abdul Aziz, King 21
Ad (city) 20, 23–4, 27, 53, 63, 89, 156, 177, 180
Ad, King 20–1, 24, 52
Aelius Gallus, Gen. 29
Ain Humran 139, 182
Akil, Muhammad 51
Al Akaf 52–3, 89
Al Ansari, Dr Abdel 179
Al Balid 12, 50–1
Al Hamdani 53, 89
al-Himyari 20, 89
al Hinai, Malik 148
Al Jasir, Hamed 179
Al Kalbi 53
al Khalas, Hamed 52, 55–8, 150
Al Liwa Al Islami 179
Al Majilla 179
Al Masri, Dr Abdulla 179
Al Rowas, Abdul Aziz bin Mohamed 174
Al Zawawi, Dr Omar 73–4, 120
Alexandria 19, 26, 28–9
Ali Mahash, Ali Ahmed 159–63, 170, 174, 182
Amr bin Said 135
Andhur 131–2, 139–40
Antarctica expedition, 121, 145
Arabian Nights, The 53, 170
Arctic expeditions 75–6, 83–8, 91–101, 107, 113–18
Armand Hammer Productions 80
Armitage, Major St John B. 46
Arzat 40, 46
Ashawq al Awsat 179

Bahn, Paul 26, 122, 163–4
Bakalla, Prof. Mohammed 179
Bakheit 164
Bayley, David 58
Bedr bin Tuwairiq 60, 137
Beni bu Ali 76–7
Bennett, Eric 74
Bil Rizat 174
Bin Ishaq 53
Blom, Ronald 81–2, 89, 107–8, 123, 126–7, 129–30, 134, 148, 151–3, 167
Bomberry, Russ 83
Bowring, Anton 74
Brasher, Chris 121
Breitenstein, Rick 162, 169
British Aerospace 103, 142
Brook, Patrick 75–6
Brown, Harold 112
Burton, Charlie 90

Challenger space shuttle 81–2, 89, 107
Charles, Prince of Wales 80, 104–5, 109–11, 120, 142
Childs, Tony 106
Chukov, Col Vladimir 115
circumpolar expedition 72–4, 80, 88, 90, 115
Clapp, Kay 123, 127–8, 131, 145
Clapp, Nick 80–2, 88–90, 103, 107–9, 119, 121, 123, 126–30, 135, 139, 141–2, 145–6, 150, 152, 154, 163, 170, 177–8
Cleary, Paul 83–4, 88
Crippen, Dr Robert 81–2, 89, 107–8
Crumbie, Mike 172
Curtis, Mike 147

Dahaq, cliffs of 36
Darbat 34–7
Darwish, Mohamed Haider, Sheikh 120
de Silva, Felix 74
Dehedoba Trail 52, 55, 57
Dennison, Malcolm 176
Departures 76
Dhofar 9, 13, 27, 32, 38–40, 47, 50–1, 72, 78, 88, 159
Dhofar Force 46
Dickson, Col H.R.P. 24
Douglas-Home, David 119
Dunsire, Andy 149, 151, 153, 155, 162–3, 167, 170–2

Eades, Peter 167
Eden, Garden of 156–8
Elachi, Dr Charles 81–2, 89, 107–8, 167
Empty Quarter 19–21, 23–4, 28, 63, 108, 154, 180
Encyclopaedia of Islam 53
Etienne, Jean-Louis 87, 91–92, 94

Fairfax, Rupert 105
Fasad 15–16, 60, 121, 136–7, 151, 154
Feather Men, The 143, 172
Fiennes, Ginnie 69–72, 74–6, 87–8, 92–3, 102, 106, 124, 160
Fotheringham, Alan 90, 106
Fuchs, Sir Vivian 106–7

Gall, Sandy 70
Gorbachev, Raisa 101–2
Greenfield, George 70–2
Greening, Tom 40, 42, 46, 67–8, 70, 73, 103, 113
Grogan, Gene 120
Groome, Nigel 168
Guinness Book of Records 101
Gumma Rashid al Mushayki, Lt 147–8

Habarut 14, 24, 57, 67–8
Hadhramaut 13, 28, 52, 159
Hadhraumi Bedouin Legion 67
Hamilton, Captain 51

Hammer, Dr Armand 74–5, 80, 85, 87, 90, 97, 101–6, 109–13, 119, 123–4, 142, 146
Hammer, Frances 112–13
Hanun 136, 140
Heath, Edward 119
Hedges, George 108, 119, 123, 126–7
Heilat Araka 137, 139, 155
Hempleman-Adams, David 94
Henry, Major Trevor 109, 123, 128, 131, 134–6, 139, 149, 155, 158, 170
Herbert, Wally 84, 86
Hirschfeld, Amy 164–5, 168–9, 174
Hoover, Mike 88
Horobin, Don 70
Howell, Laurence 86–8, 91–3, 100–1, 107
Howell, Morag 107
Humaid Khaleefa 128, 132, 134, 147
Hussein, King of Jordan 73

Ibn Jiluwi 21, 152
incense trade 13, 29, 32, 49–50, 132, 140, 175–7, 180
Independent Television News 70
Iôbaritae 19, 26
Irem 20, 52–4, 81, 89, 136–7, 170, 177, 179–80

Jabreen 21, 179–80
Jebel Ali 10
Jebel Kasbah 135
Jet Propulsion Laboratory 81, 89, 107, 139, 146, 154, 167, 177–8
Johnson, Beverly 88
Johnson, Clive 94
Jones, Prof. Barri 181
Journal of the Central Asian Society 21
Jutze, Alan 81

King, Lord 110
Kohr Rori 10–11, 48–50
Kohr Sawli 139
Koran *see* Qur'an

Landberg 53
LANDSAT 82, 103, 107–8, 157, 178

Lawrence, T.E. 20, 23, 164
Leeat 161
Lloyd, Terry 88

Mabhowt, Mohamed 151–2
Macleans 90, 106
Majid, Gen. Ali 121, 128
Mantell, Bob 100
Marbruk bin Ahmed 155, 164
Marib 29, 32, 39, 82
Masriy, Dr Abdulla 123
Maxwell, Robert 142
McConnell, Jackie 115–16, 119
Meares, Roger 93
Miles, Col S.B. 51
Mirbat 10, 50–1
Mistahayl, Said 47
Mohomed, Imam of Fasad 153
Mubarreq 35–6, 38
Mudayy 136, 140
Mugshin 154
Mugtot, Abdulla Salim 60
Murad 16–17, 60, 65–6
Musallim bin Nuffl 15
Muscat 126, 173
    Sultan of 20

Najran 180
NASA 81, 107, 121
Naseeb 47
Nashran bin Sultan 11–12, 16, 19, 55–6,
    58–60, 150
Nashwan Said 63
National Geographic 86, 145
New York Times 177
Nightingale, Roy 73
Nile, White 26
Nordair 90, 107
North Pole *see* Arctic

Obet 68
O'Brien, Kevin 148
Ollen, George 148
Oman 9, 20–1, 26–8, 32, 41, 74, 127–8
Oman International Bank 120, 148

Omanum Emporium 19, 26, 52, 82, 166,
    175, 180–1
Oracle of Diana 150
Ord, Col Ian 140
O'Shea, Raymond 20
Ovington 51
Owen, Jana 164–5, 168–9, 174, 176

Peary 86
Periplus of thed Erythraean Sea 29, 180
Philby, H. St J. B. 21–3, 152, 181
Phillips, Dr Wendell 11, 22, 24–5, 49, 54,
    60–2, 81, 132, 137, 155
    Unknown Oman 146–7
Piper Alpha rig 111
Powell, Spike 'Muldoon' 55
Ptolemies, Kings of Egypt 28
Ptolemy, Claudius 26, 29, 52, 54, 81–2, 150,
    175, 180–1
Pullar, Judith 155
Purdon, Brg. Coran 14

Qaboos bin Said, Sultan 40, 67–71, 73, 78,
    90, 103, 108, 113, 121, 173–4, 177, 181–2
Qafa 15
Qatn, Sultan of 23
Qismeem, Pass of 57
Qur'an 19–20, 24, 27, 39, 52–3, 153,
    179–80

Rakhyut 78
Ramphal, Sonny 105
Raynor, Bob 111
Raysut Hemara 139
Robat 50
Royal Geographical Society 21, 73, 103
Royal Oman Police 143
Rub al Khali 20, 22, 82, 139, 152, 154, 181

Said bin Ghia 43–4, 47–8
Said bin Taimur, Sultan 9, 22, 24–5, 40–1,
    46, 54, 59, 67–8, 137, 160, 168
Said Musallim Abu Saidi 149
Salalah 11–12, 40, 51, 73, 78, 128, 149
    Plain of 10, 26, 32, 34, 139, 163, 180

Salim, Said 34–5, 38, 40, 56, 65, 79
SAS 71, 73, 109, 143
Shanfari, Dr Ali 123, 170, 174
Sheba, Queen of 29, 32, 38–9
Shepard, Oliver 75–6, 83–6, 88, 92–3, 96,
    106–7, 110
Shis'r 24, 59, 75, 136–40, 149–50, 154, 156,
    162–4, 166, 173–8, 180–2
Shparo, Dr Dmitri 115, 117, 119
Simpsons 94
SIR-B radar 81, 89, 107–8
sponsorship 69–70, 72, 85, 90, 103, 108, 110,
    119–21
SPOT satellite 82, 108, 178
Sprenger 180
Stark, Freya 23
Steger, Will 86–7, 91–2, 94, 100
Stroud, Dr Mike 93–101, 106–7, 113–14,
    116–19, 121
Sultan's Armed Forces 9, 14, 48, 67, 69, 77,
    143
Swann, Robert 93

Tawi Ateer 170–2
Thamrait 52, 55, 57, 65, 67–8, 78, 131
Thatcher, Margaret 120, 142
Thesiger, Wilfred 23–4, 58, 75, 132, 138,
    155, 161
Thomas, Bertram Sidney 20–4, 54, 58, 61–3,
    80–1, 126, 132, 137–8, 155, 161
Thwaites, Col Peter 14, 32–3, 73
trade, Arabian 13, 27–9, 167, 175
    see also incense trade
Transglobe Expedition 106–7, 146
Tufft, Roger 94

Ubar 12–13, 17, 19–27, 44, 52, 54, 81,
    89–90, 103, 128, 136–7, 140–1, 150,
    155, 166–8, 173–4, 177–80
    Committee 182
Umm al Ghawarif 10–12, 42, 46
Umm al Hadid 21
Umm al Shaadid 58
United World Colleges 104, 110, 142
Uruq al Hadh 151
Uruq bin Hamooda 69

Viturakis, Eddie 56
Vlassova, Nina 102

Wabar 20–3, 52–4, 63, 89, 152, 180
Wadi Atinah 15, 24, 61
Wadi Darbat 160
Wadi Deefan 15
Wadi Ghadun 24, 55, 59
Wadi Mitan 12, 16, 23–4, 52, 58, 60–3, 90
Wadi Naheez 43–4, 134, 151, 159
Wadi Thimreen 47
Well of the Birds 170–2
Weston-Baker, Charles 75–6, 81, 103, 146
Whitcomb, Donald 178
Wilford, John Noble 177
Williamson, Andrew 122
Wolper, David 145

Yaqut 53, 89

Zarins, Dr Juris 121–3, 126–32, 134–42,
    149–50, 153–8, 160, 162, 164–9, 172,
    174–8, 180–1
Z'berg, Karl 86